Brett Halsey:
Art or Instinct in the Movies...

Brett Halsey:
Art or Instinct in the Movies...

by John B. Murray

Midnight Marquee Press, Inc.
Baltimore, Maryland, USA

Copyright © 2008 by John Murray
Interior layout and cover design by Susan Svehla
Copy Editor: Scott A. Nollen

The opinions and views expressed herein are those of the writer and interviewees, and do not necessarily reflect the opinions or views of the publishers.

Without limiting the rights under copyright reserved above, no part of this publication may be reproduced, stored in or introduced into a retrieval system, or transmitted, in any form, or by any means (electronic, mechanical, photocopying, recording or otherwise), without the prior written permission of the copyright owner or the publishers of the book.

ISBN 13: 978-1-887664-83-7
ISBN 10: 1-887664-83-1
Library of Congress Catalog Card Number 2008926646
Manufactured in the United States of America
First Printing by Midnight Marquee Press, Inc., May 2008
Revised Second Printing by Midnight Marquee Press, Inc. October, 2008

I have known Brett Halsey since we were students together at the Universal Talent School. I have always considered him a highly talented and versatile screen actor and was not surprised at his great popularity when he went to Italy and established himself as a movie hero, a couple of years before I went there for Sergio Leone. We have remained good friends and I have enjoyed reading Brett's scripts and novels over the years. I am glad he is the subject of this appreciation, which is well-deserved. — Clint Eastwood

Brett Halsey always had a fine reputation as a gentleman. There's not a lot of gentlemen in this business. He's a "please" and "thank you." He's royalty. To be successful in Hollywood, you need strong friends. To be very successful, you need to make enemies. Brett couldn't make any enemies...I have always considered Brett Halsey to be Hollywood royalty. — Jay Bernstein, Hollywood star maker

To the memory of two filmmakers:

Tulio Demicheli, 1914-1992, director of *Espionage in Lisbon*

Stefano Rolla, 1937-2003, assistant director of *Spy in Your Eye* and *Web of Violence*

Table of Contents

8	Acknowledgements
10	Foreword
11	Brief Chronology
12	Childhood Days
15	Admiral William F. Halsey
16	School Days
18	First Work Experiences
19	Early Interest in Show Business
20	In the Navy
22	Early Acting Jobs
24	First Big Break
27	Universal Studios
34	Ma and Pa Kettle at Home
37	On the Stage
39	Marriage Go Round
59	Hollywood Legends
73	Freelancing After Universal
76	Working in Television
98	Working as a P.I.
101	Independents
115	Horror and Sci-Fi Pictures

123 Big Time Hollywood
129 Offscreen Scenes
145 Stardom in Europe
164 Secret Agent Man
174 Contemporary Thrillers
184 Spaghetti Westerns
196 Lost Opportunities
199 Producing
202 On Teaching
205 Soaps
214 Italian Renaissance
221 Lucio Fulci
228 The Desert Lion
235 Canada
240 El Profesor, Costa Rica
253 Creative Writer
265 It Ain't Over 'Til it's Over
270 Afterword: Brett Halsey —
      Art or Instinct in the Movies...
274 Filmography
282 Bibliography

Acknowledgements

I would have written it anyway, but this book would have been immeasurably less worthwhile without the agreement and co-operation of its subject, Brett Halsey.

On my first visit to consult with him, I was very touched by his kindness. A short interview was all I expected but Brett regaled me with endless stories until late into the night. In the coming months, he was always accommodating, kind and humorous during my persistent raids on his archive of cuttings and photos. I was to learn this is typical of Brett's generosity to others.

Unexpectedly, my decision to write a tribute to his life and career lead to an immense change in Brett Halsey's life. When I went to see *Espionage in Lisbon* as a child, Brett's performance influenced my life, I suppose; now, I was returning the compliment. I invited my close friend, Victoria de Korda, granddaughter of film producer Alexander Korda, out to Los Angeles to help me interview Brett. Brett and Victoria gradually fell in love. I began to recognize their growing mutual attraction when we all three went on a trip to Kernville to check the condition of his parents' home, which he had bought as a peaceful retreat in which to write, though he later decided it would be impractical and sold it. Victoria de Korda became the fifth Mrs. Halsey in December 2006 at a register office wedding in Beverly Hills with a reception in a five-star hotel afterward. They stayed with me when they came to London in May 2007.

Many of the choicest illustrations in this book come from Halsey's archive, supplemented by posters, stills and lobby cards I have collected over many years. I am especially grateful to Brett for letting me incorporate some of his own witty and informative written memoirs of aspects of his life and career. Some of these appeared in magazines but most are unpublished.

Brett also opened the door to interviews with friends and celebrities, giving them license to speak freely. I am grateful to him, above all, for providing an extraordinary insight into more than half a century of movies and television from Hollywood, Italy, Spain, Germany, Canada and Costa Rica.

For interviews and comments about Brett, I wish to thank a number of people. Particularly helpful were those who gave me long interviews: Tracy Avildsen, the late Jay Bernstein, Frank Caruso, Gene Corman, Cesar Delgado, Clayton Halsey, the late Dorris Halsey, David Hedison, Gabrielle Houle, Ron Joy, Sandy Lieberson, the late Julian Ludwig, Adriana Mora, Edward Palmer, Marianne Rogers, Kathy Shower and Henry Silva. Useful comments about Brett and/or his career were given by: George Bacos, Angie Dickinson, Clint Eastwood, Jess Franco, Richard Gordon, Clu Gulager, Douglas and Gordon Halsey, Christian Halsey Solomon, Guy Hamilton, Michelle Jones, Norman Kahn, the late Jean Negulesco, Nancy Parke-Taylor, Russ Tamblyn, Robert

Vaughn, Susi and Philip Waddilove, the late Mel Welles, William Wellman, Jr., and Brett's close friend Stanley Winston.

Practical help was given by some well-wishers: Jeff Burr, Roger Corman, Jacques Goyard, Clint Eastwood's Executive Assistant Deana Lou and Frederick Muller. Jeff Burr was also involved in filming the interview between Brett and Bob Murawski of Grindhouse Releasing for Bob's U.S. DVD of Lucio Fulci's *Cat in the Brain*. My thanks to Bob and Brett for letting me attend and suggest a few questions.

Special thanks to Sir Christopher Frayling, Rector of the Royal College of Art in London and author of the definitive study *Spaghetti Westerns* as well as studies of Clint Eastwood and Sergio Leone, for providing the Foreword.

I am grateful to Ray of Video Unlimited for supplying 20 rare episodes of *Follow the Sun*, which I would not otherwise have been able to see; to Kata Varszegi for the beautiful coffee mug that helped me through those twilight hours of textual revisions; and to Gary and Susan Svehla of Midnight Marquee Press, who recognized right away that the fantastic career of Brett Halsey was worth celebrating.

Photographs are courtesy of Brett Halsey and other various sources during my months in Hollywood, including Larry Edmunds Cinema Bookshop and Backlot Books & Movie Posters. My thanks to Victoria Halsey (formerly de Korda), Photoface in London and Imagexperts in Hollywood for their help with the photographing of posters. Editorial suggestions were made by Victoria and also by Brett, who read several drafts and only occasionally sighed.

I requested interviews with Luciana Paluzzi and Marilu Tolo but they declined, probably for reasons of privacy as both are retired from screen acting. Mention should be made of those writers whose recent magazine profiles of Brett aided my understanding of his life and career: Dennis Capicik, Steve Fentone, Mike Ferguson, Michael Michalski, Tom Weaver and Tony Williams. Their work is listed in the Bibliography and I salute them for realizing how important Brett's career has been in the face of such long critical neglect.

Sadly, three of Brett Halsey's closest friends, Dorris Halsey, Jay Bernstein and Julian Ludwig, passed away before this book was published. I would have liked them to see it.

—John B. Murray
London, 2008

Foreword

On the day Clint Eastwood arrived in Rome, to make the Western which would eventually be called *A Fistful of Dollars*, one of the first Americans he met was his old friend Brett Halsey. Halsey had first arrived a couple of years before, to make the costume adventure *Seven Swords for the King* for Riccardo Freda, and he was already in a good position to let Eastwood know about the ins and outs of Italian genre filmmaking. They had known each other since being fellow students on the short-lived Universal Talent Program in 1952. In retrospect, Brett Halsey was to recall mid-1960s Rome as "a time and place which would turn out to be as memorable as Paris in the '20s, Hollywood in the '30s—and Greenwich Village and North Beach in the '50s." It was the era which Fellini dubbed "Hollywood on the Tiber," the era of the paparazzi and of economic miracles which produced a whole series of assembly-line popular films, many of which have since became cults. Between 1962 and 1970, Halsey acted in swashbucklers, post-James Bond spy films (notably *Espionage in Lisbon*, from a story by Jess Franco), some comedies and five Westerns.

In his best-known Italian Western—originally called *Today It's Me—Tomorrow You*, now retitled *Today We Kill...Tomorrow We Die* (1968)—he played a brooding, more menacing variation on the Man with No Name, complete with designer-stubble, dark scarf, cool black hat and close resemblance to Tyrone Power: this was a stylish riff on *The Magnificent Seven* ("Five men against fifty.... and a hundred ways to die!"), written by the young Dario Argento and partly filmed in a forest north of Rome rather than the usual Almerian desert. Brett Halsey was for some reason given the pseudonym "Montgomery Ford"—more usually, it was *Italians* who hid behind American-sounding names. At a time when one Italian actor answered to the name Clint Westwood, another to George Eastman, and one director became John Fordson, I guess anything was possible. Brett Halsey subsequently wrote a novel about his colorful experiences in Rome called *The Magnificent Strangers* (1978). He was invited *back* to Italy in the late 1980s to work for Lucio Fulci, Duccio Tessari and others. As Mark Twain once observed, in Europe they have long memories for names and faces—for your greatest work rather than your latest work.

This book, the first to be written about Brett Halsey—and not before time—covers in detail the years in Italy, but also goes back to the Universal Talent Program, the contract with Universal which lasted 13 films, the part he almost got in *The Searchers*, the television appearances, the contract with Fox, the daytime soaps, the novels, the New Hampshire judge he played in *The Godfather III*, and the course Halsey taught in Costa Rica on "Acting for Camera."

It is an unusual story about a most unusual career. Today It's Him!

—Sir Christopher Frayling

Brief Chronology

1933 Born Santa Ana, CA on June 20
1938-1949 Attended nine different high schools in CA
1950-1952 In the Navy, first broadcasting experience
1952 Signed a contract with Universal
1953 First feature movie appearance in *All I Desire*
1954 Married Renate Hoy (two children)
1959 Signed a contract with 20th Century-Fox
1960 Married Luciana Paluzzi (one child)
1961 Lead in Fox TV series *Follow the Sun*
1962 Began an extensive Italian career with *Seven Swords for the King*
1964 Married Heidi Bruhl (two children)
1970 Returned to Hollywood and made episodic TV appearances
1972 Went to New York to appear in the first of four soap operas on TV
1978 Published first novel *The Magnificent Strangers*
1984 Published second novel *Yesterday's Children*
1985-1987 Development executive, Lou-Star Productions, Warner Bros.; acting teacher
1987-1988 Vice-President Development, Jay Bernstein Productions, Paramount
1986-1990 Revival of Italian movie career after working with Lucio Fulci
1989 March, Married Firouzeh in Rome
1989 Moved to Toronto, Canada and worked in Canadian productions
1997 Moved to Costa Rica to teach at the University of Costa Rica
2004 Returned to L.A. and resumed acting while writing *Halfbreed*
2006 Married Victoria de Korda

Childhood Days

Brett Halsey was born Charles Oliver Hand on June 20, 1933. His home was Newport Beach, California, though he was delivered at the hospital in nearby Santa Ana.

His great-great-grandfather was once Mayor (*alcalde*) of Los Angeles. His great-grandfather was friends with a famous Southern Californian bandit, Tibercio Vasquez, who has a state park, Vasquez Rocks, where he used to hide out, named after him. He operated near Halsey's great-grandfather's rancho, where he left his equipment. Halsey and his mother once went to visit her cousin and saw the bandit's saddle and lariats at her house. The cousin had inherited them from Halsey's great-grandfather. Much later, when Halsey took more interest in his family history, he went back to his mother's cousin to see the bandit's equipment but found she had given it all away.

Halsey's grandfather was running a meat market at Randsburg in the Mojave Desert in 1912, and in 1914 he operated a vegetable market in Costa Mesa, adjoining Newport Beach. In the 1930s, he was living in a house in Kernville, north of the Mojave Desert. Halsey visited him there for the first time when he was four and occasionally thereafter. His grandfather was a gold prospector in the nearby mountains, but only as a hobby.

Randsburg meat market owned by Brett Halsey's grandfather.

On his mother's side, Halsey was descended from a family that came to California on a land grant from the King of Spain. At one time, they owned half of the San Fernando Valley, between Encino and Ventura. Halsey once wrote (for a network publicity sheet for *The Millionaire* television show in 1957): "My ancestors brought the first orange trees into the San Fernando Valley from Chile." They would have brought these on the journey from Spain to California via the Cape, stopping at Santiago.

Halsey's mother, Rose Marie Rinaldi Hand, had a cousin, Ana Begu de Packman, who was General Secretary of the Southern California Historical Society. She researched the history of the family, tracing his ancestry back to Juan Francisco Reyes, a Spanish King's Colonial Soldier from New Spain, Mexico, who was in California from 1769 and called on to serve as *alcalde* (Mayor, Chairman of the Council) of Los Angeles in 1793, and Carl Rinaldi from Berlin, who married Reyes' granddaughter and whose father was a court painter known all over Europe.

Halsey at age 15

Halsey's mother was a famed local beauty. She had lovely skin and was Miss San Gabriel in 1930 and appeared as Queen of the California Missions in the Rose Parade in January 1931. She was once offered a studio contract but turned it down. Halsey remembers there was a Justice of the Peace in Newport Beach who was old and crotchety and "mean to young people" and feared by them. Halsey was 16 and got a ticket, which landed him in front of the Judge. The Judge looked at him and said, "Are you Rosie Rinaldi's boy? Get out of my court. I don't want to see you here again…By the way, give my regards to your mother."

Halsey's father, Edward Lott Hand, was a roving building contractor, working between San Francisco and Los Angeles, but always in California. Edward

Hand was a native of Lake Forest, Illinois. He came to California at the age of eight and lived there until his death at the young age of 38. Halsey felt that growing up in California he was essentially "born into the movies."

Halsey was the eldest of five children. His brothers were Edward, Jr., Douglas and Gordon, and his sister was Patricia. Halsey would not be that close to them for years because he was away working in other countries. His sister died in her sleep ("the kind of death I would like," said Halsey) and Edward, Jr. died of "walking pneumonia" which he neglected.

As a boy, Halsey loved the smell of tar. He sometimes tore a strip of fresh tar and chewed it like tobacco. His love of the smell still remains. Walking down Pico Boulevard in 2005, Halsey led me over to a lorry with lumps of soft tar for road repairs and broke a little piece off and rubbed it between his forefinger and thumb. I pointed out that tar was carcinogenic and Halsey reflected ruefully on the years he had chewed it as a boy, remembering too how he used to hold a wad of tobacco under his tongue when he was breaking horses for his father, in emulation of other ranch hands.

Douglas recalled another embarrassing incident from Halsey's youth. Halsey told the story: "Dad bought a donkey for the kids but it was a mean sonofabitch and wouldn't let anyone ride him. It was so bad-tempered, one day Dad hit the donkey on the head with his fist. It died. So I had to bury it. But I didn't dig the hole deep enough. That was awful. I had to chop the legs off." Halsey grimaced at the memory.

Halsey and his father had issues and Halsey was to be closer to his stepfather, Jim, when Rose eventually remarried.

Sadly, Halsey's father Edward died before he signed his contract with Universal. Halsey once said, "My father was always against my being an actor." Halsey's father, who had been ill for the last several years, was living at 438 Newport Blvd., Costa Mesa, when he died at the young age of 38 from hypertension and high blood pressure, which in those days were not aggressively treated as they are today. He died at St. Joseph Hospital and was buried in Westminster Memorial Park. His mother, Mrs. A.H. Hand of Anchorage, Alaska, survived him.

Admiral William F. Halsey

On his father's side, Halsey's family originally came over with the Hudson's Bay party from England, before the pilgrims landed. Through them, Halsey is related to a distinguished line of Americans: a naval captain who served under George Washington, a famous jurist called Augustus Hand, a Civil War doctor also named Augustus Hand, who had a town in Illinois named after him, a famous judge, Justice Learned Hand and, most notably, Admiral William F. "Bull" Halsey, his great-uncle from whom he derived his stage name: "Admiral William F. Halsey is my paternal grandfather's first cousin."

Once Halsey enjoyed the glory when the Admiral turned up to have lunch with him while he was in Arizona for Columbia's Tab Hunter film *Gunman's Walk* (made in 1958 after Halsey left Universal). The studio top brass were envious of this little-known actor who did not even warrant a screen credit in the picture. In fact, although Halsey was present throughout the shooting, he is only really visible in the background once, when Tab Hunter is being accused of edging the half-breed off the cliff.

Admiral William F. Halsey
Below: Admiral Halsey (left) visits Brett Halsey (right) on the set of *Gunman's Walk*.

Art or Instinct in the Movies...

School Days

Due to his father's work, Halsey went to many different schools up and down the California coast: "I started school when I was four—kindergarten, that is." Halsey once commented, "I used to say I was older, because, starting school early I was always with an older group." He started grammar school in Long Beach and went to mostly Los Angeles grammar schools. He attended nine high schools, one twice, as a freshman and a senior. He was at Aptos Junior High School in 1947. At 15, he was attending Tomales High School, north of San Francisco, where he acted in a school play, *Strictly Formal,* by William Davidson. Halsey played Jim, Sally's boyfriend. A girl called Genelle Williams played Sally.

Program for the high school play *Strictly Formal*

It was the school plays that gave Halsey the acting bug: "I played in grammar school plays, high school plays, sometimes lead in high school plays, sometimes character or bits or walk-ons." His earliest role was as King Midas in a church play while he was in kindergarten. He told *TV Guide*: "I was just five years old but I can still remember the powerful feeling it gave me to be pretending I was someone else. I didn't realize it at the time, but I know now that it was right then and there that I became an actor." From that point, he wanted to be an actor and "as time went by, I acted in school plays, and even sang in various talent contests."

Halsey's best subjects at school were English Literature and social sciences and his worst was mathematics. He lettered in football, basketball and track, where he received minor injuries, but nothing serious.

Halsey's final school was Lincoln High in San Francisco, from which he graduated in 1950, aged 16. Unusually, Halsey also graduated at the same time from Santa Cruz High School near his home in Rio del Mar. Halsey explained,

"This fact is reported in both high school yearbooks. The truth is that my family moved from San Francisco to Santa Cruz, shortly before graduation time. Therefore, I officially graduated from both schools." The entry for Halsey in the Lincoln High School Senior Class June 1950 Yearbook is amusing: "…'Charlie' likes women, football, movies…ambition is to be a nightclub entertainer…dislikes school…Variety Show."

Abraham Lincoln High School in San Francisco

Halsey's future is there in microcosm: his reputation as a lady-killer, his love of moviemaking, his desire to be more of an entertainer than a classical actor, his aversion to the academic in favor of more spontaneous self-expression. And success would not take long.

Halsey almost went into singing rather than acting, he recalled: "First time I ever appeared on a stage alone, I sang. It was in a Tomales High School talent contest. I won a $10 gift certificate." In his teens, Halsey thought he wanted to be a singer and took singing lessons in San Francisco from Bill Hayes. But he changed his mind in due course: "After I became an actor, I didn't like the way singers lived. They're on the road, so I kind of scrubbed that as an ambition." He did have a good voice, "but I think it's something you have to be driven to do. It's a really difficult life."

He never sang in public again, despite making some musical shorts at Universal and a French musical comedy, *Bang Bang*. He limited himself to fooling around with a guitar and ukulele, occasional singing at parties, sometimes only in a group and, while in the Navy, singing duets, calypso and rock 'n' roll with roommate Don Kennedy, also an actor, A Paramount biography of Halsey relating to the film *Anyone Can Play* (1967) claimed Halsey's singing won him "a big reputation among the personnel at the base."

First Work Experiences

At six years old, Halsey earned his very first dollar by working in the family's garden. During WWII for about a year he lived in Concord, across the bay from San Francisco. After school he did odd jobs and cleaned up at a local newspaper office. Concord is about six miles from Port Chicago. On July 17, 1944, Halsey was blown out of bed by the Port Chicago ammunitions explosion:

> During the war, they used to load ammunition ships in Port Chicago. One of the loaders got a little careless and apparently dropped a bomb, or dropped something he was carrying, and three ships just blew up and blew the whole city. Port Chicago was destroyed. Fortunately, there was a small range of hills between the two. It would have destroyed Concord as well, except for this range of hills. At the newspaper, the linotype machine was in the window and it blew the window out. It blew all the windows out. But the linotype machine was full of shards of broken glass. The job I had for three or four days was picking broken glass out of the linotype machine. It was the worst job I had there.

In high school he worked for his father as a horse trainer. His father raised show horses as a hobby. Halsey recalled, "I was thrown more times than I can recall but only broke my arm once and sprained my shoulder a couple of times. I was thrown the first time when I was five years old. I was 12 when my arm was broken." His father also had racing sailboats and Halsey crewed on his boats when he was about 14.

In his teens, Halsey was a Standard Oil gas station attendant in Newport Beach (the gas station is now gone). He had a wide variety of jobs: as a soda jerk on summer vacations from school in San Francisco; clearing brush stumps of trees; in the Hotel Rio del Mar, near Santa Cruz, California, as an assistant manager without the title, doing everything—desk clerk, bellhop, lifeguard, even in charge of the kitchen for three or four days.

His most unusual job was one he couldn't tell his parents about: "One summer I had a job as an usher at a burlesque house on Main St. in L.A.—it was called the Burbank in those days, it's now the New Follies. I was 15 at the time and it was a liberal but not highbrow education."

Burbank Theatre

Early Interest in Show Business

Halsey has written his own memoir of his early interest in show business:

> Back when I was eight or nine years of age, my family was living in Laurel Canyon, in the Hollywood Hills. My best friend, and school mate, Danny McLaughlin, was a nearby neighbor. One evening he called me on the phone to tell me that Dagwood (Arthur Lake) had come to their house for dinner. I, of course, didn't believe such an incredible statement. Dagwood and Blondie were among the biggest stars in my make-believe universe. *Blondie* was one of those weekly radio serials that, like *Jack Benny* and *Fibber McGee and Molly*, gathered the entire family around the radio. It had also become a popular Saturday afternoon movie series. I saw them all.
>
> After a stream of "Yes, he is," "No, he isn't," exchanges, I asked for proof. I insisted that Danny put the great man on the phone and identify himself. After a suspenseful pause, a vaguely familiar voice came on the line. "Yes, I really am Dagwood," the voice cheerfully assured. I still couldn't believe it. I suddenly remembered that Dagwood's signature was the way he would yell plaintively for his wife, "BLONDIE!" whenever he was in difficulty. At that time, Dagwood's "BLONDIE!" and Tarzan's thunderous jungle yell were equally well-known to America's vast radio-listening public. So I blurted out, "If you really are Dagwood, give a yell for Blondie." Danny's parents later told mine that he gave such a full-voice yell that their neighbors must have thought their radios were playing some sort of trick on them.
>
> I have to confess that, at that moment, I didn't understand how or why, but I was convinced that the great star, Dagwood Bumstead, really was on the other end of the line—but, being the little conniver that I was, I pushed for further proof. I asked him for tickets to his show...for many years my most prized possession was Arthur Lake's hand-written note that allowed me and my party to attend a performance of *Blondie* at the CBS Radio Center. I can never forget how, after the show, he graciously shook my hand and introduced me to Blondie (Penny Singleton), Mr. Dithers (Hanley Stafford) and some of the other cast members. I don't know how anyone else might have reacted, but this eight-year-old little boy was starry-eyed for days afterward.

In the Navy

Growing up in Newport Beach, Halsey first wanted to be connected with the water, either as a lifeguard or on the Harbor Patrol: "I didn't really know what being an actor was, but I knew I wanted to be one and never lost that ambition, though there was a time I considered a naval career, but only briefly." His brother Douglas recalls that Halsey was once literally connected with the water when he fell in the harbor. Halsey explained: "I had signed on as a deck seaman for a cruise ship to Tahiti. I had the job. On Sunday I took a girl out to the boat but I fell off the raft. I didn't know it but the skipper was watching. He said 'What are you doing bringing a girl on board?' I was fired for bringing a girl on board."

When Halsey was drafted, he chose the Navy rather than the Army, perhaps because of his memories of crewing aboard his father's racing sailboats.

After basic training, the recruits were sent to the Airman's School in Jacksonville, Florida, for naval air training. Halsey recalled how green they all were: "For breakfast, we were served eggs, bacon and grits, but no one ever showed us how to eat grits—with butter. No one knew what they were. At the end of breakfast, 200 guys got up, all with the grits on the plate."

One event Halsey vividly remembers is getting his nose broken by a Marine in a barroom brawl. His friend Don Rader got up and decked the Marine. When they left, they realized they could not go back to the base: "We knew the Marines were on guard duty back at the base. The Marines guarded the air stations and they'd be waiting for us, so we had to wait until there was a shift change."

While in the Navy, Halsey was able to indulge his performing interests by becoming a radio disc jockey. In boot camp Halsey found a friend in Ed Smith, who had been a radio announcer in San Francisco. When Halsey was stationed in Memphis, Tennessee, Smith lied about Halsey's experience, which opened the door for him to become a disc jockey at the Navy radio station there. They gave Halsey a spot as staff announcer and Smith taught Halsey the ropes before his inexperience could be discovered. Halsey later reflected that this solidified his ambition to try for a career in show business.

Nothing technical at Navy Radio Station WRTI was required of him, just sit at the microphone, play pop music records and read station announcements and news. He also got to choose some music. This job lasted about a year of his two years' service.

Halsey had actually been assigned to a ship but wound up never serving on it. His ship went to Korea and earned ribbons for all the crew. Halsey noted, "I got all the ribbons, but didn't go." Halsey was lucky; when entertainer Dick Contino refused to go to Korea, his career was ruined.

When his two years in the Navy were up, Halsey went home to Newport Beach. He was not quite 19. He recalled, "I bought a sailboat and lived on that for about six months. I worked for my uncle now and then doing construction work. I had an offer to work on a radio station in Alaska." Halsey did not think, however, that Alaska was likely to provide the opportunities he sought: "I didn't want to go to Alaska. I wanted to work in the U.S., so I felt I needed a little more education and went to the Don Martin School of Radio and Television Arts and Sciences in Hollywood." He did this with the help of the G.I. Bill. There he studied, among other things, to be an engineer.

Later in his career, Halsey made two submarine pictures for director Spencer Bennett, who had helmed many Saturday morning serials. He recalled him only as "extremely efficient." Asked if his naval experience was of any use in these pictures, Halsey said, "No, not at all," because he had never gone to sea.

Early Acting Jobs

Halsey has described what led up to his first big break into show business after leaving the Navy:

> Those were pretty lean times. Having lost my bag with all my civilian clothing, my wardrobe was pretty thin. I had no money for anything except school supplies. My Aunt Claudia allowed me to live in a converted shack in the back of her home in North Hollywood. I drove a tired but functional old, green, Ford sedan. I worked for a short time at a parking lot; then I lucked into an after-school job as a page at the CBS Radio headquarters on Sunset Boulevard in Hollywood. A page is a uniformed usher who is responsible for herding audiences into the radio shows, as well as serving the talent and other higher-ups at CBS.

This put the good-looking Halsey in the right place to get noticed. His agent Dick Clayton once said to Halsey, "You know, you're too pretty. You'll have to wait until you mature to get the good parts."

There were other pages just as ambitious, Halsey reminisces:

> I remember once when we had a show that didn't attract an audience, one of my more enterprising colleagues, Robert Vaughn, went down the block to the NBC studio and stole an entire line of fans waiting for an NBC show and marched them back to CBS. He was, of course, fired, but was quietly rehired after NBC's rage had abated. This was, of course, the Robert Vaughn who went on to enjoy a long, successful career as a film actor.

Postcard, c. late 1940s, showing CBS, Columbia Square

Robert Vaughn commented, "Actually, I think I resigned, but after all this time, who cares?.." Halsey remembered Vaughn as "very determined—he wanted a career. I liked him. He was so determined to make it, I thought he would, him and Robert Dix, son of Richard

The 1960 Golden Globe Awards were attended by a multitude of young Hollywood actors including: (LtoR) Brett Halsey, Mark Damon, Peter Falk, Robert Vaughn and Michael Callan.

Dix, the Western actor, but he—Robert Dix—left the business years ago." Robert Vaughn, in turn, remembered Halsey as "a sweet guy, Chuck Hand." Vaughn in fact predicted right away, based on Halsey's looks, that Halsey would get a contract soon. Robert's own break took longer but when Robert received an Oscar nomination in 1959 for *The Young Philadelphians*, Halsey attended the Oscar ceremony at Pantages Theatre in Hollywood: "I was sitting with Robert's mother at the Oscar ceremony. I remember the electricity of sitting beside the mother of an Oscar nominee. She was thrilled he was up for an Oscar."

First Big Break

Halsey has written a charming account of his first big break:

> My page salary wasn't much ($16 a week). I could afford a moderately priced restaurant meal only once a week. *But*...CBS, with its stable of America's favorite stars, was an introduction to the show business world that I had only dreamed of becoming a part of.
>
> I was 19 years of age, with very little knowledge of the ways of the world, and almost totally on my own. My father had recently died and my mother and siblings were in far more need of help than I was. Acting in the movies was my ultimate goal but, at the time, that seemed to be as unattainable a goal as becoming President of the United States. I made a tentative plan. After finishing school, I would work at a radio station until I could find an opening in television. From television, I would somehow springboard into the movies. It wasn't much of a plan, but it was the best I could come up with at the time.
>
> I was thrilled when my existence was acknowledged by such stars as Jack Benny and his wife Mary Livingston, even when it was only a friendly nod and hello in passing. Between school and work, I didn't have much time or money for socializing, so I spent much of my free time watching the production of CBS's comedy and dramatic shows, as well as participating in the CBS radio workshop.
>
> A major turning point came one Sunday when my crew boss said that I was to work the sponsor's booth during that night's *Jack Benny Show*. The sponsor's booth is a private room, apart from the general audience, situated above the stage with a large picture window giving its VIP guests a clear and comfortable view of the action below. When I asked my crew boss why I was selected for this particular honor, he gruffly replied that Mary Livingston had requested it, and left it at that. After a few minutes, Mary appeared. In retrospect, I realized that she had an excited gleam in her eye as she smiled, then turned to introduce me to a distinguished gentleman whose name I didn't catch. Mary continued smiling as I politely acknowledged the introduction, and then escorted the man to his seat. I didn't see Mary or Jack after the show because I was called away to other duties as soon as the broadcast was finished. The incident was tucked away in the recesses of my memory as I hurried home

after the show to work on my homework assignments, which were due the next day, Monday morning.

Monday was a fairly uneventful day. The following Tuesday morning, I was called into the school office and informed that I was to call the casting office at Universal-International Pictures for an audition. I was flabbergasted. I soon learned that no one at the school was responsible. I called a new friend, Dick Clayton, who was just beginning his career as a movie agent. Dick didn't know anything about it, but told me to go—and don't be late.

I didn't own a proper business suit, so I dressed myself in my meager best, and drove to the studio in Universal City, which is just over the hill from Hollywood—arriving early. I'll never forget what an overwhelming experience it was to enter, for the first time, a real, gigantic, world-renowned movie studio. I had no trouble finding the casting office where a casting assistant quickly ushered me into the office of the head of all studio casting, Robert Palmer. In my confusion, I was beyond nervous as I responded to his questions. Palmer wasn't very impressed by my admission that I had no professional film-acting experience, and not even any current professional or non-professional theater experience either. He said he would like for me to read—to perform an audition scene. His enthusiasm waned a bit more when I explained that the only scenes I had were from radio plays and had learned none by heart. "Okay," he said, "Come back tomorrow at 2.00 p.m., and bring one of your radio scenes."

Again, I questioned everyone I knew, trying to find out how and why Universal was interested in *me*. No one had the slightest clue. Radio scenes generally aren't designed to be performed as visual art, but a radio scene was all I had, so I prepared it as best I could. At two o'clock sharp I was nervously standing in the waiting room of the Universal casting department. After a few moments, I was called into the big man's office. I immediately began by trying to explain about the drawbacks of performing a radio scene, but Mr. Robert Palmer made a waving gesture for me to stop talking. I closed my mouth and wondered what was coming next. "Don't worry about the scene, kid," he began. "We've decided to put you under contract and enroll you in our new talent program." Again, I was stunned. My mind whirled, trying to figure out this extremely unusual turn of events. I knew things were a bit crazy in Hollywood, and because of my inexperience and any real knowledge of the way things work, I decided that, crazy as it sounds, this must be normal for these people. After all, wasn't it true that Lana Turner was discovered sitting on a stool at the soda fountain of Schwab's Drugstore, and put under contract at MGM?

The next day, the first thing I did was quit my job at CBS, and then things began in earnest. In spite of everything else, my curiosity was getting the best of me. All this may have been normal Hollywood procedure, but I had my doubts, so I went back to Mr. Palmer and asked him why he had decided to put me under contract without even so much as a scene reading. He looked at me a moment before answering that *he didn't know*. "Oh," I replied, then fumbled a "thank you," and backed out of his office. I was taken to meet the head of the New Talent program, Sophie Rosenstein, as well as the folks in publicity, and many others. Dick Clayton negotiated my contract, which had to be approved by the court because I was still a minor. I was paid the magnificent sum of $100 per week. That sounded like a lot of money in those days (Clint Eastwood, who signed a couple of months later, started at $75) but, in the end, my net was so small, I just barely made it. First of all, the $100 was to be paid for only 40 weeks, so to have a constant cash flow, they prorated the money over 52 weeks. Then, they had to advance me the money to join the Screen Actors Guild, plus enough more so that I could buy a half-decent wardrobe. The studio insisted that their actors had to look like young movie stars are supposed to look.

A couple of weeks went by before Mr. Palmer called me again into his office. He asked me if I remembered the man Mary Livingston had introduced me to at CBS? "Sure," I replied. "Do you remember his name?" "No," I answered honestly. "Well, his name is William Goetz. In addition to being a close friend of the Bennys, he is the head of this studio. It was at the Bennys' suggestion that he told me to sign you the way I did."

There is much more to the Universal story, but that's the way it happened and it's true stories like this that keep so many young people's Hollywood dreams alive.

Universal Studios

Halsey signed with Universal in October 1952, but because he was technically under age he had to go to court for approval of the seven-year contract. Halsey appeared before the court along with 17-year-old actress Marla English, who had signed with Paramount for seven years, also at $100 a week. Superior Judge Frank G. Swain approved Halsey's contract and made an order for him to save 10% of his weekly salary. Halsey was quoted saying his friends all called him "Chuck." The contract approvals for Halsey and Marla came through in December and various Los Angeles newspapers featured the pair. Halsey recalls that he had a terrible flu that day.

It was Universal's publicity department that came up with the name Brett Halsey. Al Horwitz, the Universal-International publicity director at that time, did not feel that Charlie Hand or Chuck Hand had the right ring for a leading man and felt some mileage could be gotten out of Halsey's family connection to Admiral Halsey. Halsey did not mind. He felt it "sounded good." In 1961 he legally changed his name and all his children would have the surname Halsey. In a Fox resume from 1961 he remembered the name took some getting used to: "When I first changed my name at UI, people would come up and introduce

New Universal contractee Brett Halsey in an early studio portrait poses with beauty queen Miss Colombia.

Art or Instinct in the Movies...

HAPPY NEWCOMERS

Joyous over their contract approvals today are Marla English, 17, and Charles Hand, 20. Miss English, from San Diego, starts at $100 a week with Paramount. Hand, from Santa Ana, will earn a similar amount from Universal-International. He was "discovered" by Jack Benny while working as an usher at CBS in Hollywood.

themselves to me and say 'Hello, I'm Joe Blow,' and I'd shake hands and say 'I'm…'and then got stuck, couldn't remember my new name—Brett Halsey."

The Talent School groomed Halsey for stardom. "We did a five-and-a half day week—diction, fencing, dance, horseback riding."

Universal portrait (1952)

Diction teacher Dr. Vandrogen is fondly remembered by Halsey: "Clint and I were talking about him recently. He was excellent. One of the things he would do for us, as a diction coach, is—we would read Shakespeare, but most of us didn't understand Shakespeare, so he would do more than coach us in diction, he would *translate* it for us. He was very good and well-liked." Jack Kosslyn was an acting teacher. "Jack was well-liked too. Jack was a good teacher." Clint would later give him parts in his movies.

Halsey got on very well with acting coach Katherine Warren: "She was an excellent teacher, really. As a matter of fact, when Clint won the Oscar for *Unforgiven*, I had a thing made up from 'The Katherine Warren School of Acting'."

Robert Palmer was head of the talent program. "He was very good. When I was at Fox, he was also at Fox. He went from Universal to Fox and he told me once, 'Our group at Universal was extremely unusual in the history of show business.' He said 'In this style of program if one out of a hundred of the students even stay in the business, we considered it to be a success.' And he said 'Our group, *most* of the people made it.' He said it was just extremely unusual. He wasn't a teacher. He was an executive. He was a very kind, helpful man."

Patrick McGilligan, in his biography of Clint, cited John Saxon as being regarded as the most promising of the group, but Halsey did not think so: "I don't think John was singled out. He had a lot of demons. He was very likeable, I remember. There was an actor they got behind called Race Gentry but when he left the studio, he left the business. He didn't like it. Acting embarrassed him." David Janssen was also one of the students. "He had a Clark Gable thing." He later worked with Halsey in a Universal musical short and in William Wellman's Warner Bros. picture *Lafayette Escadrille*. Halsey did class exercises with future cult actress Allison Hayes (*Attack of the 50 Ft.*

Woman) and knew Rod McKuen, who later became a famous poet and singer. Another actress, who he prefers not to name, "gave a social disease to each and every one of the male contract players during her first week under contract."

Halsey does not know whether he was regarded as promising. "I have no idea, because no one ever discussed anything with me. No one ever told me anything. Shortly before they let me go, I'd done a play and I got really good reviews for the play, so I left on a career 'up'."

Overall, Halsey's time at Universal was happy and he kept his original contract. Halsey mentioned to Clint he had found it recently, and Clint said "Yeah, I still have mine, too."

The students were assigned to small parts in pictures as part of the training program and also used as stand-ins for camera rehearsals and so on. The beginning actors would be called through the office and have to audition for the director, but the process was different than for contract players, as the directors were *told* to use the students. The students' salary was charged to the movie. Only if they were completely wrong for the part would they not get the job.

None of the movies Halsey made at Universal did much for his resume. Usually the roles in good movies were too small (*Revenge of the Creature, To Hell and Back*) or the films themselves were not much to write home about, although he started (if we discount his appearance in a Universal musical short) quite respectably by working for the acclaimed director Douglas Sirk in a more sizeable part than he later had in some pictures.

In *All I Desire* (1953), which was originally titled *Stopover*, much of the time Halsey can be seen smiling. He commented:

> It may have been just nervousness that I'm smiling a lot. I didn't know. Anyhow, I was really green. I was thinking about this the other day. We did a lot of tests for 3-D. They used the student actors for everything. I remember once there was a scene. It wasn't really a scene. They had a line of actors and they were just going down the line and I remember when I could feel that the camera was on me, I was so embarrassed. And then, afterwards, I thought "No, that's not what you're supposed to do."

All I Desire was a quality start to Halsey's cinema career. Halsey remembers a humbling moment in the high school play scene he shared with Stuart Whitman:

> Douglas Sirk said to Stuart Whitman and me at the end of the picture, talking about our performance in the high school play, "I have to congratulate you boys. One of the hardest things that

there is for an actor is to play a bad actor. You guys played it really well." We were both acting our hearts out.

Halsey learned work ethic and professionalism on the *All I Desire* shoot. He and Stuart Whitman had been on set in makeup since 8 a.m. and had not been called, so they went to the commissary for lunch at 12:30. Five minutes later, an angry assistant director recalled them to the set. Douglas Sirk stood on the high school stage and read them the riot act about being on time. Halsey vowed never to leave the set without permission again.

In 1953, Halsey was in the running for a role in Jesse Hibbs' film *The All American,* about college football heroes, starring Universal Talent School graduate Tony Curtis and Halsey's fellow student Mamie Van Doren. Halsey didn't get the part but Hibbs would later cast him in *To Hell and Back* (1955).

Halsey used his time at Universal to learn everything he could about the business. He was constantly sneaking onto soundstages and watching movies being shot. The directors never seemed to mind, and some encouraged him. Director Budd Boetticher took a liking to Halsey and was particularly helpful:

> He liked me. I never knew why he liked me. I learned from Budd. He was one of my kind of mentors. He sent me to bullfight school. When I first went to Universal, Budd was directing *East of Sumatra* (1953) starring Jeff Chandler. He let me observe. He would teach me things.

Halsey learned the importance of economy and preparation from watching working directors like Budd:

> He didn't *talk* to me about acting. He liked to just joke around. He was a great practical joker, sometimes a little cruel. I remember once that there was [an] actor he didn't like very much, [who was]playing an Arab. [He was wearing] robes, and in one scene Budd set fire to his costume. So, my relationship with him wasn't professor/student, no. I was certainly a fan. I just really liked him as a man. He was just a macho man. That was his interest in bullfighting, that he wanted to be macho.

Budd later made a documentary about the famous bullfighter Arruzza. Halsey also admired the matador: "Arruzza was great. He fought on horseback."

Halsey would make 13 pictures at Universal. Some of the more unique Universal titles on Halsey's resume are the musical short subjects he did with Harry James (*Leave it to Harry*), Andy and Della Russell (called simply *Andy and Della Russell*) and the Four Aces. Halsey recalled his first professional acting job for his fan club newsletter (#1 July-August 1977):

> I was in a musical short. [He thinks this one may have been called *Ray Anthony*, starring, unsurprisingly, Ray Anthony.] Universal used to make a lot of them. In this particular one, other students in the school were also in it. There was Stuart Whitman, David Janssen and the Swedish actress Anita Ekberg. A few weeks after that, I was in a movie called *All I Desire*.

Halsey picked up knowledge of the ins and outs of filmmaking during his days at Universal.

> In the old days, with film, you needed a lot of light, a lot more light than film needs now. I only did it once, but one of my early pictures at Universal [*The Glass Web*] where I had a small part was with the old Technicolor 3-strip camera. The camera was a monster and you couldn't move it. The dolly for that camera is like a train track. 'Cos it's a big, heavy thing and it needed a lot of light. So, you can shoot now with so little light. When I was shooting *Million Dollar Baby* in 2004, I didn't wear any makeup and normally, when I started out, makeup was generally so skin colors would be approximately the same for the photography. So it's easy now to shoot in light locations.

Halsey's contract was first up every six months, then every year. In 1954, after two years, Halsey's contract was not renewed because the Universal Talent School was disbanded due to a decline in the picture business. Clint Eastwood was also let go. Both found it a blow to the ego. It meant Halsey had to freelance, instead of being assigned to pictures. His agent Dick Clayton now had to find auditions for him. It would be five years before he would again be under contract, this time at 20th Century-Fox. Meanwhile, he would appear in an large number of television productions and B movies where he could refine his acting.

Art or Instinct in the Movies...

33

Ma and Pa Kettle at Home (Universal, 1954)

Ma and Pa Kettle at Home was Halsey's first big role as the juvenile lead and he has fond memories of the film:

> Really, it was a wonderful experience. He [Percy Kilbride, who played Pa Kettle] was just the most wonderful man to work with...and helpful. I was late to work one day. It was because my clock screwed up, not me, and he was telling a story about how he's never been late...as a matter of fact, he would reminisce. And the way he speaks in the film is the way he spoke in life, that slow drawl. And he would say, "I remember once I went to do a matinee and this terrible thing happened, the big fire, and I thought the world was coming to an end and I got to the theater and the theater was down, so I stood around there. Nobody came, so I guessed we weren't going to do the play." Even though the theater was in rubble and it was the San Francisco earthquake of 1906.
>
> He didn't drive. He never learned to drive. The studio would send a car for him. He was killed walking across Hollywood Boulevard.

Marjorie Main had a lengthy film career playing irascible but loveable characters. Halsey remembers her working on *Ma and Pa Kettle at Home*: "She was not a very happy woman. She had some kidney problems, so in her contract the honey wagon had to be never more than a few feet from the set so that she could run. She wasn't nasty. She just wasn't pleasant, probably because she didn't feel well...and Alan Mowbray, this Englishman, he was such fun." Halsey has sweet romantic scenes with actress Alice Kelley "who retired immediately afterward," he recalled.

It is very difficult to imagine an innocent picture like *Ma and Pa Kettle at Home* being successful today. Halsey explained:

Alice Kelley and Halsey in a posed publicity shot for *Ma and Pa Kettle at Home*

That was the substitute for television. These films were a Saturday afternoon. I remember asking the producer once, "Why didn't you spend an extra few dollars?" to do something, and he

The Ma and Pa Kettle films were a huge success for Universal.

said, "Listen, we know how much these films are going to earn right down to the penny." He said, "We could spend another thousand dollars, or a thousand dollars less, wouldn't matter. These films are going to make X thousand dollars." And they were very successful.

Today, the Ma and Pa Kettle series seems particularly dated. Halsey is effective enough in the role of the naïve but personable son and makes a stronger impression than he did in *All I Desire*.

On the Stage

Halsey was not fond of stage work and was not comfortable learning lines. He felt it was not for him, but he did tread the boards occasionally.

Halsey was given three weeks' leave by Universal to appear in a play. *The Vacant Lot* was a contemporary drama about teenagers in a Southwestern U.S. city. It was written by Paul Streger and Berrilla Kerr, produced by John Swope and directed by former actor and Hitchcock associate Norman Lloyd. *The Vacant Lot* ran at the La Jolla Playhouse as a two-week (August 25-September 5, 1954) tryout for Broadway. Dorothy McGuire, who was a member of the Playhouse board of producers, found the play for them. She was married to John Swope, who was a famous photographer and theatrical producer and the first cousin of television producer Herbert Swope. Halsey would later live with his daughter Tracy Brooks Swope, who remembered John: "Uncle John gave Warren Beatty his first job. John and Dorothy called themselves my aunt and uncle, but he was actually my father's first cousin." The cast included Eliot Englehardt, Jeff Silver, Alan Dinehart III and Cindy Robbins. Halsey later (1961) looked back on *The Vacant Lot*: "It wasn't a good play, but it was a good part. I had the kind of light comedy role I'd love to do on the screen."

Newspaper clipping promoting *The Vacant Lot*. Pictured front (l to r): Jeff Silver, Cindy Robbins; standing in back (l to r) Alan Dinehart, III, Eliot Englehardt and Brett Halsey

A contemporary L.A. press notice previewing the play specifically mentions Halsey: "Brett Halsey, whose resemblance to Gregory Peck and Gary Cooper have led many to hail him as a star of the future."

Art or Instinct in the Movies...

'Vacant Lot' Will Open at La Jolla

The world premiere and initial pre-Broadway showing of "The Vacant Lot," play by Paul Streger and Berrilla Kerr, is scheduled at La Jolla Playhouse Tuesday night for a two-week run.

Discovered by Dorothy McGuire, a member of the Playhouse board of producers, during her recent visit to New York, "The Vacant Lot" is being produced by her husband, John Swope, and directed by Norman Lloyd.

Offbeat Drama

On offbeat dramatic piece, "The Vacant Lot" is based upon the activities of a group of teen-agers in a southwestern city of the United States. Swope and Miss McGuire have gathered young actors whose talents give promise of long success.

For the two feminine parts they have cast Eliot Englehardt and Cindy Robbins, who flew to the Coast for the play, the latter giving up a role in the Shirley Booth hit, "By the Beautiful Sea," to appear in La Jolla.

Others in Cast

Also in the cast are three young men who have already made their mark in Hollywood: Alan Dinehart III, son of the character actor of the same name; Brett Halsey, whose resemblance to Gregory Peck and Gary Cooper have led many to hail him as a star of the future, and Jeff Silver, who at 17 has appeared in more than 1500 radio and 200 TV shows.

"The Vacant Lot" is slated for Broadway if its La Jolla production meets the test. "The Seven Year Itch," starring Don Taylor, Kathleen Hughes and Willard Waterman, will have its closing performance at the La Jolla tonight.

QUINTET — "Vacant Lot," a new play, will star, top to bottom, Alan Dinehart II, Brett Halsey, Eliot Englehardt, Jeff Silver and Cindy Robbins at La Jolla Playhouse starting Tuesday.

As it turned out, Eliot Englehardt never appeared and the *L.A. Times* (August 27, 1954) felt this had a negative effect on the play, which never made it to Broadway, though they did praise Halsey's performance: *"The Vacant Lot* played in bad luck through losing its original feminine straight lead, Eliot Englehardt, due to illness. She had to be replaced within 48 hours by Sara Harte, who could not conceivably carry off a very difficult role to the best advantage…Jeff Silver gave a surprisingly bright comedy portrayal, while Brett Halsey showed himself a thoroughly capable young actor throughout…Each of the young players appeared to register a positiveness [sic]about what he or she was doing which was salutary." Halsey became the most well known of the cast, although Cindy Robbins was later a popular singer.

The reviews for *The Vacant Lot* raised Halsey's stock at Universal, although he would soon leave the studio.

Marriage Go Round

In 1954, Halsey married Renate Hoy, a former Miss Germany, who would be the first of a number of glamorous partners. She was born in Ludwigshafen, Germany. Halsey met her when she was in the U.S. for the Miss Universe contest. He was obviously smitten—he went to Germany to persuade her to return to the U.S. as his wife. She was 22 and Halsey was 21 when they wed and had a brief honeymoon in Europe. Their first home was on Argyle Street in Hollywood. The couple would have two children, Charles Oliver and Tracy Leigh, who was named after actress Janet Leigh.

Tracy got her middle name from Janet Leigh, "because Janet and Tony Curtis are good friends, have been ever since my second picture *Walking My Baby Back Home* (1953), in which Janet starred and I just played a soldier in it, but Janet was so helpful to me on that picture, we've been friends ever since." Janet Leigh passed away October 3, 2004.

Miss Universe 1952 winners: Renate Hoy, representing Germany (fourth from the left) was the fourth runner up.

The marriage lasted five years and Renate later told *TV Guide* that being married to Halsey "was like raising a child." Halsey smiled when reminded of this and said, "I don't think she has ever said anything too bad," and is still on friendly terms with her. Today he recalls with amusement how he was surprised when actor Hugh O'Brian was once "hitting on Renate" because he "seemed old." O'Brian was then 28.

Halsey's first child, Charles Oliver Hand, Jr., was born on February 5, 1956 at Queen of Angels Hospital in Los Angeles. Renate and baby were photographed for the *Los Angeles Examiner* but Halsey was not there because he was on location in Costa Rica, a country he would come to love and which would later loom large in his life.

Luciana Paluzzi was to become Halsey's second wife. She was the only child of a retired Italian Army officer and had no ambitions to be an actress when she was signed to play Rossano Brazzi's little sister in *Three Coins in a Fountain*, which was her first part. She told Hedda Hopper (*L.A. Times*, July 26, 1959): "I

Art or Instinct in the Movies...

was studying to become a marine engineer at the Scientific Lyceum at Milano. I was also taking ballet at La Scala. A strange combination, but I think I would have been the first woman naval engineer had I stuck with it."

Luciana had little dramatic training. She went for about six months to a school in Rome operated by an Italian-American who had studied at the Actors Studio. Luciana made her way first to England, where she acted with Stanley Baker in Cy Endfield's *Sea Fury*, and then to Hollywood. Television producer Herbert B. Swope saw a screen test of Luciana and cast her when he was assigned to produce the series *Five Fingers*, based on the novel *Operation Cicero* by L.C. Moyzisch. The novel had previously been filmed in 1952 by Joseph L. Mankiewicz with James Mason.

Luciana told the press how she met Halsey through his friend Gardner McKay:

> Where did I find time to fall in love? Well, I had a few hours off one Sunday, and Gardner McKay—he works next door in another TV series *Adventures in Paradise*—asked me to come to his house for a party. I went, and met Brett Halsey. He's an actor on this same lot. We started going together between scenes. I guess that's how we fell in love.
>
> I don't mind working hard so long as I can fall into the arms of a man I love at the end of a day. What a wonderful country America is. I come here unknown and all of a sudden I am paid a good salary [$750 a week], I am made the star of a television show, and I find a tall, handsome, brilliant husband. All I need now is a little time to enjoy my good luck.

In 1960, Halsey bought a house at 2123 Ridgemont Drive, again in Laurel Canyon. It was "a California modern, on top of a hill, right on the border between Hollywood and Beverly Hills, two bedrooms, a den, three baths, living room, dining room, kitchen, no pool, no tennis court, but it's rather formal. Living room is done in earth tones, walls are white, beige carpeting, beige drapes, yellow couches, lot of wood, couple of mosaics tables I made myself with bronze and yellow and red mosaic. Bookcases and records are in the den. My bedroom is white and beige, super-king-size bed." Occupying a whole wall was his favorite possession, a four-by-six feet painting by Burt Shonburg, a Southern California painter, an impressionistic harbor scene, which possibly reminded Halsey of growing up in Newport Beach.

Renate had filed for divorce from Halsey in 1959. The decree was not granted until 1960 and, because of California law, the divorce was not final until approximately 1961. Halsey was free to marry Luciana in January 1960. Looking back, Halsey feels that he and Renate married too young and did not have enough in common. At the time, he told the *Sunday News* (November 26, 1961) that they "just didn't get along." For her part, Renate complained at the default divorce hearing that "he was out every night." Renate had always preferred the life of a beautician to that of an actress and began working at the studios as a hairdresser. Later she opened her own beauty salon. Halsey saw their children every week, often taking them to his Laurel Canyon home.

He married Luciana in Las Vegas just days after his final divorce papers came through, on January 25, 1960. All of Halsey's family turned out for the civil ceremony, which was performed by a federal judge at the Sands Hotel. Later, there was a church wedding because Luciana was Catholic. Ironically, Halsey's final divorce decree from Renate "hadn't been picked up," he told the *Los Angeles Mirror* (December 19, 1960), and they found they were not legally married after all and they had to get married all over again. Luciana moved into Halsey's new home in Ridgemont Drive.

Sadly, Halsey's marriage to Luciana soon fell apart and they separated after almost a year on November 10, 1960. Luciana returned home to Rome and cabled "Lt. Halsey" at Ridgemont Drive to inform him of the birth of a son, Christian, on June 13, 1961. Friends put it down to Luciana's mother, a typical Italian mother-in-law, being always there in the picture. Luciana denied Halsey access to Christian and they had no contact until he grew up. They now enjoy a warm relationship. Luciana was not too complimentary afterward but, after 15 years away from Los Angeles, Halsey bumped into her by chance in 2004 and visited her house.

Luciana Paluzzi appeared as Bond girl Fiona Volpe in *Thunderball* (1965).

After separating from Luciana, but before they divorced, Halsey briefly dated actress Barbara Steele.

Steele was set to play Halsey's wife in *Return to Peyton Place*, but Luciana went to producer Jerry Wald and complained, "She's trying to break up my

Art or Instinct in the Movies...

marriage" and bagged the role for herself. By the time they did the picture, they had been divorced, which made for an unusual situation. Halsey told Lee Belser of the *Los Angeles Mirror* (December 29, 1960), "We didn't speak to each other for the first three days. We finally got around to talking." Eventually, they became friendly and tried to repair the relationship. The sad thing is that they really were still strongly attracted to each other, but there were too many obstacles, including her mother Maria. Luciana was quoted in the *Los Angeles Mirror* (August 12, 1961): "Next time I will marry an Italian. We just could not get along. We had different views on family life. We had different educations."

In the divorce proceedings, Halsey told Superior Court Judge Roger Alton Pfaff that his mother-in-law trouble got so bad that he finally bodily threw Maria into the street and told her never to enter his house again. Luciana countered that Halsey went alone to the premiere of the movie *The Alamo* the night she told him she was pregnant and described Halsey as "very temperamental." It was a typical, bitter divorce, all the sadder because Halsey still liked Luciana. They also made history for being the first Italian divorce. Luciana explained to *The New York Post* (September 29, 1971): "My husband and I were first because our American divorce happened to be filed first in Italy. It was an exchange thing."

Halsey humorously tells of how two of his wives once joked about him: "Heidi and Luciana were on the same plane to Rome. They were friendly. Luciana said, 'If this plane goes down, the sonofabitch loses two wives.' She's funny, Luciana." Looking at photos of her in 2005, he said, "Good-looking girl. I always liked Luciana. Even though we divorced, we divorced because of her mother, who tried to break up our marriage from the very beginning. As a matter of fact, when her mother died, I called Luciana and I said, 'Shall I come to the funeral?' She said, 'No, you two hated each other, but I want your kids to come.' It was my son Clayton she meant, really." Indeed, even after their separation, Halsey nominated her in a 1961 profile as one of his favorite actresses: "I think Luciana Paluzzi, my former wife, is a very good actress. Very, very good."

Harrison Carroll reported Halsey's melancholia in the *Los Angeles Herald-Examiner* (March 20, 1961): "At the Foreign Press awards, Halsey was awarded a Golden Globe as one of the outstanding newcomers of the year. He came to the festivities alone. 'It would have meant a lot more,' he says, 'if Luciana had been with me.'"

They were finally divorced on March 19, 1962. Luciana, who had earned $20,000 that year and $30,000 the year before to Halsey's annual $50,000, waved alimony but accepted $200 monthly support for Christian.

Halsey began seeing Tyrone Power's widow, Debbie Power Loew, who was 29, and awaiting divorce from film executive Arthur Loew, Jr. Louella Parsons

Heidi Bruhl and Brett Halsey

reported in her *Los Angeles Herald-Examiner* column: "Before he left for Italy, Brett Halsey called to say that not only will he make two movies in Rome, he will be married to Debbie Power Loew there in December. Should keep him pretty busy during '63. 'Debbie comes over soon to join me in Italy,' Brett told me, 'and we'll be married in December when my divorce from Luciana Paluzzi is final in California.' These two have had a more or less stormy romance but now all seems rosy." Eventually, the marriage was called off, though they remained friends.

However, Halsey did marry during his time in Italy. He married the famous German singer and film actress Heidi Bruhl and left his home at Via Sasso Ferrato and moved to a comfortable two-level apartment at Piazza Stefano Jacini 5: "I decided to settle in an exclusive apartment complex in the chic Vigna Clara section which the Italians had cynically dubbed the American ghetto. They called it the American ghetto because, they said, only Americans were rich enough to live there. But, in fact, of the hundred or so families who resided in the four-building complex, only about 15 or 20 were actually American. I suppose I could have found a place in one of the older, more romantic quarters of Rome, but I felt comfortable in the company of my compatriots.

"Most of these people weren't involved with the *dolce vita*/Via Veneto scene. They followed pretty much the same nine-to-five, get the kids off to school existence they had lived back in the States."

There was an outside gate leading to a little piazza. Halsey's friend, actor Henry Silva, was impressed:

Brett earned a lot of money but he always lived like a multi-millionaire. His apartment was more like a house. It was on two levels. He threw dinner parties there. The house was always full of food. I knew Heidi. She was a good cook. We got along extremely well. We had a lot of fun. Rome and Paris were the places to be.

It was making *Jack and Jenny* in Berlin that brought Halsey together with his third wife, Heidi Bruhl. She had starred in the popular *Immenhof* series of movies, beginning with *Die Madels vom Immenhof* in 1955, and youth-oriented movies like *The Young Go Wild* (1959). They would be together for 12 years and remained friendly after their divorce until her death.

At the time of their first meeting, Heidi was starring in *Annie Get Your Gun* on the Berlin stage, and was a friend of *Jack and Jenny* star Senta Berger. Actress Brigitte Mira (who later starred in Fassbinder's *Fear Eats the Soul*) took Heidi to watch Halsey act on the set and that is where they first met. Halsey's friend Lex Barker facilitated their next meeting. Halsey told the *L.A. Herald Examiner* (November 6. 1963): "She's starring on the stage in West Berlin in *Annie Get Your Gun* and she is sensational. I've fallen madly in love and want to marry Heidi." He proposed in Germany while filming *The Avenger of Venice*.

The marriage of Brett Halsey and Heidi Bruhl made the front page of a German paper.

The ceremony was held on December 30, 1964, in Starnberg, outside Munich and made the front page of German papers. It was even reported in newspapers as far away as Israel. Halsey remarked with a laugh, "Heidi and I were on a lot of German newspaper front covers when we married. One paper said 'He's only marrying her for her money.' And another said 'She's only marrying him for his money'."

Initially they had planned to marry in Italy. On May 19, 1964, Louella Parsons reported in the *Los Angeles Herald-Examiner,* "His mother, Mrs. Rosemary Hand, says Brett is arranging to fly her over for the ceremony which will take place in Rome."

Marrying in Germany and then returning to Italy added a bit of confusion to the legal details of the marriage. As foreigners married in another country, the Italians had to recognize they were married. However, in Italy there is no divorce, so the Roman Catholic Luciana and Halsey were still considered wed. So in Italy Halsey was legally married to both Heidi and Luciana. A lawyer said there was no need to worry, although if Halsey died, who would be the wife who would inherit? Halsey and Heidi had two children, Clayton and Nicole. Their first was born on August 31, 1967, at the Salvator Mundi Hospital in Rome. The baby was a dark-haired boy who was named Clayton after Dick Clayton. In Italy the father has total say over naming a child and Halsey also chose Siegfried. Heidi objected because Clayton wasn't blond: "You can't call him Siegfried." So Halsey, in a spirit of fun, changed it to Alexander Siegfried. This was because his initials spelled out CASH.

Clayton was baptised at St. Peters Cathedral in Vatican City on October 15, 1967, by a priest who was a chancellor of the Sacred Rota. The Pope attended the baptism. As Halsey explained to Caroline Drewes (*San Francisco Examiner* February 6, 1978):

> The priest was holding the baby. When he exclaimed, "Turn around, turn around," we did, and there was Pope Paul in his palanquin, stopping to watch. A photographer from the German magazine *Stern* was photographing the ceremony because my wife at the time was German actress Heidi Bruhl. He was so startled he missed the shot.

The Pope came to Clayton's baptism although neither Halsey nor Heidi were Catholic (Heidi was German Protestant). However, Clayton would be brought up as a Catholic. Halsey, who had several connections in the Vatican, wanted his children to be baptised there because the association would prove useful in Rome. But then the family would leave Italy, and when Halsey returned in the late 1980s, there had been a regime change at the Vatican and all was for naught.

Brett and Heidi pose with baby Clayton.

From the age of three Clayton was raised by a nanny while Halsey and Heidi pursued their careers in both Rome and Munich, where Heidi was the bigger star. Clayton and his sister Nicole lived at home all the time and were never sent to boarding schools. They later went to the International School near Lake Starnberg where Halsey's old friend Tony Curtis also sent his children. Clayton explained, "We lived in Rome until 1970. Between 1967 and 1970 we stayed in Munich for extended periods of time but lived in Rome. Of course there was much traveling throughout this whole period."

Halsey and Clayton would not be close during Clayton's teenage years—Clayton was left-wing then and disagreed with his father's conservatism. Halsey liked Ronald Reagan, whom Clint Eastwood also supported. Although Halsey liked Jimmy Carter as a person, he did not think he was a good President. Things loosened up later. "We've smoked pot together," laughed Clayton. This was when Halsey was staying in London for a year working on a project called *Silverworld*. He was living in a house in Flood Street in Chelsea, opposite Prime Minister Margaret Thatcher's home. Halsey and Clayton were amused to be smoking pot with just a window separating them from Special Branch policemen.

Clayton commented on his parents' marriage:

> Brett's favorite place when he was living in Munich was the Hofbrauhaus, to sit and have a beer. He and Heidi had really good times. She was recognized everywhere. He was happy during those years, on the whole. For a long period of time, they were very happy.

Halsey confirmed he loved the Hofbrauhaus:

> I liked the atmosphere. It wasn't the beer. It was really the atmosphere. I really like the Hofbrauhaus. As a matter of fact, I had my 70th birthday party there and I gave a little Christmas party there this year [Xmas 2004]. The last time I was there with Heidi, we'd been divorced a long time but we were very friendly and when I was in Germany I always stayed at her house. There was some German magazine that wanted to do an interview. I said, "I don't know." She said, "Oh, come on." I said, "I'll do it under one condition." She said, "What's that?" "We do it at the Hofbrauhaus." For Germans, it's a bit of a dive. She said, "Oh, no." I said, "Okay, forget it." "Oh, come on." "No, I don't care about German magazines." "Well, okay." So, we did it at the Hofbrauhaus. The German journalist was happy to be there, because Germans of a certain…I don't want to say class because I don't believe in class…don't go there. It's a fun place to go.

Halsey with children Nicole and Clayton

Art or Instinct in the Movies...

Ed Sullivan greets guest Heidi and Brett.

Halsey was wary of the English press, too: "Heidi went to London. She had a record coming out in London. The Press called her a 'Nazi.' I said to the reporter: 'How can you call her a Nazi? She's Jewish, for God's sake.'"

Heidi seemed to keep Halsey on a short leash. When Halsey and his friends wanted to go and run with the bulls in Pamplona, Spain, Heidi found out and confiscated the airline tickets. Clayton was sceptical: "He probably didn't want to go."

Heidi also controlled Halsey's impulsive spending. Halsey gave an example:

> Maserati came out with a model called the Mexico. I remember driving home with the Mexico and Heidi came out on this balcony we had made. She said, "What's that?" "That's a Maserati Mexico." She said, "Take it back. You've just bought a car." I said, "Heidi, this is the first one in Italy. This is the first one…" "I don't care which one it is. Take it back or I'm going back to Germany." So I took it back. Well, I had another car.

Halsey had a sad story about the balcony: "We had a cat at the apartment block when we were living on the second floor. The cat would jump from the balcony to the ground. Then we moved to the penthouse and the cat jumped and got killed. It seems cats don't have spatial awareness."

Halsey's conversation today is continually peppered with affectionate references to Heidi. One of his friends told him, "You must really have loved Heidi, you talk about her so often." It was Halsey's longest and happiest marriage. Looking back, Halsey agrees that they had many happy years, apart from the breakup, which was "a bad time."

David Hedison met Heidi a few times and commented, "Heidi was very nice." Sandy Lieberson knew her better. "Heidi was really cute, full of energy and personality. But tough."

Heidi controlled the family's money but Halsey earned extra doing looping for other actors and kept this for himself. He laughed, "I looped one famous actor and the critics said it was his best performance."

Halsey only shared the screen with Heidi on one occasion, for a German television show called *Vico auf der Donau* (1968), in which he is credited as appearing "as himself." Halsey vaguely recalled it: "Vico Torian was a very well-known Swiss musical star. And that must have been the thing we did on the Donau, it was on a ship going down the Danube or something from Vienna to the Black Sea. I haven't seen it. It was a German musical show. Probably a one-hour show." Halsey did not sing: "No. My wife was in the show, so I was there as her husband, so 'as myself.' " When they stopped in Bucharest, Halsey admired the "lovely, Paris-style architecture" that existed then.

When Halsey left Italy, he and his family moved to Las Vegas for a year while Heidi headlined the Casino de Paris at the Dunes Hotel. On one occasion, in Vegas, Halsey went up a tower with Heidi, they looked at all the lights shining brightly, and Halsey said, "Heidi, do you realize who's paying the electric bill here?"

In 1971, they moved to Studio City in Los Angeles. In Hollywood, Halsey found his European stardom did not count for much there and he almost had to start again, needing to audition once more. As he explained to Suzy Kalter of *People* magazine(May 29, 1978): "My contemporaries had either made it or failed. I had done neither. Being a European star didn't count."

The marriage between Halsey and Heidi unraveled in the early 1970s. They lived happily together at a house in Dona Lola Drive, on the Studio City side of Laurel Canyon, from 1973 to 1974. Halsey landscaped the garden and had a bar in the living room. But Heidi was reportedly ambitious and Halsey was not performing financially to the same degree he had in Rome.

The patterns of their careers also drove them apart. Heidi was doing well in Las Vegas but not so well in Los Angeles. Her most notable appearances were in *Columbo* on television (Halsey did an episode, too, an okay appearance as a golfing instructor, which Halsey deemed typical Hollywood casting as he does not play golf) and in the Clint Eastwood movie *The Eiger Sanction*. The Halseys and Eastwoods remained close friends and Clayton played with Clint's son.

It was during Halsey's stint on soap operas, which were filmed in New York, that his marriage to Heidi was under increasing strain. They separated and later divorced. Halsey's personal life took a turn for the better when he met Tracy Brooks Swope, with whom he was to have a steady relationship for several years and whose friendship he has retained to date. Actually, it was a case of re-meeting her, as he first met her on the set of *Five Fingers* when she was six years old, as she was the daughter of the producer of the show, Herbert Swope, Jr. Halsey is always amused to tell this story. Tracy did not recall that first meeting in Hollywood, although she had seen him in *Return of the Fly*: "I didn't remember. Brett told me that we had met before and then my father told me as well. My father had brought Brett's second wife Luciana Paluzzi over from Italy to star in *Five Fingers*."

Tracy has a clear memory of meeting Halsey as a young adult:

> It was in the hallway at CBS in New York, while I was starring in a soap opera called *Where the Heart Is*. I got that role right after graduating from New York's The High School of Performing Arts, when I was 17.
>
> I remember what he wore. It was a soft powder-blue zipper velour short-sleeve shirt. He had a little piece of Kleenex around his neck because he had just had makeup put on and his eyes matched his shirt. Those eyes...those incredible eyes. We made an instant connection. We had been told about each other because a mutual friend of Brett's and my father, Nancy Holmes, had said, "Oh, you've got to meet my friend who is coming to New York to do a soap, he's never been there. You're doing a soap too, and I should have him call you." At that time, I was very young, and still living with my parents. It wasn't meant to be a fix-up or anything, because he was so much older than I. Then, by accident, we met, in the hallway at CBS...It was magical...instant chemistry. We didn't actually start dating for about 10 months. It was quite a long courtship.

When Halsey moved back to L.A. after his soap stint in New York, Tracy also came out to Los Angeles:

> Gardner McKay had asked me to star in a show with Richard Dreyfus and Geraldine Fitzgerald, so they flew me out here to meet Norman Lloyd to star in the show for KCET. Brett had introduced me to Gardner. First I stayed with my aunt, actress Dorothy McGuire, then I lived in an apartment complex called the Andalusia, where you weren't allowed to have men spend

Halsey, Tracy Swope and her father Herbert Swope, Jr.

the night. It was the first time away from my parents' house. I was 21. I was here, dating Brett, but he wasn't allowed to smoke cigars or sleep over while I was in that apartment.

He spent his time writing. He lived at the Malibu Bay Club, where he had bought a condominium facing the beach in January 1978. He hoped the solitude would help him write. One day he ran into Ginger Rogers in the local supermarket. He ran on the beach and spent a lot of time thinking. Halsey's desk faced the ocean and he found there was "too much to distract me": "I didn't write a damn word." One day he saw a hawk land on the top of a pole. It had a squirrel or some small creature in its claws. Halsey watched fascinated as the hawk dismantled its prey piece by piece for what seemed like hours. Tracy stayed there on and off ("It was really beautiful," she commented) until Halsey lost the place in a court action by Renate for back child support.

Halsey also stayed at Tracy's house in Sherman Oaks because "Malibu is so far out of town." It was at 1445 Dickens Street and Halsey continued to visit when he moved to Pasadena. In 1981 they lived for about a year at 1119 1/2 Hacienda Place, off Santa Monica Boulevard, although Tracy kept her own place. They also briefly shared another place nearby. Halsey chose these locations because they were close to everywhere he needed to go.

Art or Instinct in the Movies...

Halsey's mother Rose spent time in Kern Valley, in Kern County, near Bakersfield in California, with her father Charlie Rinaldi until his death. He had lived in Kernville for many years. During that time she met Jim Neff, formerly of Sacramento, where he was with the Corps of Engineers. She married him in 1974 and they went to live in Wofford Heights, close to Kernville. She was working for Hughes Aircraft and in 1972 was secretary for the art association. She always stayed in touch with Halsey, even when he was in New York. Halsey was Grand Marshal and led the Early California Days Parade in Kernville on October 8, 1977. He was most famous then to Kernville residents for the Old Spice Sailor commercials and the soap *General Hospital*. He wore a Spanish costume during the event. His stepfather Jim won a Trophy in his Original Indian Costume. Jim would pass away in 2007.

When Halsey lost the Malibu home, he moved to Pasadena. His lawyer had a gatehouse free at 141 N. Grand Avenue and Halsey told him, "You've lost me every house I ever had, so you'll have to put me up."

Tracy and Halsey separated around 1978, after about six and a half years. They had been happy but Tracy wanted to move on: "I'd never really dated anyone else and I wanted to. He wanted us to stay together but I just couldn't." They remain good friends, though, and Halsey rings her from all over the world:

> He calls me and we talk for hours. We've always stayed in touch. We went to Cuelebra together. It's an island off the coast of Puerto Rico and we loved it there. There are about 1,200 people on the whole island. Brett would flop on a hammock and just relax. He really enjoys quiet time where he can think.

Halsey's relationship with Tracy was quite different from the sometimes-stormy relationship with Heidi, Tracy said:

> We never fought. It was fantastic. He taught me so much. We spent time in Rome together and Brett helped me to speak Italian. We went out food shopping and I had to communicate in Italian to get bread or we couldn't eat. We made a game of it; it was great fun.
>
> We went to Italy for a holiday, and also Yugoslavia—Split and Dubrovnik. We went to Yugoslavia with some of Brett's Italian friends. That was exciting. Brett speaks many languages and is very sophisticated in a very down-to-earth way.
>
> He taught me how to bite off the tip of the cigar with my front teeth and how to properly light a cigar. He's the sweetest man, very smart, too. He doesn't show off his intelligence, he is so secure he doesn't need to, but he's very smart. He observes and he watches and he's always in the moment.

> We got along so well because we were both able to be completely ourselves with each other. There was never a power struggle. We were comfortable in who we were, and we never let what we were doing define who we were. It was wonderful.

Halsey's son Clayton went to film school and asked his father to appear in one of his student films in September 1986. Halsey was amused to remember Clayton's independence: "I acted in a short film directed by Clayton and started to give him advice. He said, 'Dad, I'm the director. You're the actor. You act, I'll direct'." Clayton confirmed the story:

> I did direct my father in an eight minute 16mm black-and-white Western for film school titled *When Money Talks*...He played an evil family leader who is shot in the back by his daughter [because he killed his daughter's lover]. He had suggestions for me, which I was thankful for, but I needed to go my own creative direction. He did take my direction well. The daughter, however, played by Laura Walters, needed most of my directorial attention. But my father died very well in a beautiful long shot. I'd say his best death since *Four Fast Guns*...

Clayton went on to a busy career as a film editor, working for Irwin Winkler and others. He also edited and starred in a movie, *Bikini Squad*, produced by his half-brother Christian, later in film distribution at Cinecitta. Christian had taken on his stepfather's name and was now known as Halsey Solomon (from movie producer Michael Solomon). Halsey recalls that they hired a woman director, who balked at Clayton both acting in and editing the picture and went to the producer, who was his brother. He told her he quite understood why she was not comfortable with it and he would have to replace her, which quelled her objections.

Halsey remembers Christian once driving him around Milan "like a maniac" in a small car, even though Christian is taller than Halsey. Dorris Halsey told a story about Christian:

> He tried very hard to make a movie out of my *Love Boats* novel, which became a series [*Love Boat*]. It's still playing all over the world. So I was in business with Christian and I met Christian because Brett invited me to the Dome restaurant when it was open for lunch along with his boys Clayton and Christian. Christian said, "Now, tell me about yourself" and I said, "I was happily married for 26 years." And he said, "Ha, so was my father. To four different wives."

Christian moved his family to Los Angeles in 2006 and began to see more of Brett than he had before.

Sadly, Heidi died of cancer in 1991 when Halsey was living in Toronto. Halsey has written about his grief:

> When we received the call in early June that my ex-wife Heidi Bruhl was very ill and might be dying, our children, Clayton and Nicole, caught the first available flights to Munich. Clayton from Los Angeles, California, and Nicole from our home in Toronto, Canada. At first I was advised that I should come immediately as well, then I received another call saying it might be too much of a shock for Heidi if we all arrived together. Although she passed away only two days later, I was informed at the time that she did not know how ill she really was.
> The children were with her at the end. I arrived the next morning.
> Heidi had left instructions for her body to immediately be cremated. Therefore, even though I arrived a few hours later, I was unable to see her remains.
> The children, some of the family and I remained together in Heidi's house to help one another cope with the shock of our unexpected loss.

Looking back on this in 2005, Halsey said:

> She really didn't know how ill she was. On the Friday the kids were told she would probably never leave the hospital but Heidi was talking about leaving on Monday as she had to do some recording and prepare for a new musical tour. She had this way of looking at things the way she wanted them to be. We used to argue about that.

It was on his second Roman adventure that Halsey had met his fourth wife, an Iranian princess Farideh Asgharzadeh-Parsa, who liked to be called Firouzeh. She was Westernized, blonde and very much Halsey's type, and the attraction was mutual. Clayton recalled:

> I was Assistant Director on a miniseries in Germany. He told me about his engagement party. I told him I could not be there but there was a break and, without telling him, I flew from Hamburg to Vienna and on to Rome and turned up by surprise

Firouzeh and Halsey

and it's the only time I've seen my father burst into tears of joy. Mind you, he was a little drunk.

A letter survives which Halsey sent to Dorris Halsey on May 22, 1988, commenting on his life in Rome with Firouzeh. It provides a colorful portrait of the life of an expatriate actor in Rome. He wrote from Via Teheren 15, Int 35, 00135, Roma:

Dear Dorris,

It has been too long since we have been in touch, so I thought it is time for me to write. In fact, I *have* been writing (a script and two treatments). After a whole day in front of this machine, my head, my back and my shoulders tell me to leave it alone and write to Dorris in the morning. Well, this is the morning.

All is well here in the eternal city. I mean, all is well for me and Firouzeh and her kids. I am afraid the eternal city is going to hell. Civilization and progress are irresolutely moving ahead and poor old Rome just can't handle it. Neither physically nor emotionally.

I don't know if in the last 20 or 30 years anyone has given any thought to Rome's future, but if they have, no one is translating those thoughts into action. Traffic is impossible and can only get worse. Most of the principal access streets into the center are still the narrow country lanes which were laid out before World War I and these few narrow streets are clogged with double-parked cars.

A trip by car which a few years ago would take ten or 15 minutes can now easily take an hour. And this is not a pleasant hour. The monstrous traffic is making monsters of a people who are normally the most gentle and courteous in all Europe.

As far as getting things done, each of us who has ever cursed the inefficiency and rudeness of American civil servants, should be subjected to the sweat and humiliation of trying to accomplish even the simplest of tasks involving the Italian bureaucracy. Days can be wasted chasing the most ordinary of documents. And when you finally have the document in your hand, you can almost be certain it will be wrong and you have to start all over again. What can be particularly irritating is when you have to re-bribe the same person who is responsible for making you repeat the process.

Italy has always been famous for its inefficiency, but it has gotten to the point where even the Italians have had enough.

But, what the hell, Italy is Italy (whatever that means) and everything has its price (which, except for Switzerland, is today the highest in all Europe), so we are all still here. I read the other day that there are over 60 thousand Americans residing in Rome alone. What keeps us here? I wish I knew. If I did, being a typical American, I would wrap it in a pretty package and try to export it.

As a lifetime expatriate, I am sure that you know better than I that one of the difficulties of living the expatriate life is that wherever we are, we tend to forget the negative aspects of the place we left behind and miss the positive. On the other hand, just to turn around and go back...Well, things haven't gotten *that* bad. (At least, not yet.)

We are at that time of year when spring is trying to blossom into summer. It will rain for a few days, then the sun will come out and everyone will decide that summer has finally arrived. Then, it will start to rain again and everyone will wonder if it will ever stop. The month of May is like that. It is the same almost every year and almost every year the rains stop when June rolls around and everyone soon forgets they ever doubted the inevitability of a long, hot, sunny summer.

I have been feeling pretty good these past weeks. I am quite satisfied with the script I just finished (which I will send you) and I think I have another good one in my head, which I intend to start putting on paper in the next few days. I already have offers to act in two different Italian films this summer. I haven't decided which I am going to do, but I have a little time before I have to make up my mind. I am disappointed with the reaction to Nicky's cookbook, but I am sure you will find the right publisher before long. How about *Players?* (Or is it *Yesterday's Children* again?) [*Players* was a TV pilot Halsey acted in, which was shot but never sold. *Yesterday's Children*, his second novel, was rejected by its original publisher.]

My health is fine. I have to go to the gym regularly and pay attention to my bathroom scale, otherwise my addiction to Italian food in general, and pasta in particular, will mean the destruction of my waistline. My weakness for the tasty, high calorie, local wines doesn't help much either. The older I get, the more I am learning to respect (not like) the word, moderation. Sometimes I feel like many of the other ruins of Rome: still in pretty good shape, but in need of a little extra care and attention.

On this happy note, I will close for now. I hope you are well and happy and that I will hear from you soon.

Love and kisses,
Brett

Halsey moved to Toronto with Firouzeh and her two children. They had an apartment at 4 Forest Lane Way in Willowdale, in Toronto's upscale Bayview Village. The family settled on Toronto because Firouzeh did not like Los Angeles and she had relatives in Toronto. Toronto worked for Halsey because he was looking for a city where he could continue his career. Film production was lively in Toronto because it could double for New York City and was much cheaper than the U.S. Halsey also worked on Canadian television and commuted back to Hollywood and to Rome for work.

The move to Toronto eventually brought Halsey's second period of living in Italy to an end and in early 1990 he returned to Rome to sell his apartment. He bought a house at 99 Page Avenue, Willowdale.

With his fourth marriage, Halsey had acquired two teenage stepchildren, one boy, one girl, both at a difficult stage of adolescence. Clayton observed: "He wanted to be a good father, as he hadn't been there that much for his other children. It was hell for him. That weighed on him heavily." Halsey thought, "The son was spoiled rotten by his nanny." Clayton recalled, "Then the difficulty began with Firouzeh, too. Brett fitted in with cultural differences fine. He's very adaptable. But maybe Firouzeh was too conservative in her attitudes. She was rigid in her opinions." Firouzeh was a Muslim but not a practising one. She sent the children to Catholic schools. They wanted to fit in but didn't feel they did. And she kept encouraging Halsey to abandon his show business career. She particularly disliked his work with Lucio Fulci.

Whether or not Fulci's movies were to blame, Halsey's marriage to Firouzeh did not last. The divorce was easy. Halsey simply ignored the first set of court papers and four weeks later found he had been divorced. There were a number of women in his life in Toronto. At a party, a mutual friend introduced him to Nancy Parke-Taylor, who was an admirer of his career, and they lived together, off and on, for a few years.

With Halsey spending a long time in Costa Rica apart from Nancy in Toronto, the relationship slowly unraveled. Halsey explained, "It's difficult to keep a relationship going with someone if you only see them two or three weeks a year." Clayton's opinion was, "Their interests diverged and then, when she went to law school, things diverged more. They were planning to move to L.A. and Brett didn't want to have a circle of lawyers as friends." Nancy herself pointed out that she was studying law when she first met Halsey and that there was a considerable age difference between them. They finally parted when Halsey moved back to Los Angeles in January 2004.

After assisting in the interview process for this book, Victoria de Korda became the fifth Mrs. Halsey in December 2006 at a register office wedding in Beverly Hills. A reception was held afterward in a five-star hotel. Halsey and Victoria have traveled together to places like Prescott, Arizona, where he visited the local university to discuss joining the teaching staff, gone to the horse races at Santa Anita, and explored some of Southern California's coastal beaches. The couple visited England where Halsey was introduced to Victoria's family and then they continued on to Germany where she met Halsey's daughter Nicole and her family.

Hollywood Legends

Clint Eastwood

In 2004, Halsey reminisced with Clint about their early days at the Universal Talent School. Clint said he also actually was signed for $100 a week, not $75 as Halsey wrote earlier. Halsey could not then predict the huge star that Clint would become: "No, Clint was so laid-back. The thing he did that I was most impressed by was when he won the ping-pong championship at the fire department." The years on the television series *Rawhide* were what made the difference, Halsey thought, "He became a part of the business. He got interested in it."

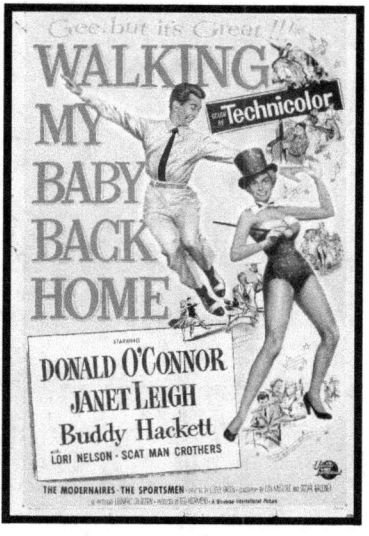

Janet Leigh

> I admired her. There was an incident when I was working on *Walking My Baby Back Home*. I was really new in the business and didn't know anything about filmmaking. They called for second-unit in the scene and I said to a friend of mine, "What's second-unit?" And he said, "What's second-unit? Ha, ha, ha. He doesn't know what second-unit is." And Janet Leigh came in and just really ripped him. So from that time on, I was her fan.

Audie Murphy

Halsey's final picture at Universal offered him a supporting role in Audie Murphy's real-life war story *To Hell and Back* (1955). Halsey's part is fairly passive. His best scene is as a terrified soldier in a foxhole. The film is a minor classic but slightly disappointing to modern audiences. Halsey agreed:

> That was remarkable, but they shot too much. We went on location with a three-hour script. They cut it and ruined it. The things Audie did were remarkable. I read the book. I was there when he did those scenes with the burning ammo carrier, the ten German tanks coming, attacking the string of German machine-gun nests.

I learned a lesson about war in that movie. There was a scene where we were running up a hill shooting at this farmhouse where the Germans were. At the end of the scene, Richard Long came over, mad as hell because I'd shot him five or six times in the back with these blanks. I wasn't shooting at him, I was shooting at the farmhouse. But it just goes to show you, in war, you wonder how many people got killed accidentally.

Halsey knew Audie personally:

At the studio, we used to spar. Although Audie was very nice, I popped him in the nose a little hard. His nose got red. He lost his temper. The red went up from the neck. The warrior came out...If I'd hurt him, my career was over. I said, "Fuck you, Audie, this fight's over." Then he was fine. His childhood was very poor, growing up on the Texas plains. He would shoot rabbits to feed the kids.

Audie was making a picture in Spain, a Western called *The Texican*, and one of the producers, Bruce Balaban, was late every morning and complaining about everything. Audie walked up to him and popped him. He said, "Come to work when the rest of us do."

Julian Ludwig produced *The Texican* and revealed that Halsey was "indirectly responsible for *The Texican*," because in Rome in 1965, "Brett knew everybody and introduced me to a producer in Rome who became my partner." Ludwig first met Halsey during his years at Universal and they became good friends. He described Halsey as:

> A terrific friend, a terrific cook, a good carpenter—he could fix things in the house—and a good actor. He was not a star when I met him; he was a working actor, a romantic lead. He was well liked by everybody. All the major stars became his friends. He's one of the nicest actors that I've ever met. I remember I was in New York to get myself established. I was sharing an apartment there with another actor friend. Brett had gone to Germany to marry his first wife Renate and came back the next day and stayed with me in this small apartment. Brett had more money than us. It should have been his honeymoon. He flew back to Hollywood the next day for a picture. We did a lot of fun things together. No one's ever said anything bad about Brett.

Over the years, Halsey would try and get various projects and scripts off the ground in partnership with Ludwig, although he never gave him one of the scripts he had written himself: "No, he was dealing with bigger producers."

Jeff Chandler

At Universal, Halsey was delighted to meet many of his favorite actors: "Jeff Chandler was one of my heroes. At Universal on the first or second day, he came up to me and said 'Hi, Brett, welcome to Universal.' We co-starred later in *Return to Peyton Place*."

After *Return to Peyton Place*, Halsey listed Jeff Chandler among his favorite actors but "as a person more than as an actor."

Randolph Scott

Randolph Scott had been a favorite of Halsey's since childhood:

> Randolph Scott wanted to join the L.A. Country Club. It did not allow actors to join, but he'd retired. He applied. They turned him down. One committee member said, "I saw you on TV the other night." It was a rerun of 15 years before. Howard Hughes was a member. They kicked him out for landing his helicopter on the golf course.

Tyrone Power

Growing up, Halsey's biggest movie hero was probably Tyrone Power:

> He had a *smile*. He had a kind of tragic life. He had a business manager and he bought a yacht, *The Black Swan*, which he had shipped to Barcelona to have with him when making the movie *Solomon and Sheba*. He rang his business manager and told him he'd paid $35,000. The business manager said, "You don't *have* $35,000." What the business manager had done was just put the studio check in the bank. He never invested the money. Tyrone was broke when he died. He paid a lot of alimony, too. The only thing he had to leave was the income from his rights in *Solomon and Sheba*, which he produced.

Tyrone Power died at the young age of 44. He had a heart attack while filming a dueling scene in *Solomon and Sheba* and was replaced by Yul Brynner. Power's father had also died at an early age of a heart attack.

Halsey was delighted when he became friends with Tyrone Power in the early days of his career. They met through mutual friend, Mike Steckler, who was Tyrone's stand-in:

> I was invited over to his house, about five years before he died. He died in 1958, so it was about 1953. We spent some time together. We were together when he met Debbie [his last wife]. It was a pool party at his house. She came with a girlfriend…
>
> I don't recall us ever talking about the business.

Halsey recalls one intimate conversation with Tyrone that he will never forget:

> I remember once, three of us were on his boat in Newport Beach, watching the sky. It was just dusk and he looked up at the sky and there was a single-engine plane. And he said, "I would never fly at night in a single-engine plane." He flew double-engine planes in the war. He was in the Marine Corps. He turned to me and said, "You know, you'll be replacing me one of these days." He knew his days at the top were drawing to a close.

Halsey told me this anecdote as we went for a walk down Pico Boulevard and I scribbled it down in my notebook, but later asked him if the quote was exact and he was slightly indignant: "Do you think I would not remember Tyrone Power saying that to me?"

Halsey feels Tyrone Power never received the critical acclaim he deserved:

> He was a good actor. He did a reading of *John Brown's Body* with Charles Laughton and got good reviews, but he was not well respected for his film work, like Tony Curtis.

Later, Halsey and Tyrone's widow Debbie, whose marriage to Tyrone had only lasted a little over six months, became close friends. The prospect of marriage was even on the cards at one point. Halsey would later appear opposite Romina Power, daughter of Tyrone and Linda Christian, in one of his more interesting pictures, *Perversion Story*.

Tony Curtis

Halsey became friendly with Curtis when he was working in small roles on two Universal pictures, *The Black Shield of Falworth* and *Johnny Dark*. He especially admired Curtis' work in *Some Like It Hot* and *The Sweet Smell of Success*. Halsey felt he was not sufficiently valued for his film work: "He's a good guy. I liked Tony."

Romina Power and Brett Halsey in *Perversion Story*

All those years after *Johnny Dark* and *The Black Shield of Falworth*, Halsey bumped into Tony Curtis again a few times, most recently at a celebrity signing event in Burbank in 2007, at which Tony seemed pleased to see him. He spoke of Tony's problems and his admiration for his talent:

> I was in a party and Tony came and he was really stoned out of his mind. He came with this great big white 10-gallon cowboy hat. He wore a toupee. He came up to me and put his arm round me and he was talking to these people and was telling all these stories, all these things we'd done throughout our life—none of which were true. He was going on and on and on, all these things, total, *total* fiction.
>
> Then, a couple of years later, I saw him. We had lunch together. I remember after lunch we were walking down Sunset Boulevard and he took his shirt off. He said, "Look at this. I'm in such great shape. I've never been so healthy in my life." He said, "I've quit that." He said, "The doctor told me, had I gone another week, I'd be dead. But I'm clean, working out, look." He said, "I've got more money than I ever had in my life. I thought I was broke but my business manager found that I had a property up in the desert somewhere. I made a lot of money with that." So, after that period, he hit a period of reasonably good health. He *said* the best time of his life.

> I think he's one of the most underrated talents in the business. I think he's a *wonderful* actor. *Some Like it Hot*—he was fantastic. He's done a lot of really good work. *What Makes Sammy Run*, he was wonderful in that. *Sweet Smell of Success*. If he'd died young, he'd be a James Dean. Now I don't think he's acting so much. He's doing so well with his painting. He travels a lot, has exhibits and sells.

Rock Hudson

Halsey's social life during the Universal days was filled with acting acquaintances including Rock Hudson, whose homosexuality was a closely guarded secret. Halsey recalled:

> At Universal, there was an annual party with a show on stage. Universal had a stage to show contract actors what to do. I stared down, and there was Rock Hudson's agent. Rock's agent was Henry Willson, a notorious homosexual. His clients were known as "Henry's boys." Henry Willson tried to get me to sign. I said to Rock, "I don't know, Rock. I don't like to be known as one of Henry's boys. How do you feel about everybody calling you a fag?" He replied, "Well, Brett, you know, no one's ever called me a fag to my face." I thought, "Rock's not gay." A couple of months later, Rock drove into the car park with a guy. He got out of his car. I saw him look around to see if anyone was watching and then he kissed the guy. So then I realized he was. Producers knew.

Halsey recalled that he had a friend who was an actor and baseball player and who knew nothing of gay men. He went to a Rock Hudson party and, when the guests were all gone, he was left alone with Willson. It was raining and he got soaking wet pulling down the garage door when he tried to leave and Willson invited him in to take off his wet clothes, "Then Henry took my friend out to show him the swimming pool. Henry grabbed my friend by the balls. He grabbed Henry by the throat and lifted him up. He was choking him. At the same time, he was thinking 'If I kill him, my career is over.' In the end, he reached over and dropped him into the pool."

While in Rome, Halsey encountered Henry Willson, who died in 1978:

> It was in the restaurant of the Hilton in Rome. It wasn't a social event. It was just the middle of the day. I looked at him and I thought the evil he contained came out in his face...like Dorian Gray in reverse. He was near the end of his life.

Broderick Crawford

Halsey recalled particularly learning from Broderick Crawford, as he has written:

> I was in high school and living in Rio del Mar, California, when I met a woman who had been an associate producer on Broderick Crawford's Oscar-winning film, *All the King's Men*. Having direct contact with a person connected to the film somehow reinforced my desire to become a movie actor and made my first meeting with Crawford all the more meaningful. It was early in my career when I was hired to play a guest role in his hit TV show *Highway Patrol*.
>
> I was never comfortable learning lines and I was always envious of actors like Crawford who, with his photographic memory, could give a glance through his script and have it, letter perfect, locked into his memory. His problem was, at the time his alcoholism was totally out of control.
>
> I'll never forget my first face-to-face meeting with the great star. I had been mentally rehearsing our scene all morning. Finally he came staggering onto the set. I don't think he had me clearly in focus when we were introduced. Then, as we were about to begin the scene, he leaned his arms on my shoulders and gave me a light spray of spittle as he kindly gave me his

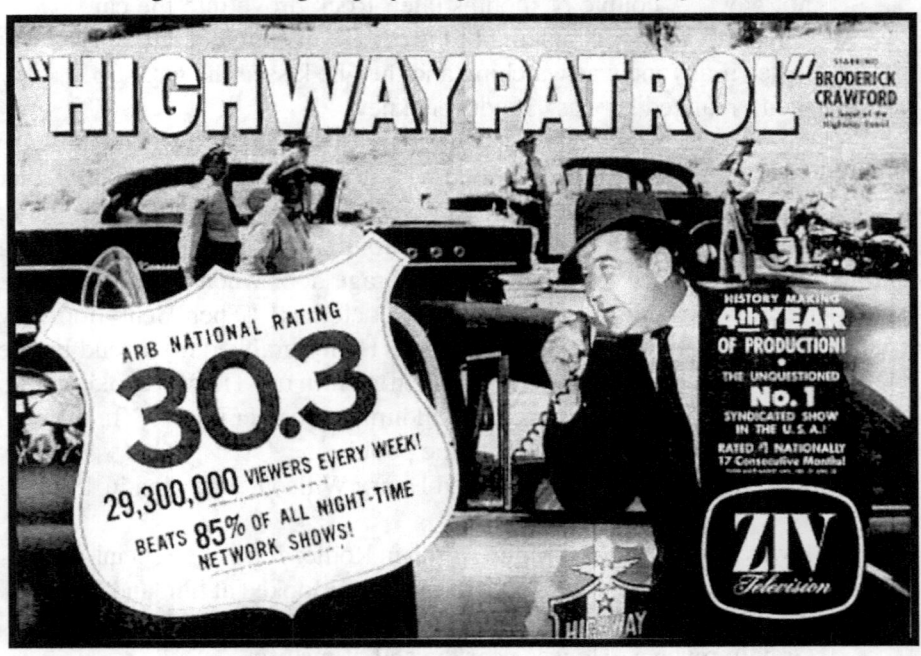

instructions how to play the scene. "Listen, kid," he slurred, "don't pay any attention to what I say. Just start talking when I stop." It wasn't exactly the way I had anticipated that I would be playing my first scene with an Oscar-winning actor...

Some years later, after he had stopped drinking, I learned a valuable lesson while acting with him again.

We were both guest actors on the TV series *City of Angels*. The male and female stars of the show were very energetic with their on-set rewrites and thoughtful preparations for each of the upcoming scenes. Of course, the guest actors were seldom invited to become a part of the stars' arm-waving, artistic machinations that they felt were necessary to improve the show. I sat watching Broderick Crawford, as he sat quietly, observing with little apparent interest. Even though he gave the appearance of being barely awake, I had the impression that I was watching a large cat, silently poised to pounce on its victim. Sure enough, when it came time to play, our stars had used up their energies with their preparation, but Crawford was fresh. He had been sitting quietly, conserving his energy for when it was important. It wasn't as though he stole the scene from the stars; it was more like he buried them with his massive talent. It was then that I learned the importance of an actor being able to pace himself and conserve his energy for when it was really needed.

Miriam Hopkins

In 1958 at the Sombrero Theatre in Phoenix, Arizona, Halsey performed the role of the young American artist in the light comedy *Time of the Cuckoo* with Miriam Hopkins. He was only paid expenses. He did not do it to be seen by casting agents, "so much as expanding my talent." He remembered one time he had coffee in his room, which cost a dollar and came in beautiful tableware. He decided to keep the cup and saucer: "I felt entitled to, as they were paying so little."

Miriam Hopkins had been a huge movie star in the 1930s and was nominated for an Oscar for her performance in *Becky Sharp* in 1935. Halsey, who usually always remembers his fellow thesps pleasantly, could find nothing positive to say about Hopkins: "My memories of her are not very good. She'd done the play before. She'd come in just for dress rehearsals. It's hard to act without your leading lady. She was grumpy. Not pleasant to be around. Too sour. And she was working at half-speed. But it was a good show." Halsey felt she had been employed purely for the marquee value of her name and she may have felt the show was beneath her.

Dennis Hopper

Halsey worked with future stars of the new post-*Easy Rider* Hollywood, Dennis Hopper and Jack Nicholson. He knew Peter Fonda ("a hippie") and particularly his sister, Jane Fonda: "I knew Jane since we were kids."

Halsey did not become a pal of Dennis Hopper: "We didn't become pals. I was always friendly with him. I wasn't into the drug culture. It just never appealed to me. I was always afraid of it. I was afraid that what happened to them might happen to me and I just didn't want to have to face that."

James Dean

Halsey was a friend of the now-legendary James Dean:

> I knew him pretty well. James Dean recommended me for a TV role on *General Electric Theater* he couldn't do. He told me he was recommending I do it. But then at the last minute he did do it. We had the same agent [Dick Clayton]. He was trying to help me. We used to hang around with the same group of kids. We hung out at a coffeehouse, a famous one called Googie's. It doesn't exist any more. Googie's was right next door to Schwab's Drugstore on the corner of Sunset Boulevard and Crescent Heights. We used to laugh at Clifford Odets, the icon of U.S. theater, who was hanging around the young guys, hoping to meet the young girls.
>
> I was with his girlfriend, Maila Nurmi [who played *Vampira* on television], when we got the call he was dead. It was a great shock. We were waiting to hear he had arrived where he was going. He was probably tired when he had the accident.

Halsey did not remain in touch with Maila Nurmi after Dean's death:

> No. Well, she was kind of weird. I remember the apartment she had *before* the one that she was living in when Jimmy died. I used to live almost next door. It was a one-roomed place and she had 17 cats and they never got out, so when she moved, they had to renovate the place. It was months before they could just get the smell of the cats out. Even though she was the host of this movie channel that was one of the minor channels, she was so well known and imitated because she was very good at what she was doing.

Halsey's story of how Dean tried to help him is interesting by way of contrast with the account by former actor Andy Milligan (in *The Ghastly One* by

Maila Nurmi

Jimmy McDonough) of how Dean tried to eliminate rivals. Milligan acted with Dean on a television show and had been getting a lot of work on CBS Television until it suddenly dried up. A bigwig later told him Dean had been spreading it around town that Milligan was saying the only way to get a job with CBS was to "keep your legs uncrossed." Milligan described Dean as "not a nice person," who had a "grudge against anybody in his way."

Halsey, though, never actually went on any auditions where he was competing with Dean for the same role. Halsey saw *East of Eden*, *Rebel Without a Cause* and *Giant*:

> I thought he was very good in *East of Eden* and I think that is when I started to admire his talent. Some people, Dean, Valentino, Marilyn Monroe, conveniently died young and at the height of their stardom.

Halsey does not feel Dean would have survived into middle age as this iconic figure:

> I don't think so. I don't know how he would have survived it, because he was *special*—and he thought of himself as special.

Art or Instinct in the Movies...

He wasn't overbearing about it, but he did. I can't imagine he would have retired, but he would have quit acting. Maybe directing, he probably would have gone into directing.

Halsey also scotched the persistent rumors that Dean was bisexual:

> I was having lunch at Warners a couple of years ago and met a Warners historian. We sat and talked a while and discussed the stories that Dean was gay. I told the historian I never saw anything like that and I knew him pretty well. The historian said the people who knew him all say that. Only those who *didn't* know him say he was gay.

Marlon Brando

James Dean and Marlon Brando are usually bracketed together as revolutionizing screen acting during the 1950s. Halsey only ever had passing contact with Brando but had views on his squandering of his talent:

> In his early films, he was great. He still esteemed the profession. There was a thing I resented about Brando, his habit of not learning lines, his disdain for the craft. I felt that he was paid enough that he could have taken the time to learn his lines. I felt that the Screen Actors Guild should have fined him or something for his dishing the profession. I think he would just do whatever he could get away with, because he was a genius. He was a great actor, but he would get away with too much. They would give him too much. He was too wrapped up in himself to direct. I think that's one of the reasons many actors can't write, because they focus in on their character and it's hard to see the broader vision.

William Wellman

Halsey had some friends around him in his first Warner Bros. picture, *Lafayette Escadrille* (1958), which starred Tab Hunter and also featured David Janssen and Clint Eastwood. In this WWI airman picture, Halsey worked for one of the great veteran directors, William "Wild Bill" Wellman (*Wild Boys of the Road*, *The Ox-Bow Incident*), who had personal experience of the subject matter. Wellman's son, William Wellman, Jr., was also acting in the picture. William Wellman, Jr. recalled Halsey coming in and out of the six-week shoot and getting on well with his father. It was Wellman, Jr.'s first film and when I asked him if it was difficult being directed by his father, he replied, "No, he'd been directing me all my life."

Halsey agreed that Wellman, Sr. was "very nice, very affable to everybody," although he had a fearsome reputation:

> William Wellman had quite a reputation as Wild Bill. He got involved with fights with actors, physical fights, as a younger man. He was very subdued. His wife was there most of the time.
>
> The picture was set in WWI, so I had the moustache and long hair. After the location shooting, we had a one-week break before going into the studio to do the rear projection for the flying scenes. I had the chance to go to New York to do a television show called *West Point* on location at West Point Academy, in which I played a cadet, which meant short hair and no moustache. I was worried what Wellman would say, because of his reputation. I went to the makeup man and explained my problem.
>
> I asked him if I could wear a flying helmet and maybe he could put a moustache on me and we said, "Maybe Wellman won't even know."
>
> What happened was, I was late coming back on the red-eye. The plane got into L.A. just before my call. I had to run from the airport to the studio. I put the helmet on, the moustache

Art or Instinct in the Movies...

and the uniform, but I was very nervous because he did have that reputation. But he didn't notice anything and I got away with it. I never told him.

In the end, Halsey said, the picture was "not very successful." "It was a group of young airmen at flying school, who were together all the time. It should have been fun and high-spirited, but it was based on a true story and I think Wellman was too close to it. It was too dark."

Portrait of Halsey from *Lafayette Escadrille*

Freelancing after Universal

Halsey recalled the period after leaving Universal as his "greatest struggle" and "toughest time" of his career. He wrote in the 1961 Fox profile:

> It was four months before I got another acting job and they were few and far between that first year after I left UI. I didn't starve because I had saved some money, but I kept doing more tests at more studios for more parts I never heard anything about. I did a test right here at Fox [that] I hope they haven't got and have forgotten about. I tested at Metro, Paramount, Warners, 20th Century-Fox. The test at Paramount was funny. The girl we tested was going to test as a dancer and they wanted me to test for her. I wasn't a dancer but the choreographer insisted I could do it. I think the most embarrassing moment of my life was when I saw this test, because I looked like a big ox, no grace whatever.

The brilliant composer Elmer Bernstein (*The Magnificent Seven*), as a personal favor to Halsey, provided piano accompaniment during the test. Halsey was saddened when Bernstein died in 2004. "He was a very nice man."

In 1954 Halsey made his first TV appearance in an episode of *Waterfront*, which starred Preston Foster as a young soldier who was engaged to a girl. He had a fight scene in this show with Charles Bronson, who was then virtually unknown. Bronson hit Halsey too hard and for decades Halsey bore Bronson a grudge until they met again later at a time when Bronson was much older and very frail. A huge number of TV appearances followed. Halsey learned a great deal from television where he worked for some classic movie directors such as John Brahm (*Hangover Square*) on Ziv-TV's *Dr. Hudson's Secret Journal*. He also got to appear with a number of big stars such as Peter Lorre and Broderick Crawford.

Halsey's career might have taken an entirely different turn but for an abortive encounter with Walt Disney, as Halsey has written:

> One day in the late 1950s, I was called to the Disney Studio to discuss a role in an upcoming Disney project. Whatever the job was, I didn't get it, so I can't remember what it was called or who was involved.
>
> The head of casting had accompanied me to the producer's office in the main administration building and, after the meeting, he and I left the office to return to the casting office on the floor below.

While walking along the corridor towards the elevator, I spied the legendary, great man himself, walking in our direction. "Wow," I thought, "I'm going to meet Walt Disney."

I was quickly gathering my thoughts, trying to come up with something appropriate to say to him, when the casting director looked up and spotted him, as well. "Oh shit, here comes Walt," he gasped, then grabbed my arm and steered me through a nearby door to the stairwell. "Thank God," he said with a sigh of relief, after having avoided a face-to-face meeting with his boss.

That was it. That was as close as I ever got to meeting the idol of almost everyone in the world. I say almost because Mr. Disney was obviously not the idol of his casting director.

Halsey's movie career was beginning to lift off in Hollywood. First he got a small role in a cinema classic opposite Susan Hayward and then graduated to leading roles in cheap independent films. It was the films Halsey made during this period that began the cult movie career for which he will be most fondly remembered. Juvenile delinquent dramas, Westerns, soaps, hot rod dramas, war movies, science fiction, horror. You name it; he was in it. He was

Halsey and Susan Hayward in *I Want to Live*

constantly working for small studios like Allied Artists, usually getting paid a modest $500 a week. Most of the B pictures did not demand any great acting and the directors did not have time to work much with the actors, though Halsey always did his best.

Because he needed the money, Halsey never minded taking small, unbilled roles in big pictures like Robert Wise's *I Want to Live* (1958), starring Susan Hayward. Even that was not easy to come by and Halsey was flattered when he learned the extent of the competition: "Robert Wise told me he interviewed 200 actors for that part. I only worked there two days."

Jay Bernstein was Susan Hayward's manager and said of *I Want to Live*: "I watched it recently. It's one of his best performances. Brett stands out in the movie. Susan Hayward got an Academy Award for that. She was nominated four times."

Halsey remembered that Susan Hayward was "very high-strung." He has two main memories of the shoot. In his scene at a party with Hayward, Halsey had to fetch hamburgers and Cokes: "I put the Coke down but knocked it all over the front of her dress." Halsey was mortified but she made no fuss, he recalled: "She looked down and said, 'Brett…did you get any on you?' I said 'No.' 'Okay, I'll go change my dress.'"

At the end of the scene, Halsey was supposed to throw the hamburger away but the lessons of economy he had learned on low-budget Bs were ingrained: "I was supposed to throw the hamburger away. I put it down. Wise said 'Cut. Throw the hamburger away.' We went again. I put it down. Wise said 'Cut. Why won't you throw down the hamburger?' I said 'Well, do you have another one?' Wise, he laughed." Halsey was not used to the resources of A-budget films. In the release print, there are no Cokes or hamburgers at all; perhaps as a result of these problems, just a wistful expression by Halsey at the end of the scene.

Working in Television

In those days, reputations could sometimes be made overnight in Hollywood with one prestigious television appearance. Unfortunately, Halsey never experienced overnight success:

> I did a show with Dennis Hopper for *Studio One* called "The Last Summer," a version of the Scott Fitzgerald story *Winter Dreams*—the poor kid in the golf club falls in love. Dennis Hopper was destined to be a star, from this. I was the rich kid. In those days, the town [Hollywood] was so small, you could become a star in one go. I did the dress rehearsal with Dennis Hopper and it was perfect. He was brilliant. We went out live on Sunday night. It was a disaster. We had blocked the show for three cameras and one of the cameras went off and the backup camera locked up, so we had to shoot it all with two cameras, so Dennis' big career was delayed, 'cause it was just a mess.
>
> I had already done the same show for *Playhouse 90* with John Cassavetes, for the same director. *Winter Dreams*. Same story—same role. It was basically the same script. It was the poor boy at the rich man's country club and I was the rich young guy.

The director was John Frankenheimer, who once stated in interview that he had a particular fondness for the work of Scott Fitzgerald. Halsey tells the following Frankenheimer story:

> He was *the* biggest star in live television. I remember once, one scene was a ballroom at the country club and he had two cameras on cranes, one going this way and one going that way and there were a lot of extras. The assistant director came and said, "John, we have to be careful we don't run over the extras" and John said, "Fuck 'em, let them get out of the way."

Halsey seemed to do all the popular television series of the day: *The Millionaire*, *Studio 57*, *Mackenzie's Raiders*, *Tales of the 77th Bengal Lancers*, *U.S. Marshal*, and so on. In fact, he had continuing roles in three episodes of *Raiders* and *Bengal Lancers*. Halsey commented, "I used to go from one to another so fast, I can't remember them all—these were all done between pictures." One of the more eventful shoots, for Halsey, was on *Bengal Lancers*. Halsey recalls that he was on horseback, with his rifle in his left hand and a pennant in his right hand, charging toward the Indians, and realized that, with both hands occupied, he would not be able to stop his horse. He tried to get the horse to stop but instead he fell off and landed in a spiny yucca bush. Halsey had done enough television and B movies to know it was virtually a sin to do retakes, so he decided to continue the charge towards the Indians on foot. So it took an hour before he could get the spines out of his rear end.

Halsey appeared three times in Keith Larsen's Western series *Brave Eagle*, which was filmed from the point of view of the Indians. Halsey played a young brave and recalls having to turn his feather headdress away from the wind, which was ruffling his feathers. One of Halsey's most prominent and widely seen early television guest appearances was in the highly popular *Gunsmoke* starring James Arness ("Helping Hand," 1955). The show was popular not only in the U.S. but in Great Britain, which had only limited U.S. imports on television, and worldwide. Halsey recalled the show: "The *Gunsmoke* that I worked on was on stage. They didn't go outside. Dodge City was built on a stage." The construction of the town made shooting a "little bit cheaper:"

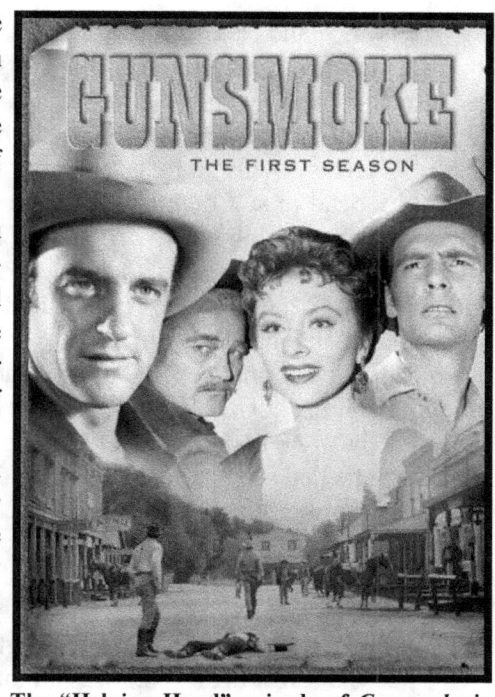

The "Helping Hand" episode of *Gunsmoke* is on the First Season DVD.

> They used the set they shot everything on. It was black-and-white. They would only go out when they had to. It was control they needed. When you shoot outside, you depend on the weather—the sun. One problem with shooting outside in a town is the sun moves—the shadows move—so when you match shots, sometimes you have trouble matching shadows.

It is likely they had an outdoor set as well:

> They must have, but not the town. Later they did but when I worked on it, the town was all on stage. What they would do with those permanent sets, like this, was they would have a wire on the top so they could put screens across to soften the shadows.

"Helping Hand" is a sad story of a misguided kid who is not really bad but too immature to avoid trouble. Halsey is very impressive in the role, partly because he looks so young, about 18. This helps him convey the kid's naivete. He is also good at being angry, as when he warns Marshal Dillon (James Arness), "Maybe I ought to be out looking for a gun." Dillon at the end has to shoot him dead in self defense. The kid was too stubborn and hotheaded to accept Marshal Dillon's help and advice and Halsey's affecting performance gives the show a tragic impact. Halsey commented, "Only thing I remember about that, he [Arness] had to grab me and lift me up. He lifted me up *like that*, no trouble at all, and I wasn't light."

Excellent performances like this revealed something of Halsey's extensive dramatic training at Universal and did not go completely unnoticed in the business. Producer Gene Corman told me he cast Halsey in a feature because of something he had seen him do, probably on television.

Halsey was seen as a firefighter in an interesting episode of *The 20th Century-Fox Hour* called "Smoke Jumpers" (1956), which Halsey clearly remembers:

> That was a film about forest firefighters and they'd parachute in to the forest fires. That was an interesting job. It was drama. We shot most of it on a stage at Fox and that was before all the protection things. At the end of the day, I'd come home and there were just gobs of black in my nose I'd dig out because of the smoke and stuff. It was a pretty good show. It was black and white, directed by Al Rogell, brother of Fox production manager Sid Rogell. It was one of those ensemble pieces. We were a group of firemen parachuting out of a plane. It was interesting.

Dick Clayton was the one who found television roles for Halsey. Like most young Hollywood actors, Halsey appeared in Lloyd Bridges' underwater series *Sea Hunt* (1958). Halsey remembered Bridges: "He was a sweet man, kind to young actors. It was shot here in the studio but the underwater scenes were shot in Florida, because the Pacific is cloudy." These ZIV-TV shows were shot in three days. He appeared in many long forgotten television shows such as *Silent Service* in which he played a young Naval officer in the WWII U.S. Submarine Service.

Halsey remembers working on the television show *West Point*:

> The assistant director on that was Erich Von Stroheim, Jr. He was very correct. He was supervising the other actors getting haircuts. He introduced himself to one of the actors: "I'm

Erich Von Stroheim, Jr." And the guy said, "Yeah, and I'm Fatty Arbuckle." That kid, his hair was cut down to the scalp.

Halsey was living a bachelor lifestyle in a house in Rosilla Place in Laurel Canyon. For a while, his actor friend Don Kennedy roomed there. Halsey remembered that Kennedy had a tense moment once on Steve McQueen's Western series *Wanted: Dead or Alive*:

> Steve was doing a TV series and drawing and playing with his pistol and pointing it at Don. Don said, "Steve, don't point that gun at me." Steve continued playing with his pistol. Don said, "Put that away—or I'll shove it up your ass." Steve put it away. Steve was the star and Don just a guest, but Steve put it away...Steve was a good actor, not as versatile as Paul Newman. I knew him, but he was less grounded, he was self-destructive.

Between B pictures Halsey remained highly visible on television. In 1959 Halsey had a small role as an artist in an unsold pilot for a detective series called *Brock Callahan*, starring Ken Clark. Clark had been an athlete but was a rather wooden actor, even when he went to Italy and starred in Westerns and spy pictures as Agent 077 Dick Malloy (Halsey would play another Agent 077, George Farrel). Halsey remembered that, in Rome, Ken "did a lot of pot." His main memory of *Brock Callahan*—he had no recollection at all of director George Blair or executive producer Harry Ackerman—was working with actor Leo Gordon: "Another crazy guy. He pointed a gun in my face. It was loaded with a blank. He said 'Don't worry, I won't fire.' I knew he was nuts, so I put my arm up in front of my face. The gun went off. He said 'Oh, Brett, I'm sorry.' I said 'Oh, I'm not sorry I put my arm up.' He would have shot me in the eye."

Halsey got to work with the great Peter Lorre when they both appeared in an episode of *Five Fingers* in 1959. *Five Fingers* was an NBC series starring David Hedison about a double agent who poses as a talent agent. Hedison remembered Halsey's appearance in the show: "His work was quite wonderful. But then, I'm a fan."

Halsey is indeed interesting in the show. He made a creditable stab at an impossible accent:

> The problem was presented to me, an Arab educated at Oxford pretending to be an American. So I thought, "Well, I'll just play an American." When I played a *Mike Hammer*, I played a Bulgarian diplomat and they asked me, "Can you do a Bulgarian

accent?" I said, "Sure." So I did this general Slavic accent and afterward the director said, "You did a wonderful job with that Bulgarian accent." I said, "Come off it. You wouldn't know a Bulgarian accent if it came up and bit you in the ass." And he laughed and said, "I *don't* know a Bulgarian accent."

Lamont Johnson directed that episode of *Five Fingers* and did not say anything to Halsey about the accent:

We were kind of friendly. I knew him when he was an actor. The one thing about that show that has always stayed in my mind was that we had a scene with Peter Lorre shot at the Bel Air Hotel, which is a pretty posh place, and the director said, "Well, Peter should be eating." He said, "Go ahead, Peter, order something." And Peter ordered this big bowl of caviar. The Production Manager nearly died when they got the bill for this caviar. Peter Lorre was a lot of fun.

There appears to be genuine flirtation between Halsey and his future wife Luciana Paluzzi, co-star of *Five Fingers*. Halsey acknowledged this: "Yes, we were living together. It was an odd time because actors couldn't live together unless they were married, so she rented a house across the street from my house in Rosilla Place and that was her official home, but we lived together."

It is formula television, but it has a few interesting moments for the student of Halsey's work: his hesitation at having to shoot his protector David Hedison, his (apparently genuine) fascination with Luciana and her reference to Halsey's height, which he acknowledges. Halsey and David (Fly and Son of) work well together on screen as a team.

Fox had faith in Halsey and then starred him in a television pilot called *White Hunter*, set in Africa but shot at Fox's ranch in the West Valley. The pilot did not sell and Halsey was not surprised: "It didn't sell because it was kind of stupid." His main memory of the shoot is how cold it was at night. Co-star Felicia Farr, Jack Lemmon's wife, sat around with Halsey drinking because of the cold. "I had to do this run towards the group. It was a long run and then I'd get to the group and she'd break up and start laughing. It happened three or four times. She was fun." The show upset sponsor Henry Kaiser as it featured stock footage using Land Rovers. He was furious because he made Jeeps. Halsey was amused that the highly paid television executives would make such a foolish mistake. Halsey never knew Gregory Peck but wore his jacket from *The Snows of Kilimanjaro* in this show, and some stock shots from the film were also used.

Halsey in the TV pilot *White Hunter*

Halsey succeeded in becoming a recognized television star when he landed a lead role in a show called *Follow the Sun* (1961). Fox had already shot a few episodes starring Barry Coe and Gary Lockwood but decided they needed a bigger name and persuaded Halsey to do it. They then inserted some short sequences with Halsey into these episodes. Halsey was pleased, because he was paid for the entire episode. *The New York Times*, October 15, 1961, Sunday edition featured a big advertisement with a slightly melancholy picture of Halsey and the text: "An exciting new star co-stars with Hawaii. Say Aloha to Brett Halsey, a sun-loving free lance writer who likes to pound his typewriter to the rhythm of swaying palms and hula hips."

Halsey remembers how Fox got him to sign up with the show:

> When I did *Follow the Sun* at Fox, the studio chief Peter Levathes had been in banking. I had a "no TV" clause in my contract. They wanted me to do this TV series. I said, "No." They kept asking me. Finally, Peter Levathes called me into his office. I felt like getting his goat, knowing he was not a show person. He asked, "What's the problem? What can we do?" I said, "Gardner McKay has a bigger dressing room than mine." He said, "Would you do the show if we gave you

Art or Instinct in the Movies...

Follow the Sun with Cesar Romero, Elsa Lanchester and Halsey

a bigger dressing room?" I said, "Yes." "Okay, we'll give you a bigger dressing room." He was all prepared for a conflict about money and couldn't understand an actor could make an issue about a dressing room.

Halsey had some wild parties in his dressing room. One was so raunchy that the director broke his ankle. Halsey was given a bill to repair the hallway of the dressing room, and he and Gardner McKay were both fired but later reinstated. Fox told Halsey, "We've decided not to fire you." One actor guesting on *Follow the Sun* came to the party with his wife, took one look and said on the way out, "No, I can't do this any more."

Despite going on to earn big fees in his years of Italian stardom, Halsey was not exclusively motivated by money: "Self-fulfilment is most important, because actors don't make any money. $5,000 a year is the average."

Follow the Sun's pilot sold but the show was short-lived, as it was too dark to get large ratings, though it spawned a Dell comic book. Every week the show alternated between each of the three co-stars and Halsey starred in only 11 episodes, but worked hard, spending one or two hours each night on the script. The show employed veteran director Jacques Tourneur on a Halsey episode. "Sgt. Kolchak Fades Away." Robert Vaughn appeared with Halsey in the first episode, "A Rage for Justice," and also in another episode without Halsey.

When the series was canceled, Halsey was philosophical, telling *TV Guide*:

> I learned a lot from practically every B picture role I ever did. I don't regret the series either. It started out as a dark show. Everything seemed to take place at night and it was all pretty downbeat and heavy-handed. We finally got things changed but it was apparently too late. The show we have now is the show we should have had when we started last fall.

Looking back today on *Follow the Sun*, Halsey feels it was doomed because it was badly produced. "It was set at night. It should have been light and airy, pretty people in Hawaii, not a heavy drama." The show only existed because Jeep manufacturer Henry Kaiser sponsored some shows on ABC for Jeep ads. Jules Bricken directed the pilot, starring Halsey, who was not impressed.

> *Follow the Sun* was in the time of *Hawaiian Eye*. You figured you're going to see nice-looking people in sun, and he wanted to do this heavy drama, which was *totally* wrong. I felt it, but I didn't have the sense or the confidence to go into the production headquarters and fight with him, because he fought like hell with the people at the top. That's one regret I have. The show ended up all in the dark. The leading lady was much older. She was a New York actress. She was very nice but I thought she was too old to play opposite me then. It was just all wrong for *Follow the Sun*. It was 7:30 Sunday night. Our competition was *Dennis the Menace* on CBS and *Disney's Wonderful World of Color* on NBC. *That* was early Sunday evening. That's not

that show. That's a 10 o'clock show. It was just wrong. It was the first show. It got *terrible* reviews. So, I don't think he was very good at all.

Halsey is actually excellent in this moody drama but suffered one bad review:

Gardner McKay was not very well regarded as an actor. One of my reviews in one of the trades said, "At last there is an actor on television who makes Gardner McKay look good."

The reviewer was Cecil Smith of the *Los Angeles Times*. Amusingly, Smith was asked to play a newspaperman in a later episode of *Follow the Sun*. Director Ted Post wanted nine real newspapermen to play reporters in the episode "Conspiracy of Silence." Smith wrote in the *Los Angeles Times* (December 8, 1961):

Star of *Follow the Sun* is Brett Halsey. I once gave Mr. Halsey a dreadful review, saying his acting was so bad it made Gardner McKay look good. Brett is a pleasant fellow but didn't take too kindly to this. Now he plans vengeance by reviewing me. He even has his opening line, "Smith's acting is so bad he makes Brett Halsey *and* Gardner McKay look good." You know, he's right.

Despite the validity of Halsey's criticisms of the show, "A Rage for Justice" works very well as a television film noir, with its moody night scenes and overly romantic music, as in the hotel scene where Rita (Ilka Windish) asks Paul (Halsey) if he is a good writer: "Well, it won't go into the *Literary Review*." These scenes have a European-style atmosphere that anticipates some of the films that Halsey would go on to make in Europe, like *Web of Violence* and *Perversion Story*.

Although Halsey felt Ilka Windish was too old to be playing opposite him, they have a nice, friendly rapport. Halsey's character moves from a sorrowful demeanour as he watches Rita at her daughter's grave to a sudden forcefulness as he interrupts her shooting Robert Vaughn for the death of her daughter.

In another episode, "A Ghost in Her Gazebo," Halsey co-starred with Cesar Romero and Elsa Lanchester. Halsey recalled that when he was in the hospital having his tonsils removed, Lanchester's husband Charles Laughton was on an upstairs floor. She visited Halsey and, when asked about her husband, replied, "Oh, he's dying." Halsey always remembered the matter-of-fact way she said it. "She was so sweet, so accepting. He died a couple of days later."

A popular episode is "Night Song" due to the appearance of singer Julie London. Halsey exhibits leading man charm in their scenes together. His performance in the show makes one wonder what would have become of his film career if he had stayed in the U.S. rather than relocating to Europe

Mike Steckler landed a job as dialogue director on *Follow the Sun* with the help of his good friend Halsey—a good turn, since Steckler had accidentally damaged Halsey's $13,000 German sports car in a head-on collision as they were driving down a winding road after a party. Thankfully, no one was injured.

Halsey now had some influence in the business as star of a network television show and gave a helping hand to old friends whenever possible. He had an early break on the *Life of Riley* show starring William Bendix and, when he read the script of *Sgt. Kolchak Fades Away*, he thought the role was perfect for Bendix and pestered the producers until they signed him.

In later years, Halsey credited *Follow the Sun* writer/producer Ellis Kadison with encouraging him to write his first novel. They renewed their friendship when Halsey returned from Italy and, when he heard Halsey's stories, he offered to get him a book deal. Meanwhile, Halsey was enjoying his television fame, especially the invitations to glamorous functions and galas. Halsey has written about the way power and influence almost went to his head:

> 6:30 p. m. (12), Follow the Sun. (Premiere). "A Rage for Justice." Opening show in a new adventure series apparently set in Honolulu. This one stars series regular Brett Halsey who bears a startling resemblance in style, ability and even looks to "Adventure in Paradise" Star Gardner McKay. Halsey plays a magazine writer who, tonight, helps an opera star prove that her daughter's death was not accidental. Ilka Windish as the vengeful singer contributes a strong performance which succeeds in sustaining the hour.
>
> 7 p. m. (5), Ed Sullivan. Highlights of the show include a production number imaginatively handled by Choreographer John Butler, for songs contributed by Gordon and Sheila MacRae, singly, together, and in groups, including such old-time standards as "Daisy," "Oh Johnnie," "Sweet Adeline," and "Chicago."

Today's Best Bets

> Back when I was starring in the ABC TV series *Follow the Sun*, I was near the top of the heap as far as being a commonly recognizable showbiz celebrity. I confess that I enjoyed and took advantage of this lofty distinction; that is, until the incident that brought me back to reality and taught me a life-long lesson in humility.
>
> It all started one Saturday morning when I was to go to Phoenix, Arizona, on a publicity junket for the show. I was tired from a long week of shooting and didn't really want to go, but it was a part of the job, so what could I do? A studio limo was to pick me up and get me to the airport in time to

catch my flight. At the time, my house was near the end of one of those difficult, winding roads at the top of Laurel Canyon; and as the clock was advancing dangerously close to the zero hour, the limo was nowhere in sight.

I called the studio to demand "Where the hell is my ride?" I was informed that the driver had probably lost his way. It was too late to call a taxi, so I reluctantly agreed to jump in my new BMW 507 sports car and race down the mountain and across town to LAX. BMW had built only a few 507s. In Los Angeles only Elvis Presley, one or two others, and myself had one. I was cursing the network, the studio, and the limo driver all the way to the airport, because this was no way to treat one of their most valuable stars and, besides, I hated the idea of leaving my treasured jewel of a car in the hands of those insensitive parking attendants at the airport.

I arrived at the airport, quickly entrusted my car keys to the head attendant, and dashed into the terminal. Normally I enjoyed being recognized in public places, but this time I was late and had no time for fawning fans as I raced to the ticket counter.

"Damn," I cursed. I was too late. Too late to catch my plane, which was already on the runway. Well, I was pissed. My time was too valuable to be squandered by the inefficient jerks at the studio and network, which couldn't even properly schedule a simple limo pick up. Naturally, the first thing I did was go to a phone and call those inefficient jerks at the studio and network and tell them what I thought.

"I sure told those bastards," I thought as, puffed up with my own importance, I strode back to the valet service area. The head attendant quickly sent someone for my car. While waiting impatiently, I happened to notice what appeared to be a nondescript, middle-aged black woman standing off to one side, shyly watching me. The time was dragging by and I was becoming more agitated because my car was not coming. I gave the black woman a hasty glance, which she returned with a shy smile. Finally, after what seemed like hours, the attendant returned, apologizing because he couldn't figure out how to get my BMW started. The starter mechanism was a bit complicated; so I curtly explained the process and impatiently watched him dash off toward the VIP parking lot. A few more minutes passed by and I noticed out of the corner of my eye that the woman had gotten up her nerve to approach me. I was polite but cool as she said, "Excuse me, Mr. Halsey, but I'm a long-time fan and just wanted to introduce myself." I smiled condescendingly as she went on, "My name is Ella Fitzgerald."

"Ella Fitzgerald," I repeated as my super-ego suffered a sudden and extremely sharp deflation. "My God," I thought, "Ella Fitzgerald is shy about introducing herself to *me*." I think that outwardly I kept my cool but, underneath it all, I was awash with humiliation and in too much shock to remember much of what we talked about before my car and her driver arrived. Of course, they both rolled up much too soon, but I never forgot the lesson I learned that Saturday morning. *Nobody* (except maybe Ella Fitzgerald) is nearly so important as they pump themselves to think they are.

Halsey did quite a bit of television during the 1970s, because when he moved back to the U.S., he found that his popularity remained in Europe and did not cross the ocean with him. Gene Corman pointed out that the fate that befell Halsey when he returned to Hollywood—no recognition of his Italian stardom—was not unusual. The same happened to Stewart Granger after a period in Italy (Gene produced a Granger movie, Roger Corman's *The Secret Invasion*, in 1964). On the other hand, Gene made the point that Halsey eventually bounced back into the American public consciousness in the medium of television commercials: "He was the Old Spice man. He was very big." Although Halsey would go back to leading man roles in Italy in the late 1980s, only film buffs really noticed, as Gene observed: "Those films didn't play in the States."

Gene agreed with Jay Bernstein's view that what it takes to be a star in Italy is different from what it takes to be a star in Hollywood.

The quiet response to Halsey's return caused some financial constraints. Clayton noted, "Los Angeles in the 1970s wasn't Rome in the 1960s. It was getting a bit more difficult. There was not so much money flowing." Heidi controlled the purse strings more tightly, out of necessity. Her success in Las Vegas kept the family afloat, as Halsey did not work

Halsey as the Old Spice sailor

much for the first year after returning from Rome. Once back in Los Angeles, he turned to television and, eventually, to regular daytime roles in soap operas. Overall, he would do stints on four soap operas.

Halsey is a little bitter about the way actors are treated at auditions, especially when they have already made their name and reputation:

> Russ Tamblyn, star of *Seven Brides for Seven Brothers*, was a good friend of mine once. They were casting for a TV series of *Seven Brides* and Russ went on an audition for the series. The two producers said, "What have you done?" Russ said, "What do you mean? Haven't you seen the picture?" Neither of them had seen the picture. Veteran star Lee J. Cobb once went on audition. The company's producer asked him what he had done. Cobb asked him, "What have *you* done?"

Halsey began to re-establish himself in Hollywood, first with a couple of appearances in a good hit television comedy Western series, *Alias Smith and Jones* at Universal, starring Pete Duel and Ben Murphy.

Halsey's 1971-72 appearances on *Alias Smith and Jones* remain among his best television work. One, "Return to Devil's Hole" (1971), was released on video in the U.K. It was directed by Bruce Kessler, who had made several motorcycle pictures. Halsey recalled that working with Bruce was "fine" and he was an efficient television director. Halsey related with amusement that Bruce objected to the florid hand expressions Halsey had picked up from working in Italy: "Bruce Kessler said, 'Brett, could you put your hands in your pockets, because you look like an Italian actor.'"

Halsey's experience making Italian Westerns was more of a hindrance than help on *Alias Smith and Jones*:

> When I came back, I was really good with my gun, because you stand around and you draw your gun. There was a set-up with either Smith or Jones. I was supposed to draw first. Then he draws and kills me. He was so slow that I couldn't draw slowly enough. I'd draw long before he'd draw and it didn't work. I slowed but still drew before him. I had a Colt. I had my own holster and own Colt. My name was engraved in gold; it was later stolen. In the end, they had to do it in cuts, because I could not slow down enough.

Back in Hollywood after his years in Rome he could not hear the camera the way he could in Italy. That interrupted his performance because he thought the camera was not working.

Actor and acting coach Jeff Corey, who directed the second Halsey *AS&J*, "The Day The Amnesty Came Through" (1972), coached talents like Jack Nicholson and Robert Vaughn. Halsey remembered him with amusement:

I had known him as an acting teacher, but never studied with him. Every word out of his mouth was like Moses…very intense. It was getting late on the set and, at Universal directors get fired if they run late. Now, Jeff was someone who loved to rehearse. He had a rehearsal studio in his house. He saw it was getting dark and knew there was no getting late and he lost it. "That's it, no rehearsal." I said to him, "Jeff, how do you prepare your students for things like this?" He said, "Brett, I teach theory. The shit they have to learn for themselves."

The series never recovered from the shocking loss of leading man Pete Duel, who shot himself in the head at home at the height of his popularity. Halsey refused to believe it was suicide: "He was stoned. It was an accident."

Halsey's reappearance on Hollywood television shows failed to help him acquire a starring role in a series. Henry Silva commented:

When Brett returned to Hollywood, they gave him small parts. That's the terrible thing about the industry. Hollywood only cares about Hollywood. They didn't give a damn about Brett's exposure in Europe. Dick Clayton was one of the best agents in town but probably Brett's agents didn't push hard enough for him. I fired every Hollywood agent I had. Brett did soap opera on daytime TV and there's a prejudice against soap stars, a phony class thing. That sent him off to teach in Costa Rica.

Jay Bernstein explained that occasional appearances in episodic television were not likely to re-establish Halsey in Hollywood in any big way: "The industry doesn't watch those shows. Guest shots got no-one anywhere. I was paying $2,500 for top guest stars. Ricardo Montalban told me he might have to sell his house. He said he earned only $17,000 the last year, yet he worked every other week. Unless you are a lead, you don't earn big money."

It was certainly not that Halsey was difficult or demanded the kind of star treatment once afforded him in Rome. Jay said, "Brett's so easy to work with. I employed him twice, and I think there's no other actor I worked with twice in television."

One of Halsey's many claims to fame is that he co-starred in a television commercial with John Wayne. Halsey would accept television commercials because they were lucrative but also because "actors act—you're not an actor if you don't act." The Wayne commercial was the first:

Actors didn't do commercials. Models did commercials. But my agent said, "You'll be in it with John Wayne. For Gillette."

> We were showing the commercial in the American World Series. Four or five showings.

Years later, as a voting member of the Academy of Motion Picture Arts and Sciences (Halsey was elected in the early 1970s), he had not seen *True Grit*, but voted for John Wayne to win the Oscar. He felt it was owed to Wayne.

Halsey did not vote for director Elia Kazan's Lifetime Achievement Award because of his co-operation with the House Committee on Un-American Activities in the McCarthy era:

> He was a rat. He gave up people to save his skin. The voting members didn't vote for Kazan, although he was talented. The Board of Governors decided.

In the 1970s Halsey's Italian stardom counted for little, forcing him to turn to soap operas. Daytime television was something of a graveyard for established actors. Ironically, at the very same time, his name was appearing in big letters outside cinemas in Paris and other European cities that were featuring his Italian films, but that meant nothing in Hollywood.

Halsey kept going with guest roles in television shows. Halsey has an amusing memory of *The Bionic Woman* episode "The Antidote" (1978) in which he played a doctor: "I was going to give her a shot, and I picked up the wrong arm. The director screamed, 'Drop it, drop it. That's her bionic arm!'"

In 1976, Halsey appeared in the interesting film noir series *City of Angels*. "That was stupid for television. It was too expensive. It was set in the '30s, so they had to have all these cars and all the costumes. It wasn't a very good budget and it wasn't well-executed."

Halsey lent his talent to a number of popular television shows such as *Love Boat* and *Fantasy Island*. Although audience favorites, Halsey wasn't impressed with the shows:

> *Fantasy Island* and *Love Boat*, I always played the same part. It was either the lawyer or the doctor or this or that. I'm not sure if it was *Fantasy Island*, I got the script. I just flipped through it to my part. "Okay." And I learned my lines for that day and I was sitting there, and the director came 'round and sat next to me and said, "Hey Brett...I'm having a little trouble with the story here. I'd like to discuss it with you." He knew I was a writer. I hadn't read the script, so I didn't know the story. So I said some kind of generalities and then he had to go. But I never, ever, did a job again after that without reading the script.

When Halsey left *Search for Tomorrow* he moved from New York back to California. He did not work much for a year, though he did do a small role in the television movie *Crash* directed by Barry Shear, a lively television talent who had directed superior episodes of *The Man from U.N.C.L.E.* and *Police Woman* and an impressive independent feature, the minor cult movie *The Todd Killings*. *Crash* was not quite in that league but was deemed good enough for theatrical release in some countries including Brazil and Yugoslavia. Halsey was Eddie Albert's co-pilot involved in the airliner crash. He recalled:

> Barry was a good director. That was an interesting picture. I think I'd just come back from New York when I did that. I was working in a soap there. That was something when we crashed. They had about a ton of mud. We were just breathing this dust for hours, Eddie Albert and I. Of course we knew it was in one take, because to set that up again would take hours. I liked Barry Shear. He died young.

Halsey was strong as a con man in the *Fantasy Island* episode "The Boss" (1979), more formula television. He was often typed as suave con men in episodic television. A rather good example was the "Max Smith" episode of *Top Cops* (1993) in which Halsey relishes his role as conman Max Craven. His performance calls to mind the humor he brought to Lester in *Touch of Death* (1988) in both his mannerisms and appearance. *Top Cops* is a recreation of crime cases and its quasi-documentary feel makes this one of Halsey's more unusual television appearances. Had it featured a more extensive scripted role, it might have been truly memorable.

In the *Buck Rogers in the 25th Century* episode "Cruise Ship to the Stars" (1979), Halsey acted with Dorothy Stratten, who was murdered by her former husband over her affair with film director Peter Bogdanovich, whose career faltered afterwards. Thinking of Stratten, Halsey remarked, "I saw her as a really sweet girl. Some pretty girls have an edge. She had no edge....Her death broke something inside Peter Bogdanovich."

Halsey plays the captain of the cruise ship on the show and has a

Dorothy Stratten, Brett Halsey and Gil Gerard in *Buck Rogers*

couple of good dialogue scenes, especially an opening dialogue with Dorothy Stratten, whose voice was then dubbed by the producers.

British director Sidney Hayers, who had many impressive credits including the superb occult movie *Night of the Eagle* and episodes of *The Avengers*, directed an episode of *The Fall Guy*, "The Meek Shall Inherit Rhondda" (1981), in which Halsey appeared. He captures Halsey's wry humor as Jerry Rome, a vain movie star interested in playing the lead in a Francis Ford Coppola movie. This was years before Halsey actually found himself in a Coppola movie. Halsey registers a look of surprise at the end when Colt Seavers (Lee Majors) proves not to have died in the fall from the airplane—and, in an amusing bit of business, Jerry Rome preens himself for a police mugshot. Halsey's old friend Robert Wagner briefly appeared in this episode.

In the *Charlies Angels* episode "Attack Angels" (1981), Halsey portrays the head of a corporation who is in danger. In one scene while sitting alone at his desk Halsey's character conveys worry simply by drumming his fingers on the desktop, an economical screen shorthand that made Halsey an effective character actor in episodic television.

An episode of *Knight Rider* (1983) found Halsey working again for Bernie Kowalski, who had directed *Blood and Steel* and the *Columbo* episode in which he had appeared. This was a pleasure, as he had become friendly with Bernie after the movie was finished: "Bernie was a good director and always fun to be with. I can't remember our conversations having anything to do with show biz."

Halsey was living in Pasadena, which was a 20-minute drive to Burbank when he was working at Warner Bros. for the company Lou-Step Productions, which produced *The Dukes of Hazzard*.

Halsey was hired to write by the executive producer, on the basis of his novelistic success. He was to be involved in developing new projects for Lou-Step, which was part of Warners. Former actor Skip Ward, a long-time friend of Halsey's, was the show's producer. The two male leads of *The Dukes of Hazzard* decided to go on strike together to strengthen their bargaining position in demanding a pay rise. Halsey recalled, "They got fired. The studio said, 'To hell with them, we'll get new Dukes.'" Halsey was then asked to serve as an acting coach for the two inexperienced replacements, Byron Cherry and Chris Mayer, because of his long acting experience. Halsey recalled:

> They told me they had hired two inexperienced actors. It's Friday. I said, "When do they start shooting?" "Monday." "How inexperienced are they?" "Well, one of them doesn't know what ACTION is." I helped them as much as I could. Eventually, I quit. I said, "The kids are getting too dependent on me. They won't do anything unless I tell them, so I'm going to Tahiti."

Dorris Halsey had offered him a free ticket she had received in connection with her work as the Motion Picture Consultant to the Government of Tahiti. Halsey found Tahiti a great place to relax because it was so unspoiled. He spent over a month there with Hugh Kelly, one of the famous Bali Hai Boys, at the Bali Hai Hotel and examined the voluminous material the Boys had accumulated with a view to a screenplay about their lives. Halsey completed a preliminary treatment and Dorris tried to sell it as a television Movie of the Week to Joca Productions. She was also trying to place another unproduced script of Halsey's, inspired by his childhood in Costa Mesa, *The Girls of Fashion Island*. Today, Halsey is still considering reviving "The Bali Hai Boys" as a novel.

Byron Cherry and Chris Mayer with Halsey on the set of *The Dukes of Hazzard*

Halsey also acted in *The Dukes of Hazzard* a few times, purely to keep his screen actor's insurance benefits up to date.

His appearances in *The Dukes of Hazzard* (1979-1984) are fun in a lighthearted fashion, but the show remains irredeemable. Halsey exhibits complete confidence as a horse thief in "The Rustlers," but the story is nonsense. "The Dukes in Hollywood" is slightly better, featuring Halsey as a Hollywood producer in a caricature that prefigures his parody producer in the movie *Ratboy*

(1986), but is still basic, unchallenging fluff for an actor of his range. He was also in another episode, "Enos in Trouble (aired 11/19/82)."

Halsey wrote and developed shows at Warners, such as the spy drama *Passport to Danger*. Halsey recalled:

> There was an actor who played my son in soap opera, Terry Lester, and when we were preparing or trying to sell *Passport to Danger*, I wanted Terry to play the lead, so we took him to the executives at Warner Bros. we were trying to sell it to and when we walked in the building, the receptionists said to Terry, "Oh my God, Terry Lester's just walked in the building." It could have been a big movie star. We went upstairs to the suite with all the executives and they didn't have any idea who he was. *They* turned us down. All the women....

This story illustrates how little notice the industry takes of daytime television, as Halsey himself already discovered.

At Warners, Halsey's parking place was next to Paul Newman's, "but I never saw him." He particularly admired Newman: "That's what I like...beautiful career. Paul Newman just stole the film *The Road to Perdition* from Tom Hanks, he was so good."

Halsey played the suave villain Jason Darius in the *Airwolf* episode "Sins of the Past" (1984). It is a pity he did not appear regularly as the charismatic, sophisticated crook. Halsey remembered the show: "That was fun. The lead was Jan-Michael Vincent. He was in his bad period, with drink. He had a fight with his girlfriend, who broke his arm when she slammed a car door on him, so he had to go through half the thing with this cast, hiding it."

Halsey's friend Kathy Shower was also in this episode, playing a model, though Halsey had nothing to do with her casting. She explained:

> It was just coincidental that we happened to audition. We had different agents and everything at the time, but it was a nice surprise when we got there. The best thing was they filmed it in Catalina and they flew us over in the morning on a helicopter, if you were a guest actor on the show.

Her memories of the show are not good:

> It ran late into the evening and they told me that I had to go back on the boat. Well, the people coming over called the boat the "Barfamatic" because they were just so ill. It was so choppy by the time they got there. I was eating corn ball loops and I

just stuffed myself all day working on the set and I said, "Oh, I can't take that ride back, there's just no way" and they said, "Well, we'll give you something, don't worry, you won't be sick, we'll give you Dramamine and everything." I'm not good at that kind of stuff. So they gave me these pills and I took the pills and they came up. They said, "Okay, we got the helicopter, you can fly back." I don't remember the flight. They left me off at an airport. I fell asleep on a bench and they pumped me three hours later. It was just not a good experience, *Airwolf*, for me. It was traumatic. Brett flew over and flew back.

Halsey plays a crooked Southern sheriff in the 1984 *Matt Houston* episode "Caged." "I remember that particular show. I don't think it was very well written. I did another *Matt Houston* that I liked."

Halsey had an unannounced appearance in a two-line scene in the "Insubordination" episode of the then-popular female cop show *Cagney and Lacey*. He played a junior executive who accosted Cagney in a bar and she expressed surprise at being picked up in a gay bar. Halsey smiled and said, "This isn't a gay bar." Halsey explained his tiny unbilled appearance: "I was a friend of the producer and I probably needed the job. They would have said, 'We've got this part'."

Halsey's acting career had slowed, so he was pleased to take up an executive job offer from his friend Jay Bernstein, whose television production company was thriving. Halsey also appeared in two episodes of Jay's series *Mike Hammer* and tried to sell Jay one of his own scripts. Jay could not remember the circumstances of the job offer:

> He would not have suggested it. Probably the job was open... Brett didn't work much then, as an actor. He never sold himself—I asked *him* to work with me. He was Head of Devel-

opment for two years. That's a lot of time spent dealing with someone I don't know.

As Vice-President in charge of development, Halsey had meetings with writers and had to read four or five scripts a day, followed by socializing in the evening. He did the job for two years until finally resigning because he found it too demanding: "The work was too hard. Too much work. For me to promote a TV show, I needed a star name actor and star writers. I had to wear a mask. It was part of the selling." Halsey would consider projects from stars like Robert Culp, whose demands were too great for a company the size of Jay Bernstein Productions. "Too big a star," Halsey commented: "As I recall, he wanted the production to buy him a converted PT boat that was in Washington and shoot a series, starring him and the boat, somewhere near Seattle, Washington. He also wanted to direct and made other demands that could not be met."

Jay only paid Halsey "a modest salary," but he had a huge office and an excellent expense account: "I made money on expenses." And Jay could be very volatile. While Halsey was working for him, they had an "adversarial" relationship but after he resigned, they were "friends again." Jay carried a loaded gun, for which he had a permit, even in his own house and once took it out and waved it about at a party, until Halsey took it from him.

He also discovered that a vice-president had to "do awful things": "A man was sent to me, who had been president of a company I had worked for as a kid. He needed a job. I had no job to give him. I thought 'Oh, my God.' " Halsey was relieved to go back to the relative fun of being an actor for hire. There was a reason he appeared in two episodes of *Mike Hammer*: "To keep up my Screen Actors Guild insurance, I had to earn a certain amount even as an actor, so part of my deal with Jay was I had to work in *Mike Hammer* twice, so that's kind of illegal. Actors are supposed to audition for jobs, because the job should be available to everyone." But he was not paid more or given any special treatment.

Working as a P.I.

Halsey remembers his early struggles in show business:

> During the early days, I was often close to being broke and worried about feeding my little family. One of my fellow actor pals, Burt Nelson, was doing some part-time bodyguard work for a detective agency run by the legendary former New York cop, Barney Ruditsky. One day Burt told me that one of Barney's young bodyguards had been shot while protecting a wife from her husband. [The husband killed the wife. The bodyguard caught a bullet in his foot while diving behind a sofa.]
>
> Anyway, a job was open, and Burt arranged an interview for me with Ruditsky. I pumped myself up and looked as formidable as I could for the interview. Barney must have liked me because shortly before he hired me, he smiled and reminded me that my fly was open...
>
> At that time I was still too young to have even played a detective on TV, so I was completely on my own with my first assignment, which was to go to the house of the famous movie star, Linda Darnell, and guard against any intrusion by her estranged husband. I don't remember his name. I was also to sweep the house for any telephone bugs. I didn't have any electronic equipment, and wouldn't have known a telephone bug from a cockroach, but I went through the motions. I never saw Miss Darnell. She remained closed up in her upstairs bedroom during my entire stay. They told me she was keeping close company with a bottle of vodka, but since I never saw her or a bottle, I can't say for sure.
>
> It was a big Beverly Hills house and, after I had completed my search for a bug in the main floor and the basement, I settled in a chair in the library, where I had a clear view of the front door—just in case the husband was to come calling.
>
> Strangely enough, this experience got me started to think about writing. The library was lined with heavy oak bookcases, so, in my boredom after a few hours of quiet solitude, I began checking the book titles. I dragged out a copy of Budd Schulberg's *The Disenchanted*. It is a wonderfully told story about how old Hollywood destroys its own. Here I was, sitting in the home of one of Hollywood's fading idols, reading about a history that she certainly had some part of.

I was so caught up in the book that her husband could have come in with a blazing machinegun and I probably wouldn't have noticed.

The rest of my few days at the Darnell mansion were quite uneventful. I never did meet the famous actress, but through this book, I did meet the talent of Mr. Schulberg. As soon as possible, I picked up a copy of *What Makes Sammy Run*, which was another enthralling experience for me. I started thinking that maybe someday I could tell some of these stories—maybe not as well as Budd Schulberg, but it wouldn't hurt to try. Of course my main preoccupation at that time was getting my acting career on course but, in the back of my mind, I always knew that someday—*someday*—I would try to write a novel...

Although I'd been working at my acting career for a very few years, I regarded my stint as a private eye as in-between employment, and it was to last only a couple of months. I remember that I was offered a permit to carry a gun, but I declined. I didn't think it would look so good for my actor image if it ever were to become known that I had to shoot someone—even in the line of my in-between duty.

There was a very famous Hollywood producer who, while in the midst of a difficult divorce, hired our agency to identify the man who had been seen squiring his estranged wife around town.

For some reason, the assignment fell to me, the least experienced and least qualified for the job. They knew that most weekends he would come in from out-of-town, but that's all they knew. My job was to find out his name, what he did for a living, and where he lived. The only information I was given was that the wife was working in a local play and the boyfriend would probably pick her up after the show.

I discreetly positioned my car so that I had a clear view of the stage door and, while I waited for her to appear, I began to struggle for an idea of how I was going to accomplish my mission. I immediately rejected the thought of walking up to the man, introducing myself and asking for his vital statistics. I thought and thought and, coming up with a complete blank, I just decided to wing it.

A nice-looking man met her at the stage door, helped her into a taxi and off they went. I followed the taxi for the mile or so it took for them to arrive at the well-known Sunset Strip nightclub The Interlude. By the time I parked my car and made my way into the club, they were already seated at a cozy, intimate table. I settled in at the bar, made some mental notes about the man's appearance and watched—still absolutely in the dark about how to get close enough to them to maybe pick up a few tidbits of useful conversation. It was impossible. I sat glumly for about an hour, nursing my expense-account drink, until they got up to leave. I hung back a bit as I followed them out the door. They hesitated a moment on the sidewalk, then turned and began walking up the street toward Larry Findlay's, a popular club nearby.

There was quite a crowd waiting to be allowed into Larry Findlay's. The wife recognized an up-and-coming TV detective and his girlfriend and moved to his side. The TV actor had been a classmate of mine in acting school, so I quickly took the opportunity to move in a little closer and say hello. Although I was standing next to the subject of my investigation, I knew it wasn't the proper time to begin my interrogation.

The crowd wasn't moving and the man impatiently suggested that they go somewhere else. My heart sank. I had him almost in my grasp and I was about to lose my prey. A moment passed and then I heard a voice from the door calling my name. I looked up in surprise to recognize a close actor friend, who was working at his in-between job as Larry Findlay's' late-night doorman. "How many are you?" he yelled over the crowd. Without a glance to my four companions, I responded, "We're five." "Come on in."

Needless to say, even though the wife still did very well in the divorce, my boss and the client were quite impressed with the completeness of my report. By the way, none of the participants were ever told the true identity of the undercover private eye.

Independents

As a freelancing actor Halsey found himself on auditions at studios both large and small. He appeared in a number of features for independents. These were generally low budget but offered Halsey progressively larger parts until he became a regular leading man. They were also a great learning opportunity and almost certainly paved the way for his success both as a contract player at Fox and as a big star in Italy.

He did *Three Bad Sisters* (1956), directed by Gilbert Kay (who later helmed *Follow the Sun*), for Schenck-Koch. He played an artist who was the lover of one of the sisters. Halsey has only a vague memory of it: "I don't remember the picture very well. I liked Gil Kay. I think I worked with him a couple of times. It was another one of those cheapies. I think that was my first independent picture after leaving Universal. Leaving the comfort of being under contract was difficult because I didn't know any other."

Halsey has an uncredited role in *The Girl He Left Behind* (1956) starring Tab Hunter and Natalie Wood. He remembered Natalie:

> She was really a sweet girl…once, I was in wardrobe, a journalist was interviewing Natalie's costume designer. She was saying how tiny her waist is and how lovely it was to design

Art or Instinct in the Movies…

for her. The journalist asked, "What's her bust size?" The designer said, "We don't talk about that."

In the first of his juvenile delinquent pictures, *Hot Rod Rumble* (1957), Halsey had a large supporting role. The film is an enjoyable cult flick. The director Leslie Martinson later did much bigger pictures, including *P.T. 109* and a camp classic, the Adam West *Batman*. Halsey does not recall him coaching the actors: "I am surprised he lived as long as he did because he'd get so upset, always yelling, 'Oh, you're killing me.' There was one actor, Richard Hartunian, and he was crazy because he was full of cocaine all the time. He thought he was Marlon Brando. He died shortly after, of cocaine overdose."

Halsey's character is unsympathetic and violent in *Hot Rod Rumble*. It was a cheap Allied Artists production and not especially memorable, although it was quite popular with its target audience of teenagers. Halsey explained that the actors had no sense of despair at working on such a small picture:

> No, because we were all very young at the time. This was a stepping-stone. Of course we were going to do something better. That only happens to actors when their time has passed and they're on the downhill. "Am I ever going to do anything better?" Then, it was all optimism.

Halsey had a sympathetic role in a picture with the lurid title, *High School Hellcats*. Unfortunately, he was credited as "*Bret* Halsey." "I was heartbroken. My first major role and they misspelled my name. By the time they realized, it was too late."

Director Edward Bernds would also direct Halsey in one of his best-known pictures, *Return of the Fly*. Halsey would be credited on Mexican lobby cards for *Return of the Fly* as "Brett *Hasley*" and his son Clayton's first film-editing credit was also "*Hasley*." Halsey remarks of Bernds: "I've noticed good directors get stuck in B movies. Edward Bernds was a really good director."

The Cry Baby Killer (1959) assumes an importance in film history out of all proportion to its merit as a film and as a Brett Halsey vehicle. It does not hold up due to a weak ending, and Halsey disappears fairly early on, although his performance is intriguing. But its enduring fame is guaranteed because, at the start of the picture, Jack Nicholson, in his first big screen appearance, is a punk being beaten up by Manny, Halsey's character. Up until this film he had only done some bits on television.

Jack is rather underpowered in this screen appearance, and Halsey manages more screen charisma, but then at that time he was much better known and a more experienced film actor. It is a shame that Halsey's character disappears after providing the impetus for Jack flipping his lid. The suave ladykiller performance he gives is highly amusing and engaging. His sidekick, awestruck at

Manny's ability to inspire female obedience, exclaims, "Boy, you sure got what it takes. Man, you really move in fast—and with class." Halsey smiles in amusement. The performance is also an interesting period piece. Were Californian punks in the late 1950s really so nattily attired as Manny, so clean-cut and socially sophisticated? The film is engaging while Brett Halsey and Jack Nicholson are on screen, but foolishly dispenses with them in favor of uninteresting minor characters. Nevertheless, Halsey remembered Jus Addiss, who was credited on this film as Joe Addis, and was later a regular director of TV's *Rawhide*, as "a good director."

Roger Corman was executive producer of *The Cry Baby Killer* and it might have been assumed Brett Halsey would have ended up as a Corman regular, as did Nicholson and Ed Nelson, who was also in the film. But Halsey never appeared in any of the Corman-directed films, or any other film financed by him, probably because of the television series he landed, *Follow the Sun*, and subsequent years in Italy.

Audiences watching *The Cry Baby Killer* probably imagined superstar status was waiting for Halsey rather than Jack Nicholson. Indeed, by 1967, a frustrated Nicholson had virtually given up acting in favor of writing (*The Trip*) and producing (*Head*), until *Easy Rider* catapulted him to fame. Halsey commented, "I remember talking to Jack about it right after. He said 'This is a crazy business. I turned that picture down—acting is too tough—but Peter [Fonda] kept after me.' It made him a star." Nicholson's account does not square with the unconfirmed gossip that he maneuvered himself into his role, for which Bruce Dern was lined up, by promising to use his contacts to get the funding if he was cast.

Halsey had a sense of realism about the pictures he was making: "I wanted to work to the best of my ability but I didn't kid myself that I was making art. A couple of times I worked with directors who didn't know what they were doing." Looking back, Halsey felt he was lucky he did not get trapped in B pictures, as many actors and directors did, but he was too good an actor—and too good-looking—not to get into A pictures. Halsey mused in 1961: "Only thing I can think of that's different about *my* career—so many times you hear 'Don't take certain roles'—but I did every kind of role. So many times people

get stuck in B pictures, but I was lucky I didn't. I did plenty of them and, far from resenting them, feel I got excellent experience in them, even better than experience in stock, because I was getting paid for getting experience in front of the camera, and that's my work, my career. I learned a lot from practically every B picture I did, and I did plenty of them."

Halsey won the lead in Allied Artists' cult film *Speed Crazy*. He played a race car driver who is also a psychopathic killer. This film and others of the J.D. ilk made Halsey popular with younger audiences. Norman Kahn ran a fan mail service for actors and Halsey employed him to handle the volumes of letters. Kahn confirms that Halsey received sackloads of fan mail. Halsey would never see most of this mail. Kahn would reply to it with a mimeographed autograph on a picture. Only something special would be sent on to Halsey.

Speed Crazy, directed by former production manager William J. Hole, shows its age and low budget more than some other B cheapies. Halsey uses his natural charm in the scene where he flirts with the waitress in the café. Halsey worked with Hole on another movie and they both ended up working on television's *The Bionic Woman* in the 1970s. Hole was an assistant director on the show, though Halsey does not remember seeing him when he was a guest on the series.

Rather than being low-budget exploitation movies quickly fading into obscurity, these films remain some of the most popular titles from the 1950s.

Art or Instinct in the Movies...

Halsey remarked, "They were noticed by the target audience and they were the people who were most likely to be fans, I think. Teenagers." Halsey was able to play the lead in many B movies, unlike Hollywood big-budget A pictures:

> They were more fun in the sense that there was the urgency. You know, we'd make these pictures in eight to 10 days and you had to be so well prepared, because there was no time to stop and discuss a scene. You do that before the picture starts. So, as training for an actor, you had to really be prepared. There's no place for young actors to train like that today, because in television directors don't have time to teach and they don't rehearse with actors as we did in those Bs. Because we didn't get paid for it and you can't do that now. Especially the studios can't. We would maybe rehearse a week before. They have to pay you for that and they won't do it.

Halsey found himself working in two different submarine films. *The Atomic Submarine* (1959) is the more famous of the two, because of its sci-fi overtones, but actually *Submarine Seahawk* (1958, a.k.a. *Submarine X-2*) is the better film, albeit funny to British eyes because star John Bentley later found fame (or notoriety) in the dreadful television soap *Crossroads*.

Halsey's character has a breakdown in *Submarine Seahawk*.

Halsey agreed that *Submarine Seahawk* was the better movie because, "it had a better script." Halsey was serious about his roles, so to prepare for *Submarine Seahawk*, where his character has a nervous breakdown, he took the script to a psychiatrist: "He worked it out. He would break it down into stages of the breakdown." *Seahawk* offers a good example of Halsey's rather sulky look, which he used to full advantage in his early movies when his character was given unwelcome news. Later, this sulkiness would mature into his brooding performances in spaghetti Westerns like *Today We Kill...Tomorrow We Die*. Halsey got a good review in *The Los Angeles Examiner* for *Submarine Seahawk* (Lynn Bowers, January 22, 1959): "Best of the bunch who play out the drama are Brett Halsey, who should attract a lot of the younger crowd, and Paul Maxwell."

One of the best of Halsey's early films was *The Girl in Lovers Lane* (1959), which was released as a support feature in Britain. *The Girl in Lovers Lane* offers a more civilized picture of disaffected youth than *High School Hellcats*. Halsey plays drifter Bix, a character rather like James Dean with a college diploma. It adds to the charm of a well-modulated performance.

The current DVD of *The Girl in Lovers Lane* regrettably utilizes a poor quality print that does not do justice to director Charles R. Rondeau's appealing visuals. Seeing it for the first time on the big screen, I was impressed by the

spatial composition and fine contrasts in the black-and-white cinematography. The distinguished cinematographer Edward Cronjager had an alcohol problem, and after falling off the crane on one picture, found A pictures harder to come by, so they got him on their little B movie. "He was sober when doing our picture," Halsey pointed out.

Nevertheless, there is still much to savor and, in 1961, Halsey selected it as his favorite film role to date: "I liked the transition—a tough character who spent a lot of time alone, very self-sufficient, and through love of a woman he finds no man is an island unto himself. She's murdered and he is accused of the murder, which he has not committed, and is finally vindicated. Trouble is, not many people saw the picture, as so often happens with Bs."

Pressed today for his favorite picture, Halsey *still* chooses *The Girl in Lovers' Lane*: "I liked that. It was a quickie. We worked hard on that. *The Girl in Lovers Lane* was a very small production that we were barely able to finish because of financial problems. I believe that it was the first and last film by the producer, Robert Roark." The film was shot at the small California Studios, across the street from Paramount.

Halsey remembered the director: "Charles R. Rondeau was a good director. He did a lot of TV. I chastised him, he should have made more features. I got him his first job in television, directing my wife Luciana in *Five Fingers*."

Even though Halsey was never directed by Roger Corman in a movie, *The Girl in Lovers Lane* was distributed by Corman's Filmgroup company. *The Cry Baby Killer* was part-financed by Corman, and Halsey was in his brother Gene's production *Blood and Steel* (1959), a modestly-budgeted WWII picture.

Gene Corman had his own small unit within 20th Century-Fox and had guaranteed distribution by Fox, but he also had creative freedom, as he explains: "My little unit was autonomous at Fox. I could cast anyone I wanted." It was Gene, not director Bernard Kowalski, who cast Halsey. Gene had seen Halsey in *The Cry Baby Killer*, and liked him in that, but that was not the reason for casting him: "There was something else he did, I don't recall what it was, maybe on TV, but I was very taken with this. I always thought he was an actor who should have had more appreciation." Gene was on-set throughout the filming:

> I was a hands-on producer. I would know if we had any problems. These are difficult pictures, where you need the support of the actors. Otherwise you are in a deep hole, as it is not possible to get added financing for these movies.
>
> Brett was easy to work with. He's a good guy. I wished all actors were like Brett. Sometimes a little bending of the rules is necessary in pictures like this. Brett was very flexible in terms of working late. This picture was a little complicated but everyone went out of his way to accommodate if, for some reason, we had to basically move things around.
>
> Bernie Kowalski got on well with Brett. Bernie was always easy-going, conscientious, and had a good way with people.

Halsey confirmed that "Bernie was always in good spirits." Kowalski later did a stint on Clint Eastwood's television series *Rawhide* as associate producer.

The photography was by the brilliant Floyd Crosby, who shot *High Noon* and worked on many Roger Corman projects as well as *Follow the Sun*.

Halsey's memory of the shoot was his concern for getting home when a fire threatened his home in Rosilla Place . He raced home, which took longer because access roads to the mountain were being closed, only to find his neighbours sitting on their balconies with daiquiris, watching the fire.

Gene Corman remembered the Canyon fire; his home was also threatened: "I had a house in Bel Air—we all went through that difficult period. It was a very dry period then. It was a small brush fire, which just got way out of control. Then there were torrential rain and mud slides." About a half-day of shooting was lost on *Blood and Steel*, which was unfortunate for a tightly budgeted picture. The movie begins well and promises to be as good as a Sam Fuller war picture but ultimately reveals its limitations in a hurried ending. Halsey is effective throughout, never seeking to elicit audience sympathy.

Thanks to its distribution by Fox, *Blood and Steel* did well financially both in the U.S. and abroad.

In 1960, Halsey portrayed a rich doctor in a George Raft picture *Jet Over the Atlantic*, which was shot in Mexico City. Halsey respected Raft, who had been a big star in Halsey's youth. The plot concerns a plane on which a bomb is discovered during a flight from Spain to New York. The director was the talented Byron Haskin (*War of the Worlds*), who went on to make *Captain Sinbad* with Halsey's future wife Heidi Bruhl. Halsey commented:

> Haskin was very efficient. I think he had had an alcohol problem early on in his career but he didn't have it on this picture. The picture was made as cheaply as possible, so they probably got him on his way back. George Raft wasn't very well, but it turned out all right. We brought the picture in on time. And shooting in Mexico was interesting at the time. It was made really on the cheap.

Jet Over the Atlantic, a minor entry in Halsey's filmography, is much more dated than other B movies of his from this era, largely due to an obviously rock-bottom budget which leads to some unconvincing contrivances in plot and execution. It also does not give Halsey very much to do but look competent and concerned as a young doctor on board the flight. Halsey would go on to play a doctor in the rather better *Desire in the Dust* a year later and at one point it seemed his clean-cut looks were moving him out of the delinquent roles of *Speed Crazy* and *The Cry Baby Killer* and into being typed as a young professional. It was first television, and then continental movies, that renewed his leading man status (until his return to Hollywood in the 1970s, when, as a more mature actor, he would be back to playing doctors).

Publicity pose for *Desire in the Dust*

Returning to the Western field, Halsey again worked for William J. Hole in *Four Fast Guns* (1960): "I was the second fastest gun in the West." The film came about in a strange way when builders, deciding to build some houses in the desert, also constructed a movie studio to attract people to the houses. So they hired Hollywood moviemakers and made *Four Fast Guns*. In the end, they made more money from the movie than they did from the houses, so "they decided they were moviemakers" and they made a second movie and lost the lot. Halsey said, "They didn't have the sense to rehire the same people."

Halsey's main memory of shooting *Four Fast Guns* involves the star James Craig: "James Craig kills me and has to pick me up. I was kind of heavy, he was kind of old, so I had to help him." Halsey's son Clayton nominates this movie as his father's finest screen work.

For years, Halsey was friendly with B-movie actor-director Mel Welles. They regularly played chess. "He beat my ass every time," recalled Mel.

A mutual friend was screenwriter F. Amos Powell. He adopted the "F" for famous—like Famous Amos Cookies. Halsey explains Amos got started in screenwriting through actor Leo Gordon, who wrote a number of fine Corman pictures such as *The Wasp Woman*: "Leo took on more assignments than he could handle. Leo would farm them out. He brought Amos in."

Amos' screenwriting credits include some low points like Jerry Warren's *Vengeance of the Stone Hand*. Halsey said of Jerry Warren: "He made Z pictures, for a lower price than anyone ever made them. I don't know how he got them released or shown." And there were high points, usually in conjunction with other writers, such as Roger Corman's *Tower of London* and Michael Reeves' *Revenge of the Blood Beast*.

Halsey reflected on his friendship with Amos: "Amos had an unfortunate career. He thought everything he wrote was gold and resisted rewrites. He had a script called *The Cottage*, which needed a lot of work, so I took it to Jo Heims, who wrote *Play Misty for Me* [as well as *The Girl in Lovers Lane*]. Jo rewrote it. Amos was furious and had the original copyrighted so no one could change it." Amos later ripped off his own script for S.F. Brownrigg's low-budget movie *Keep My Grave Open*.

Powell's career turned into a great disappointment and, when he learned he was ill, he shot himself in the lobby of St. Joseph's Hospital in Burbank, California, after being refused admittance because of inadequate insurance. Halsey elaborated:

> His co-writer Leo Gordon told me that, before Amos killed himself, he put post-it notes all over his flat on what to do with his things. He had some cancer. He had no social security. When he was young, he was a printer, breaking strikes. That

ended when linotype went out. Then he was a bookie for a long time. He had no government credit for welfare. He went to St. Joseph's, which is a private hospital, and they wouldn't admit him. So he blew his brains out. It was as if he was saying "I'll show them." He had a sour personality. I liked Amos but he was not a real good people person.

Gardner McKay, an actor making a name for himself at Fox in the television series *Adventures in Paradise*, was one of the group of people with whom Halsey went to Ensenada each year, primarily for the yacht races. Halsey and Gardner met at Fox and became close friends. Gardner was handsome but not really a very talented actor, and he knew it. He told Halsey and others that he was an artist who makes money by acting. Later in his career, he wrote plays and a novel. Halsey once talked him into doing a life story of Gardner's grandfather and great-grandfather, who designed and built clipper ships. He got producer friend Julian Ludwig involved but, as Ludwig explained, "the story never came to pass."

Halsey also went to Tijuana for bullfighting, for Jai-Alai and dog racing. He commented: "I went to bullfight school for a movie that was never made. Budd Boetticher sent me. I went to bullfights every weekend. Budd, who directed *The Bullfighter and the Lady*, was a big fan of mine. He promised me a job in that film, but this other actor had lost a lot of money to him. Budd had to give him the job. It was the only way he could get his money back."

Halsey was in the same group of friends as Gary Cooper's daughter and, as a result, became "kind of friendly" with Cooper. Halsey recalls going to his house with David Hedison, and Cooper was tired and cantankerous, saying to them: "I worked at Paramount day and night. You guys are all a bunch of faggots." He said he was once so tired from doing one picture after another, he just left and took a plane or a boat to Africa. The studio said, "You can't do that." Cooper replied,"What can you do about it?"

On another occasion when Halsey visited, Cooper answered the door in dinner jacket and black tie with his trousers rolled up, barefoot. He was fixing the toilet in the powder room, as he couldn't get a plumber.

Halsey remembered another real character was director Henry Hathaway. Halsey went to his house for parties. Halsey recalled, "Hathaway was a very civilized, educated man in private but a tyrant on set. When he was getting ready to do *Niagara*, Hathaway had Robert Mitchum into the office. 'You know, Bob, when I work, I shout at people and call them a dumb son of a bitch. I don't mean it. That's my way of working.' Mitchum said, 'Okay, when someone calls me a dumb son of a bitch, I just punch them in the nose. I don't mean anything by it. It's just my way of working'." Halsey admired Mitchum despite his apparent lassitude: "Actors like Mitchum, beneath all that, have great energy."

During the 1970s, Halsey worked in a controversial feature, *Coon Skin* (1975), produced by his friend Al Ruddy of *The Godfather* fame. The film was produced by Ralph Bakshi Productions in association with Paramount. However Paramount dropped the film after pressure from various groups and the movie was theatrically distributed by Bryanston Distribution, whose title list includes cult flicks such as *Andy Warhol's Frankenstein*, and *The Texas Chain Saw Massacre*.

This was a Ralph Bakshi animated feature with live actors, including Tracy Brooks Swope. It was the only time Tracy actually appeared on screen with Halsey. She recalled: "Ralph Bakshi created *Coon Skin,* and we worked in a sequence with animated characters. It was later banned because it was considered racist. Brett and I did it as a favor for Al Ruddy and Ralph Bakshi. It was an enjoyable experience to perform with Brett." Swope and Halsey were uncredited in the film.

There was an outcry by a political action group called *CORE* and a bomb threat against the theater that first showed it, and Paramount Pictures yanked it from cinemas within a week of release. It remains very difficult to see, even to this day, although it is available on VHS under the title *Street Fight*.

Horror and Sci-Fi Pictures

Halsey's first excursion into the world of genre pictures was a bit part in Universal's *Revenge of the Creature* in 1955. Halsey had a close encounter of the scary kind with the Creature when his character Pete is killed on a moonlit beach.

His next film was the sci-fi flick *The Atomic Submarine* in 1959. Alex Gordon produced both submarine pictures in which Halsey appeared. After Alex's death, Halsey was quoted in *Fangoria* magazine saying what a nice man he was, "a wonderful personality, always smiling." Alex's brother, producer/distributor Richard Gordon, who had once considered Halsey for a role in one of his British pictures, much appreciated this and wrote to Halsey to thank him. Richard Gordon testifies that Halsey was one of Alex's favorite actors to work

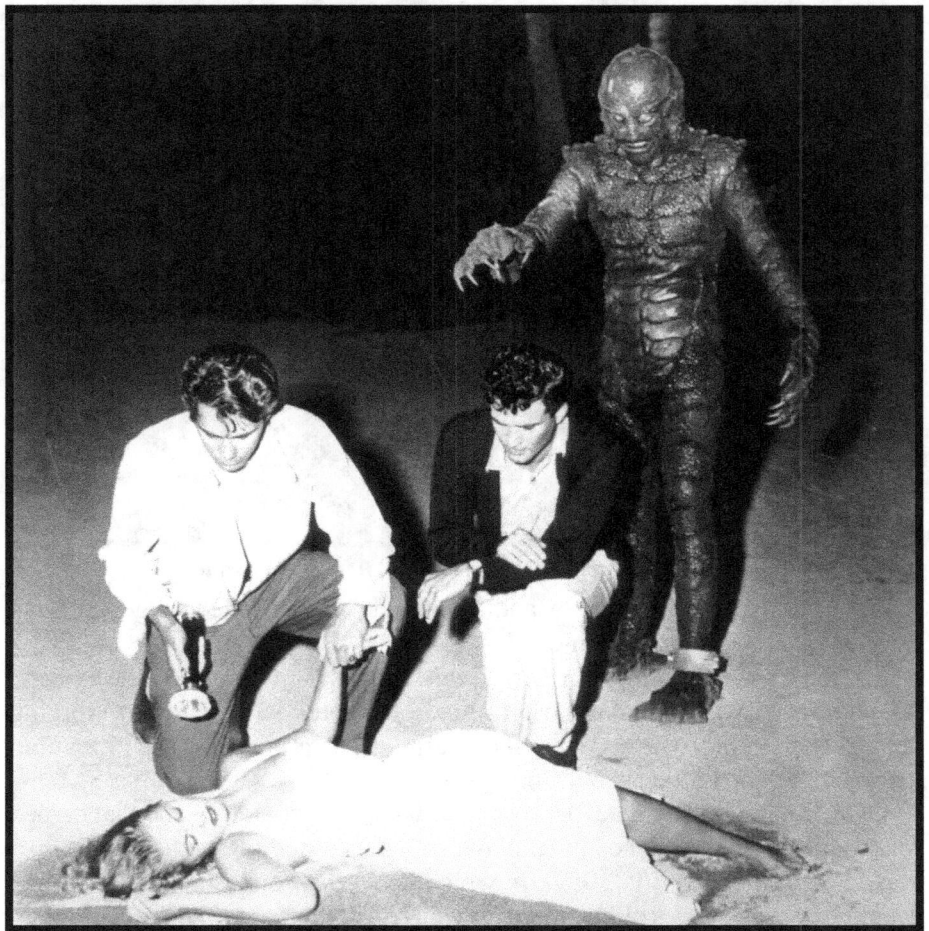

Halsey learns to never turn your back on a Universal monster in *Revenge of the Creature*.

Art or Instinct in the Movies...

Halsey in a studio portrait for *The Atomic Submarine*

with, and Halsey feels that Alex and Richard are "two of the true gentlemen I have encountered in this business."

Halsey was pleased to be in *The Atomic Submarine* because of his co-stars, whom he had idolized when he was a kid: Bob Steele, star of Saturday morning serials, Dick Foran, who had starred in Warner Bros. musicals in the 1930s, and George Sanders' brother, Tom Conway.

The film that really made Hollywood take notice of Halsey and that helped make him a fully fledged contract player at a major studio was the minor sci-fi classic *Return of the Fly* (1959), in which he worked opposite Vincent Price. Stepping into the shoes of his friend David Hedison, who starred in the original *Fly*, Halsey was second billed under Price.

With Vincent Price in *The Return of the Fly*

Halsey was still a minor movie star after making a string of low-budget teen pictures. His salary was still modest, approximately $1,000 for a two-week picture. When he was offered the lead in *Return of the Fly*, it must have seemed like just another low-budget picture. But he had seen the original *Fly* and thought it was a good picture, and there was the opportunity to work with major star Vincent Price. Indeed, the producer Bernard Glasser was a former Beverly Hills high school physics teacher and claimed the fly head used in the film had greater authenticity than in the original film. He told the press on August 27, 1959:

> The Fly mask is entirely accurate. It's a scale model of a microscopic photograph. We feel, though, that our new head has more horror-impact than the one used in *The Fly*. It's bigger and, like a real fly's head, it will pivot on a 360 degree axis. It will also drool as we have perfected a more realistic effect by a newly discovered formula that combines glycerin and liquid cement.

Halsey would be working for the independent production company Associated Producers, who did all the Fox B films. The film was to be shot on the

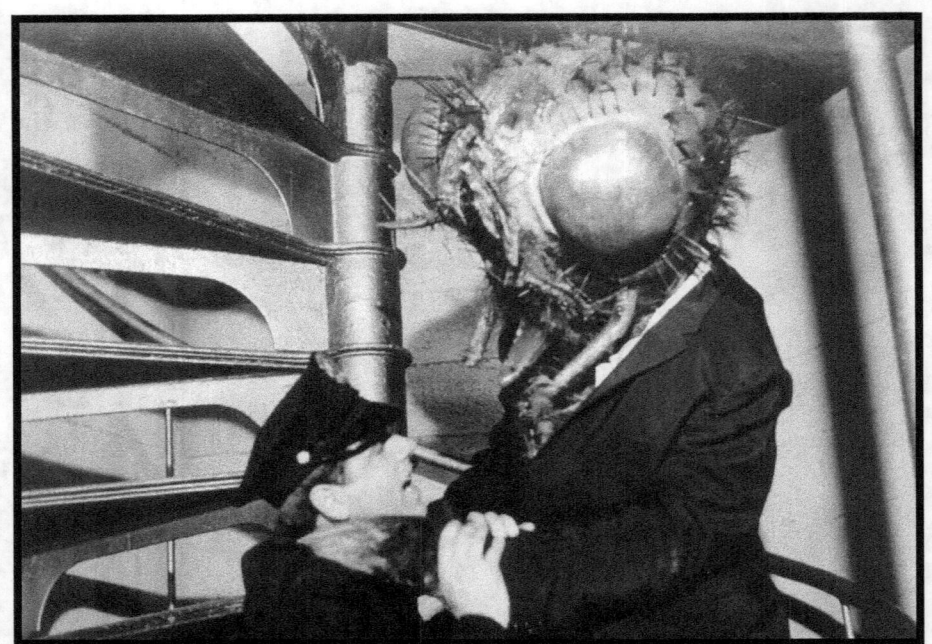
A stuntman filled in for Halsey once his character became the fly.

Fox lot. Halsey was getting tired of his modest earnings and felt the film had some potential, so he demanded a raise. When they refused, Halsey declined the role. After a lot of negotiation, Robert Lippert, the head of Associated Producers, called Halsey to his office and told him he should do the picture, as it would be very good for his career. But he would not pay him any more money. Halsey was persuaded that it was perhaps the break he had needed and agreed to do the picture for no more money, but the final sweetener was that, as soon as his character was transformed into the fly, Halsey did not need to work because a stunt man in the fly mask replaced him. So he only worked five days but was paid for 10. It was a good move, because his work in the film led to a contract at Fox.

In the first of two screen appearances with Vincent Price, Halsey is paired with a more experienced performer with whom he clearly enjoyed some rapport. Price had starred in the original hit *The Fly*, directed by Kurt Neumann, and was brought back for the cash-in sequel. Halsey had worked for the sequel's director, Edward Bernds, in *High School Hellcats,* but was probably cast because of his striking facial similarity to actor David Hedison from the original. In the sequel *Return of the Fly* Halsey portrays the son of Hedison's character.

In some critical quarters, such as Dennis Meikle's book *Vincent Price: The Art of Fear*, *Return of the Fly* is regarded as a crass cash-in on the original *Fly* and as greatly inferior. I beg to differ. Indeed, I am not so sure it isn't in the final analysis a better film than the original. It is a very satisfactory B monster movie and quite different in tone and texture from the A-movie original. The

sequel was shot in black-and-white for budgetary reasons, whereas the earlier film was in glorious color. This was a decision later condemned by Vincent Price in *Cinefantastique*: "It wasn't a bad film, but it was ridiculous to shoot it in black-and-white. I love black-and-white, but you do two pictures in color—not one in color and one in black-and-white."

There are several reasons for the film's success. The more serious treatment of the plot enables a greater suspension of disbelief (important in fantasy films) than in the original, which Price always maintained was the funniest film he had ever made and certainly strays into camp toward the end; the resultant higher level of tension in *Return of the Fly* enriches Halsey's natural earnestness on screen.

As the protagonist, Halsey does have a more sympathetic air of vulnerability than the more ruthless character portrayed by David Hedison in *The Fly*. Halsey is also a more expressive actor than Hedison. The collaboration between Halsey and Price has a nice chemistry, something Hedison was unable to do since he shared no screen time with Price.

As one of Halsey's most widely seen pictures, *Return of the Fly* occupies an important position in his pre-Italian credits, and this author ranks it among his 10 best films.

David Hedison argued that *Return of the Fly* was not as good a picture as *The Fly*. Halsey smiled: "Well, then, I say the opposite." For Halsey's friend Jay Bernstein, this exchange is typical Halsey: "David took the offensive. Brett took the defensive." All light-hearted, though, as David Hedison explained in remembering his friendship with Halsey:

I had done *The Fly* in 1958 and I heard they were doing *Return of the Fly*, so I was curious to visit the production. I remember going on the set and meeting Vincent Price and Brett Halsey for the first time. Vincent was wonderful—we had not done any scenes together in *The Fly*. I found Brett a charming, friendly, very warm man.

Brett and I became very close friends during that period. He threw wonderful parties with his friends Don Kennedy, an actor, and Dick Taylor, a plumbing contractor, and, when he married Luciana in Las Vegas, I attended the wedding and we had a great time. Brett was a very warm fellow, very real, very down to earth—and he still is. Brett is Brett, he's never changed.

When Brett went to Italy, we lost touch. I was very busy doing the TV series *Voyage to the Bottom of the Sea*. But when he married Heidi, we saw them a few times. Later, he showed me photographs of the films he'd made in Italy and I said "Brett, these films are wonderful, they are *so* interesting."

One thing I slightly chided him about. *Return of the Fly* had a much lower budget than *The Fly*. The fly mask was ridiculous and Brett didn't want to do the picture. He refused it until they told him he would not have to appear in any of the scenes after the transformation. They could use a stunt man

to wear the fly mask. That's when Brett decided to do it. He just didn't want to wear the mask.

I scolded him after the film was made: "Brett, you have really missed out on an important part of the actor's work. You should have done those scenes. You had the opportunity to express the character's emotions through gestures and body movements and you missed out on an important challenge in the work." I felt that, for once, he took the lazy route. But perhaps if I had seen that ridiculous headpiece—I might have done the same.

I think it's true that he might have been in *Return of the Fly* because of his facial resemblance to me. Who knows?

Halsey commented, "I always denied I looked like David Hedison, until once I was in his house, his wife came up and embraced me from behind. His wife thought it was David... So, then I thought 'Maybe I do'." Halsey also remembered that once, at Norm's restaurant, he and David were at the counter talking "and this guy came up and said 'Oh my god, I never thought I'd see this. The Fly and the Son of the Fly, eating together'."

Halsey is still amusedly unrepentant about not wearing the fly mask, denying that it would have made any difference. He did concede, however, that the stuntman they used, Ed Wolff, was "uncoordinated." He was not an actor but a circus giant.

Mainly, Halsey did not want to do the mask scenes because he viewed it as a better deal, financially. As Robert Lippert would not pay him an increase in salary, he made up for it by working fewer days. Looking back on it, he said, "It's strange they didn't do it in color. It *was* in Cinemascope. I guess just to save money. Another reason may be we had a very short schedule, and, with color you need more time."

David Hedison summed up his feelings about *Return of the Fly*:

> In all, I think *Return of the Fly* was not as good a film as *The Fly*, which had a proper storyline. Recently, Brett and I were invited to the Memphis Film Festival to talk about our work in *The Fly* and *Return of the Fly*.

Halsey especially enjoyed working with Vincent Price: "He loved the business. He had such fun." They would work together again and become good friends. Halsey regards Price as one of his top three favorite colleagues out of all those he has worked with.

Halsey often socialized with his movie colleagues. He spent time with Price ("He was fun when drinking") and his wife Mary, whom Halsey also liked:

We went to Ensenada to party. We'd go as a party, six of us. Ensenada had a freer atmosphere, for bars. Mexico is dangerous. Everyone has a gun. The Americans stopped making films there, it's too dangerous.

One U.S. producer in Ensenada got back to his hotel. There was a knock on the door. There was a boy who gave him a package. Minutes later, the police arrived, doing a drug raid. They were Mexico City police and they said, "Give us $5,000 to go away." He said he didn't have $5,000 and they should ask the film company president for the $5,000. The president came to the phone and said "Keep him, we don't want him. We'll replace him." After another hour, eventually they paid $200 to free him.

Halsey would work with Price again in *Twice-Told Tales* (1963), an anthology based upon Nathaniel Hawthorne's stories. Halsey would appear in the second story, "Rappaccini's Daughter." His character is a student who tragically falls in love with a woman whose touch is deadly because of experiments performed by her mad father (Price), who poisons her because he wants her to remain pure and never know the touch of a man . The film was not a critical favorite and, as with most anthologies, never caught on with audiences. It suffers from dull direction by Sidney Salkow, who was the brother of Price's agent.

Price and Halsey in *Twice-Told Tales*

Big Time Hollywood

The attention Halsey garnered for his excellent work co-starring with Vincent Price in *Return of the Fly* led to an immediate contract with 20th Century-Fox and the step up to A pictures such as *The Best of Everything*. In August 1959, Buddy Adler, head of Fox, took one look at Halsey's performance and signed him to a long-term contract. Halsey remarked, "I went from *Return of the Fly* to *The Best of Everything* in about a week. It was a really good career move."

At Fox, their new talent program wanted Halsey to participate, but he declined. He felt it wasn't as good as the Universal program, which he deemed the best there ever was in the business, and remembered that Marilyn Monroe had not been well treated in it. Fox employed famous acting coach Sandy Meisner: "I had a run-in with him because I wouldn't take his class. I didn't like the way he taught and I told him that."

The first Fox picture was *The Best of Everything,* directed by Jean Negulesco. The film, considered a "woman's picture," was to be shot in color. Producer Jerry Wald cast Halsey as Eddie Davis, the boy who jilts Hope Lange's character. Halsey commented, "That really got me started at Fox, after the eight-to 10-day wonders. Negulesco took his time. He was an artist."

Halsey has written of the film:

> *The Best of Everything* was my first major role in a major motion picture. Although it dealt with New York subject matter, it was shot in California.
>
> In one of my first scenes with Hope Lange, who could be very intense with her acting, I had to tell her that our engagement was off because I was going to marry the rich girl. I knew she was going to slap me in the face at the end of the scene, but I wasn't prepared for the slap that came. It could be that I was a bit off-balance, but her slap knocked me off my feet, over the back of the sofa, and onto the floor behind it. Naturally we had to shoot it over again. That time I was ready, and she was a little more gentle.
>
> Rona Jaffe, who wrote the novel, had told me that the story was based on real people. I played a man who was quite a cad. After the movie came out, I was at a party where I was surprised to meet the girl Hope Lange's character was based on. I was quite pleased when she complimented me on how well I played that sonofabitch.
>
> Later still, at a party in Malibu, I met the man on whom my character was based. He, too, was very complimentary, and

told me how proud he was of the way I played him. I thanked him, of course, but I couldn't understand the reason for his compliment. The character I played really was a sonofabitch. Who knows about people?

In fact, in the final cut of the film, there is no slap, but Halsey confirms it was shot, even if it later ended up on the cutting room floor. Shortly before he died, Negulesco told me that Halsey was "very professional...the kind of actor who comes to the set fully prepared."

Halsey was now an established talent. He would go to Sunday brunches with director Don Siegel. He met Merle Oberon at several parties when he was trawling through the Hollywood social set and she seemed to enjoy talking with him. He was also popular with some of Hollywood's younger ladies, including a young Grace Kelly. Halsey is too much of a gentleman to discuss it but admitted that women always formed "a large part of my life."

Halsey played a young doctor, Ned Thomas, in a more modest 20th Century-Fox production, *Desire in the Dust* (1960), which was shot in black-and-white near Baton Rouge, Louisiana. (Halsey would later be given an honor by the Governor of Louisiana, the right to call himself a Colonel, as he explained: "It was given by one Governor, for services to celebrity, and renewed twice, but I never used it, so I saw no reason for it to be renewed again.") The crisp photography was by Merle Oberon's spouse, the distinguished Lucien Ballard.

Hope Lange and Halsey in *The Best of Everything*

Halsey's earnest performance won him the Hollywood Foreign Press Association Golden Globe Award for the International Star of Tomorrow. Robert Vaughn had also won one. The film starred Raymond Burr, who was already a friend. It was the story of a family in the South. Halsey had misgivings about handling a Southern accent: "I said 'I don't know if I can play a Southern accent. Can he be from Boston?' And the Southern accent fell on my tongue so naturally, I had to play Boston with a Southern accent."

Also in the cast was the wonderful actress Joan Bennett, veteran of the classic Hollywood era, but Halsey recalled he had "not much contact" with her and had more to do with Raymond Burr: "When Luciana and I got married, he gave us a beautiful set of candlesticks. Previously I had appeared in *Perry Mason*. All of Hollywood did *Perry Mason*. The pay wasn't so good in those days. On the Bs, I was paid $500 a week, so a two-week picture paid $1,000 a picture. On two occasions when I worked in Italy, I had a percentage deal. Each time the picture went bankrupt. In Italy, the only way to work is with cash."

Halsey is also cynical about studio accounting, citing the experience of his friend Julian Ludwig, who produced *The Texican* (1965): "That picture still hasn't broken even. It's $10,000 in the red."

Producer Jerry Wald was impressed with Halsey's work in *The Best of Everything* and gave him a prominent role in *Return to Peyton Place*, which was the sequel to the highly successful *Peyton Place*. The film was directed by actor Jose Ferrer.

Ex-spouses Luciana and Halsey in *Return to Peyton Place*

Halsey was delighted to be cast alongside actors such as Jeff Chandler, Mary Astor, Tuesday Weld, Eleanor Parker, Carol Lynley and Robert Sterling, as well as current girlfriend Barbara Steele.

Return to Peyton Place has a torpid, lifeless quality, much like a dull soap opera. The only interest is really the casting of Halsey and Luciana, who, in real life, had been married and divorced just before the picture started shooting and were to portray a couple onscreen. Halsey was in the big league now and was exposed to a much wider audience. The picture was well-received. *The Motion Picture Herald* (May 1961) said: "*Return to Peyton Place* is lifted above the average of most romantic melodramas by some fine directorial touches on the part of Jose Ferrer." *The New York Times* (May 6, 1961) found the sequel not quite as good as the original *Peyton Place*: "Slick, soap-operatic follow-up to Jerry Wald's earlier hit, though not quite equal of its predecessor."

Halsey particularly admired Hollywood veteran and Academy Award–winning Mary Astor (*The Big Lie, Meet Me in St. Louis, The Maltese Falcon*). Doing one scene with her, he was so entranced listening to her, he almost forgot to say his lines: "My favorite actress I ever worked with is Mary Astor. I learned more from her on *Return to Peyton Place* than from any other actress. Just working with her was a great lesson in acting." Halsey even saw Mary dictate to Jose Ferrer how a scene was to be shot.

Halsey retains a leather-bound copy of the script of *Return to Peyton Place* signed by all the cast and producer Jerry Wald. It is the only script he has kept apart from his breakthrough film *Return of the Fly*: "Usually, I would get through the shoot by tearing the pages out."

Spending the bulk of the 1960s away from the U.S. effectively ended Halsey's participation in big time Hollywood. By the 1970s, Hollywood movie production was in decline due to competition from television and other leisure activities, and Halsey could not expect to be as active as he had been in 1950s Hollywood. Fortunately, he was versatile enough to turn his hand to television appearances, to commercials, to teaching, and to writing and producing.

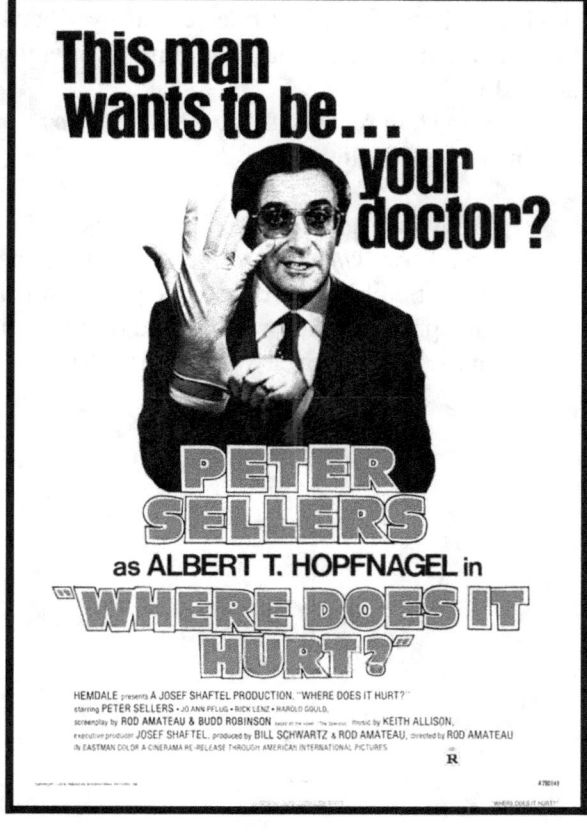

Halsey found himself with a major role in the Peter Sellers movie *Where Does It Hurt?* (1972), which might have re-established him in Hollywood movies, except for the fact that it sank without trace. The director was Rodney Amateau, a well-known television comedy director (*Dobie Gillis*), who also made the David Niven-Robert Vaughn turkey *The Statue* the year before. Halsey remembered his contact with Peter Sellers:

> He was so cool and I was so disappointed, because I wanted to learn from him, and he didn't have anything to give. I often heard that he had no personality other than the characters he played. But he was polite. He did it for the money. I've never seen it. It ended up in some sort of bankruptcy. I talked to Rodney Amateau about it and asked, "Where is the picture?" and he told me it was caught up in a bankruptcy court.

The film subsequently got a belated minor release and has been seen on television, though it is not one of Halsey's better pictures. His role is not showy enough to have brought him much attention, even if the film had been successful.

Jay Bernstein recalled *Where Does It Hurt?* mainly because Peter Sellers was one of his PR clients:

> We would double date. We interviewed a hundred girls to do an ad for *Where Does It Hurt?* where they would carry him on a stretcher. We chose five girls and paid them $100 a day. The photographer was a friend of mine and there was no film in the camera, ever. We got laid a lot.

Offscreen Scenes

In the 1950s and '60s, bachelor Halsey cultivated the image of a lady-killer and a playboy. Halsey smiled when he told the story about his Fox colleague Gardner McKay: "Gardner McKay gave me a cigarette lighter engraved 'To Brett and whichever lady he is with at the time'."

A *TV Guide* profile stated: "He is a bona fide member of William Holden's exclusive Mount Kenya Safari Club (complete with blazer emblem to prove it), but has never been to Africa. He owns a $13,000 sports car but hasn't raced since 1958, when he almost went over a cliff at 105 m.p.h. He plays a well-above-average game of tennis but boasts no tennis court at his home."

Halsey loved to drive fast in sports cars. In fact, he cited automobiles as his pet extravagance and wrote that he "always loved fine cars." In June 1961, he owned three cars, a $13,000 BMW (German), an $11,000 Facel Vega (French) and a 1943 Army surplus Jeep. He told William Homick of the *Waterbury Sunday Republican* (December 10, 1961) that he was convinced the Army had used it where the fighting was fierce: "There are bullet holes and shrapnel marks on it." He sold the Facel Vega the following month and planned to sell the BMW while awaiting delivery on a new $8,000 Continental (American) in black with black leather upholstery.

The near-accident happened in a race in Mexico when Halsey lost control of the car. Halsey remembered the incident for the 1961 Fox profile:

> I used to race cars but after I nearly got killed in Mexico, in 1958, I quit. I was driving a Jaguar. I was on this mountain road doing 105 miles an hour on the curve and hit a wet spot and lost control of the car. I thought "It's all over," but I regained control of the car just before it went over a steep cliff, got back on the road and that was the last time I raced.

After that experience, Halsey turned to safer sports such as tennis, watching baseball, swimming, sailing, horseback riding, fencing and tournament chess, winning a local Hollywood tournament in 1959. Around this period, Halsey also dabbled in sculpting human figures from life, heads from imagination, and continued to work in mosaic.

At home, he would listen to Broadway musicals such as *Camelot*, *Carousel* and *The King and I*. He collected Harry Belafonte records and went to see him live with his friends Gardner McKay and Skip Ward at the Greek Theatre in July 1961.

Halsey was friendly with William Holden but was friendlier with Holden's girlfriend, actress Stefanie Powers, who he would see from time to time.

Halsey began a longtime friendship with actor Henry Silva (who usually played a heavy and portrayed Mr. Moto in *The Return of Mr. Moto*, Fox 1965). Silva commented:

> We never worked together, unfortunately, but I knew Brett at all levels of his career. I'm very fond of him. I've known him for 45 years. I first met him when I was living in Sunset Plaza Drive, a lovely area. He lived there too, and I saw him coming and going. One day we started talking. He was an extremely handsome guy. He looked like Tyrone Power. He was doing well at 20th Century-Fox. I even met his mom at his house, a lovely lady.
>
> What I found unusual about him was that he was an actor who worked hard at what he did, but he had no entourage. He didn't think he was above being human. He was a straight-shooter. What you saw was what you got. He was non-bragging.

David Hedison, Henry Silva and Halsey pose together at an autograph show in 2006.

On the whole Halsey enjoyed his celebrity. In 1961 he was invited to become a beauty pageant judge for three contests, California Dairy Queen, Miss Southern California and a regional contest for Miss World. His tongue-in-cheek comment was: "This is nice work and I like to do it." Halsey was amused when he was on holiday once in Jerusalem and a woman approached him at King David's tomb. "Oh, I know you." she said. "Probably from TV," said Halsey. "No, I know you. Your mother lives in my father's apartment block.." Later on, when he was a big star in Italy, Halsey was comfortable with having fans: "They don't bother you there."

He ran into Frank Sinatra at various social events and remembers one time when Sinatra flew to Lake Tahoe in his private jet to perform a concert. Halsey traveled along with Nancy Sinatra and her husband, who were opening for Frank. Halsey thought it was cruel that Frank did not stay to watch his daughter and her husband perform, only returning for his own performance. Halsey recalls that Sinatra could be unpredictable. When he lost $180,000 gambling in Las Vegas once, his entourage said, "We are in for trouble," but Sinatra could not have been more amenable.

Robert Goulet wanted to take Halsey on a tour of the Irish coast, stopping to have a drink in every pub. Looking back, Halsey is glad they never did it.

Halsey even socialized with Elvis Presley:

> I was friendly with Elvis. I never thought he was that big, more after he died. I just knew him socially. I had a BMW 507, a sports BMW. Elvis had one too. A part was needed and I had to wait six months for it, so Elvis gave me his BMW 507. I drove his for six months. He didn't care. He would party at his house. He felt more secure with his own people around. The last time I saw him, he was a mess, overweight.

It was during his time at Fox that Halsey first met important Hollywood mover-and-shaker Jay Bernstein, who was already a fan. Jay Bernstein recollected their first meeting:

> I met Brett in 1961. He was having lunch at the Fox commissary while doing his series *Follow the Sun*. Sitting with him were Gardner McKay and Gary Lockwood. They were showing pics of a gorgeous blonde, and I was there with a friend. Gardner had a date with this beautiful blonde, Leslie Parrish, who was Daisy Mae in *Lil' Abner* and in *The Manchurian Candidate*. I fell in love with the picture of Leslie Parrish. I was working in the PR firm Rogers & Cowan, after growing up in Oklahoma, then the Army, then college. She signed with Rogers & Cowan as a client.
>
> Brett to me was a movie star. I was younger than him, four years, and always aware of him. He had those Tyrone Power looks. I was always aware of Brett. I have no idea how we became friends. I consider him as one of my four best friends.

The friendship continued even when Halsey spent the rest of the decade in Italy. Jay explained:

> I visited him. I was always in Europe. I represented a lot of stars and it took me to Italy. He took me to parties. I knew Luciana; I was her PR during *Thunderball*. We just got along well.

> My feeling about him is—being in this business 40 years—I was trying to think who he reminded me of: Tyrone Power, Cary Grant, Alan Ladd, William Holden. He's classy like Cary Grant. Very quiet in his manner, yet he's not quite the same as Cary Grant. Cary was quiet and not quiet. Brett's more like Henry Fonda—a quiet gentleman. Brett always had a fine reputation as a gentleman. There are not a lot of gentlemen in this business. As for his personality, if you're a movie star, you're usually eccentric. Brett was never eccentric. He has good taste. He's a man of letters. He has manners. Brett is someone who can speak. That's why I hired him as a development executive, Head of Development. He has good taste; he's a writer, an intelligent man. Brett is very intelligent but not an intellectual. He's soft-spoken.

Jay reflected on the fact that Halsey never became a major Hollywood star:

> He wasn't selling himself, ever. He never sold himself to me, even when he tried to sell me one of his scripts. In Hollywood, you need friends. To be very successful, you need to make enemies. Brett couldn't make any enemies.
>
> Brett's not had strong agents. He never had guys who were the opposite of him. Dick Clayton is the same as he is, the sweetest, nicest guy in the world. He needed someone who was the opposite.

Yet Halsey was recognized continually as a star in the Italian industry. Jay explained:

> What it takes to be a star in Italy is different to what it takes to be a star in Hollywood. You need to be one-third asshole. Brett's not the only one. I employed Ray Danton as a producer on *Mike Hammer*. He also had an Italian career, not as extensive as Brett's. He, too, had that sort of look. Here, it's too hard.
>
> Brett's looks may have worked against him. Maybe people were jealous of his good looks. That may have held him back. Brett won't fight to be here. He's a "please" and "thank you." He's Hollywood royalty. To be stars, actors need someone strong behind them. In his book *Hollywood Animal*, Joe Eszterhas writes that in this town, no one roots for someone else's movie; Brett wishes everyone the best. He's never

been miserable, like most of the stars. I've had depressions but he's very steady. My ego is probably different to Brett's. He doesn't brag about anything. Not long ago, I embarrassed him. I said, "I would have liked to have been you." I admired Alan Ladd, William Holden, Tyrone Power, Brett Halsey. I don't have Brett's looks. He'd like to be happy. He wants to be happy; he wants to make other people happy. He's never said "no" to anything.

His life is very private. He looks like a leading man. He acts like a leading man. He would have done well in the studio system, at MGM, at Warners. He's like Robert Taylor, though Robert Taylor in the movies was an outdoorsman; Brett's more of an indoorsman.

He's like the quiet American. He has dignity, humility, professionalism, lack of self-importance. He's non-egotistical. I rang him and said, "They're doing a biography on you, it's authorized. How much are they paying you?" He replied, "Nothing." I said, "I got a half a million dollars advance." He said, "I just want a lot of books."

He's achieved a lot…but you can be removed from that. I don't think Brett ever had a PR [agent]. Brett's like Roger Moore, a nice, dignified guy, but Roger worked the social circuit. Brett never played the circuit like Roger Moore.

While working in Italy, Halsey lived a glamorous bachelor lifestyle. At first he had a "very nice" three-bedroom apartment in Via Sasso Ferrato in Rome. Actor Mickey Hargitay stayed there when Halsey went to Germany to make a film and see his future wife Heidi. Halsey remembered he bought a new car in Germany and drove 700 miles from Germany to Rome. He went to bed and, when he woke up in the morning, a tree had fallen on his brand new car.

Sandy Lieberson, his Italian agent, said of Halsey's European period:

> Brett loved working in Italy. He was a big deal there. He was in demand for working in films—a big star—and, in the U.S., there was not much on offer for him. Plus, he loved Rome in that period. It was wild on every level and Brett participated in it all. It was much more exciting than boring Hollywood.

Sandy recalled that Halsey's circle of friends in Rome included Clint Eastwood, Lex Barker, Gordon Scott, Steve Reeves, Richard Harris and Rossano Brazzi: "It was an actors' clique and it was great fun and exciting." In June 1964, Halsey, Ray Danton, Gordon Scott and some other actors challenged

Rome adventurers: Gary Lockwood, Barbara Parkins, Halsey and Robert Webber

an Italian football team to a soccer game on the beach. Danton broke his toe trying to kick a goal.

In Rome, Halsey met one of his closest lifelong friends, Stanley Winston, a colorful entrepreneur who had owned a casino in London and had gone to Rome to introduce the Laundromat concept to Italy. They would have many adventures together over the years. As well as being Halsey's agent, Sandy was one of his friends:

> It was one of those unusual situations where Brett was a client and a good friend. We would see each other several times a week, in Roma, on the beach at Fregene, and at weekend parties with Lily Gerini, an American who married an Italian Marquis. Her connection to the film industry was entertaining people in it. She had a particular interest in Brett.

Halsey remembered her hospitality:

> We were just good friends. She was a very wealthy woman… her husband died early on. Lily had a magnificently restored Roman villa on the Appia Antica in Rome and another, perhaps even more spectacular, with a private beach in Porto Santo Stefano. This lavish villa was built on an old Roman ruin and

still had a tall Saracen watchtower on the property, which was used as a lookout post by the Nazis in WWII. Normally I kept my catamaran docked at her place in Porto Santo Stefano and spent many summer weekends in one of her guesthouses on the property.

Lily's parties were legendary. Her guests always included the cream of Hollywood and New York society as well as the top European royalty. Some of her guests would stay for a weekend and some for a month or so. Gloria Swanson, David Niven, Princess Ira Von Furstenberg, Paul Getty, Sr. and Jr. (at different times), Gore Vidal, Rossano Brazzi and a host of others were all her friends.

Halsey said of Cary Grant and David Niven that, when they entered the room, "the lights got a little brighter; there was an aura about them."

Halsey pictured expatriate social life in Rome:

The hub of all social activity seemed to be the Café de Paris on Via Veneto, where the group would gather in the late morning for a cappuccino and the Paris edition of the *Herald-Tribune*'s daily crossword puzzle, then on to Piccolo Mondo or the Bolognese in Piazza del Popolo for lunch. Later in the evening, after dinner, they would return for a leisurely espresso and cognac while watching the late-night parade of beautiful and trying-to-be beautiful people making the well-traveled, familiar promenade: up the street, in front of the Café de Paris, across

Café de Paris

at the corner, then down past Doney's and the Excelsior, back across the street and repeating the course.

And it wasn't just parties every night of the week on offer:

There were also the public watering holes, which became regular stops on a night's prowl. There was the smart, jet set favorite Osteria del Orso, where Michelangelo and Raphael lived in earlier days. Dave's Dive, favorite spot of Peter O'Toole, Peter Finch and Richard Harris. The Taverna Flavia, made famous by Elizabeth Taylor. Oil moguls Paul Getty and George Williamson were frequent diners at George's, which was known for its marvelous kitchen and later became equally known for the way its waiters would flimflam the patrons by opening a bottle of wine, pouring a few glasses—maybe half of the bottle—then when you asked to have your glass refilled, the waiter would ignore the still half-filled bottle and open a new one.

There was Jerry's Bar, where Lex Barker and Ernest Borgnine could frequently be found in the nonstop gin rummy game, and nextdoor the legendary Brickstop's nightclub, where the world's jazz greats would meet in Rome. Jimmy Welch's disco was down the street, where we danced to the best and latest American records, and the Red Banjo, complete with a genuine down-home hillbilly band, rebel bartenders and near-American (usually English) waitresses.

The premier spot, the place nobody missed, was Jerry Chierchio's Luau. There were rumors that Jerry had left the States in a hurry to avoid being prosecuted for murder. There were other rumors that he was somehow involved with the American Mafia and that the exiled American gangsters Lucky Luciano and Joe Adonis often dined with Jerry in the Luau. But then, John Wayne or Egypt's ex-King Farouk could be found dining with Jerry, so no definite conclusions were ever drawn.

Halsey recalled one funny incident. There was a very exclusive restaurant, where a large group was dining at a long, beautifully decorated table with a friend, Bob Oliver, a rich and very generous host. He was drunk, stood up to make a toast and fell flat on the table, which must have been on casters or wheels because it moved across the room with him lying on it, like a surf board. When it stopped, he turned over, amidst all the mess of what was a beautifully laid table, and continued with his toast.

Halsey has specific memories of Richard Harris and Rossano Brazzi. He and Harris frequented the same bars:

> I remember walking up the street with him about four o'clock in the morning. Halfway up the middle of the street, he shouted, "Come on, somebody, fight, come on, somebody, fight," in the middle of Via Veneto. He was quite a drunk. He told me a story years later why he gave up drinking. He said he had met Laurence Olivier and he was telling Laurence Olivier how much he admired him as an actor and how he'd give anything to be able to work with him, and Olivier said, "Richard, Richard, we did a picture together." So he said, "That's when I decided I'd better give up drinking." As a senior citizen actor, he was excellent.

Rossano Brazzi was not part of the bar scene:

> That was a different social set. Brazzi didn't hang around with the foreign set as much but he was certainly a part of the beach set. We were at the beach once and they were having an argument. I don't know why they were arguing in English, but they were. She was a marvelous woman, big, way overweight but with a personality. Anyway, Rossano said to her—her name's Lydia—"Lydia, when you talk to me, shut up."

Steve Reeves was partially responsible for all the American expatriate actors being in Rome, due to his success in the Italian film *Hercules*. Halsey did not know him well but recalled: "He was a very nice man. He was very quiet. One of the things I learned later on was that he didn't speak until he was seven years old, because his parents were deaf and dumb. He's one of the few who got very lucky. He married a Swiss woman, and she took care of his business and he was one of the few who came back with some money. Quite a horseman, too."

Halsey afforded *la dolce vita* by adopting the philosophy of spending as he went. If he wanted a new Ferrari or Maserati, he would buy it, using the simple logic that he would have to get a job to pay for it.

Halsey made many friends among the local Italians, as well as those expatriates living there. They enjoyed:

> A good quality of life. It was magnificent. Things were cheap. There was lots of money. Life was a big long party. The world

isn't the same. We went to a party in London. Five days later, we were in Athens. I didn't know how I got there.

Halsey would later base the character of the agent Sandy in his 1978 novel *The Magnificent Strangers* on Sandy Lieberson, though Halsey described the end result as "faction"—between fact and fiction. Sandy observed, "I think Brett made me a much nicer, caring type of person.. We all know what agents are really like.. But there were definitely certain characteristics that I recognized."

Halsey and Sandy even went on holiday together to West Berlin in 1963 and crossed into East Berlin. Sandy recalled:

> That was an adventure. We encountered a grey, depressing city full of ruin and rather depressed people, such a contrast to West Berlin that it was staggering.

Halsey vividly remembered this trip:

> It was like going into a different world just going through Checkpoint Charlie. I had bought a new car while I was there, a Thunderbird, and we drove over and then we'd go to a little café, park in front of the café and sit and watch people looking at the car.

The local populace was very poor:

> You weren't allowed to use Western money at the time, [only] East German money. But everyone wanted the West German money. Once, Heidi had sold some records in the East and had some royalties coming. So she went to pick up her royalties and they paid her in the East German money, which was no good, so she bought a sable coat.

Halsey was a single man in hedonistic Rome until he met Heidi. It is rumored he had affairs with a number of his leading ladies and women fell in love with him at parties. Halsey looked back on the years in Rome as "magical." Halsey's son Clayton concurred: "My father always loved women." Halsey remembers once walking down to the banks of the Tiber in evening dress with a bottle of champagne in the company of Tina Sinatra. He tried to open the champagne elegantly but the cork would not come out. In desperation, he hit the bottle against a corner and the top broke off neatly, saving the situation beautifully.

Rome in the 1960s: (back row) Bob Oliver, Mrs. Frank (Nancy) Sinatra, Brett Halsey, Henry Silva, (front row) Mrs. Paul (Gail) Getty, Jr., Nancy Sinatra

Henry Silva renewed his friendship with Halsey when he, too, was lured to Rome by the Italian film industry:

> We knew each other much better when Dino de Laurentiis called me and said, "How you like to come to Italy to make some films for me?" The scripts were not too bad, so I said, "Okay." Nineteen sixty-five in Rome was *never* to happen again. It was extraordinary. Major stars from Hollywood were working there...Joseph Cotten, Anthony Quinn, Gregory Peck. Peck went over to make a three-pic deal: there was a tax break then. You had to stay out of Hollywood for 18 months, so you would not pay taxes. I didn't avoid taxes but the salaries were good and you went from one film to another.
>
> Brett made a lot of movies in Italy and Spain. We all went from film to film. We played a lot of tennis. It was like being in a wonderful place. It was wine, women and song. For a single guy, you had an extraordinary choice of girls, girls who worked for Ingmar Bergman, girls from Germany. I spent 10 years in Europe, Brett not quite that long. I even turned

down pictures in America because of the food, the people and the ambience. When you worked for their directors, you worked—but only eight hours a day, and if you got the work done sooner, you went home early. In the U.S., they'd say, "Let's do tomorrow's work."

In the 1950s and 1960s, Brett was really a star. Women used to flock to him. Even now they do. He had intelligence and charm, not a put-on charm, and was big-hearted. I was partaking of his parties. I am grateful to him for introducing me to a variety of beautiful girls.

Halsey's enduring friendship with Clint Eastwood continued when Clint accepted a role in the spaghetti Western *A Fistful of Dollars*, which made him an international star. Halsey ran into Clint outside his hotel in Rome the day he arrived. Halsey and Heidi invited him to a party a few days later, where Clint was advised not to do the film because it was a project that had been around for a long time. Clint also became friendly with Heidi and later would use her in one of his pictures. Halsey recalled, "Clint used to come to our house." Halsey said that Clint had no idea what he was getting into when he agreed to work in Italy: "He said it was two tickets and he had never been to Italy."

In Paris, Halsey once looked up his pal Gardner McKay. They got together and went out to eat. Halsey told him he'd never been to Maxim's and would like to see it. McKay took Halsey to the entrance of the fabulously expensive restaurant and said, "Okay, you've seen it. Now, where do you want to go to eat?"

George Bacos, a member of the Writers' Guild, stayed at the Residence Place Hotel for four months while trying to get a production credit on an Italian Western. The film had a Yugoslavian producer, and Bacos was hoping to be the film's American producer, but there were difficulties raising the money. So while he was doing treatments and rewrites he bumped into Halsey. They became friendly, played tennis and sat around drinking coffee on the Via Veneto. Bacos took an interest in Halsey's screenwriting. He recalled visiting Halsey's apartment and meeting Heidi, and especially remembered Halsey's king-size bed, which he had imported from the States. He bumped into Halsey again in the early 1970s when they were both back in Los Angeles.

Halsey shared coffee on the Via Veneto with Buster Keaton and bumped into past colleagues from Hollywood, including Jeffrey Hunter: "I met Jeffrey Hunter on the Via Veneto in Rome early one morning. He said, 'I can't do it anymore, I just can't earn enough money. I need to earn $50,000 before I can eat.' He was paying alimony and had debts." Hunter ended up making low-budget fare in Spain like Javier Seto's *Mafia Mob* with Margaret Lee, a film he left before it was completed because the producers ran out of money and could not pay him. Halsey defended him: "He needed the money. He was a good actor, a generous actor. When Renate had to do a test, when under contract at Universal, he acted in the test with her, just to help her do a better test."

Halsey also bumped into actor Farley Granger, reduced from starring in Hitchcock films to playing psychos in low-budget Italian thrillers. As with Jeffrey Hunter, Granger needed the money. Halsey said: "He seemed down." He met Cameron Mitchell ("a nice man") at parties. Mitchell was in Rome starring in pictures for directors like Mario Bava, for whom Halsey would eventually work.

On one occasion in Rome, Vincent Price, who was making a picture there, looked Halsey up. They went out to dinner and dancing. Halsey took Price to meet a Swiss painter he knew, Kurt Poulter. Price was a connoisseur and knew Poulter's work. He pointed out one painting as the best Poulter had ever done, so Halsey bought it. A moody abstract, it still hangs in Halsey's Beverly Hills apartment above his sofa.

Halsey even encountered some Hollywood history on these foreign movies:

> I met some actors in Spain and Italy who were in Hollywood when sound came in. They would shoot the picture in English, French and Spanish; English during the day, French or Spanish at night. They brought over well-known actors from Spain and France [to shoot the export versions]. Charles Boyer was one who came over and never went back.

Halsey went back to Hollywood in 1967 but found no work. He wrote:

> One day, my mother called from Los Angeles to tell me that someone had asked her if I was interested in selling my house. "Why would I want to sell my house?," I questioned.
>
> "Well," she answered, "when are you planning to come home?"
>
> "I don't know," I replied as truthfully as I could. "One of these days."
>
> "It's been five years," she responded.
>
> Five years. I hadn't realized I'd been away five years. "Okay, Mom. Don't do anything. I'll be home in a couple of days."
>
> Elmer Valentine, who got the idea to open Hollywood's perennially successful Whisky-a-Gogo while on one of our jaunts to the French Riviera, met me at the airport. We went on a tour of my old Sunset Strip haunts and saw many of my

old pals. I was having a good time, but something was wrong. Nothing had changed, but everything was different. It must be me, I thought. Here are the same people sitting in the same places, talking about the same things as when I left.

Then I realized what was different. These people still believed the sun rises and sets on Sunset Boulevard and now I knew better. I'd been following the sun all over the world. The next day, I visited my Hollywood agents. They were friendly but evasive as hell about my prospects for getting work. After all, I'd been away an awfully long time. People said to me, "Are you still in the business?" I was depressed. The States didn't have theaters to show B movies anymore. They went straight to TV.

When I got back to Elmer's, there was a cablegram waiting from Sandy Lieberson in Rome. An Italian producer wanted me for two pictures, back to back, in Yugoslavia with top money. I called Sandy and happily accepted.

Halsey flew non-stop to Rome, which took 13 hours: "That's a hell of a flight. But I preferred to do that and stay in bed for a day." Halsey had no great respect for air travel. He was once friendly with a Swiss airline pilot and told him he was basically the same as a bus driver, transporting people in a metal tube. The pilot was very offended. He told Halsey he was more like the CEO of a large corporation because of all the responsibility.

Halsey felt great relief at arriving back in Rome where he was in such great demand. He observed that the scene was growing decadent:

> There was no way for us to be unaware of the mushrooming drug culture back home. The press was full of it and, although the Italians are great fad followers, they just didn't seem interested in drugs. There was a small group in the rarefied strata of highborn decadent nobility who were into heavy drugs, but this same group was implicated in drug and sex scandals even back in Mussolini's time. Most of the American actors were too concerned with the physical demands of their movies to get into destructive drugs.
>
> The only marijuana we saw was brought in by tourists, but hashish was cheap and plentiful. Heroin was on the outer fringes, and the first time I saw cocaine, it was the situation, not the drug, which blew my mind.

Paul Getty, Jr. gave a party for Dewi Sukarno, who was visiting in Rome while her husband was still running Indonesia. It was quite a dignified affair. The place was full of ministers and diplomats. Paul and I and a prominent American actress were having a polite conversation with the Empress (or whatever her title was), when the actress suggested that Paul show her his collection of rare antique miniature pornographic sculpture. I thought the actress was overstepping the bounds of protocol, but when Madame Sukarno expressed an interest, I shrugged my shoulders and the four of us went to Paul's bedroom. I couldn't help thinking about her eight-foot-tall bodyguards on the other side of the door as we admired the tiny works of erotic art. I almost dropped my drink when I heard the actress offer Dewi a snort of coke. I felt like I'd just taken a high dive into an empty swimming pool. But the biggest shock came when she didn't refuse.

There was also a brief flirtation with LSD. A doctor, who was a former neighbor of mine in Hollywood, came to Rome with a small bottle of the clear, harmless-looking liquid. One night he decided to give everyone what he said was half the normal dose. He said that if no one reacted badly, the next time he'd give a full dose. It was kind of fun. Everyone was watching everyone else, waiting for some weird reactions. But the worst thing that happened was, we all got a little silly and laughed a lot. The silliest part of the evening happened later when a Roman producer showed up at the door with Shirley Jones on his arm. I didn't know Shirley Jones very well, but she always had the reputation of being a pretty straight lady, so everyone did his or her best to appear normal until she left. She must have thought we were all crazy.

Later experiments without the doctor's supervision turned out to be not so harmless. One of Britain's superstar actors had to be forcibly restrained from attempting a dive into the fountain of Trevi from an apartment terrace five floors above.

Another held a party in terror into the night while he was deciding whether or not to disembowel one of the world's outstanding businessmen. Some of the excursions into serious narcotics ended in dark tragedy—the demise of Paul Getty, Jr.'s second wife, Talitha, from an accidental overdose and William and Carol Berger's drug-related arrest, which resulted in Carol's deplorable death in an Italian jail.

Hasley's spy movie *Espionage in Lisbon* was shot at the newly built Estoril-Sol Hotel near Cascais. Halsey considered investing in some of the local real estate:

> We had a deal with the Estoril-Sol, which was not open yet. It was publicity for the Hotel. I considered buying a villa in Estoril. There were great villas in Estoril available for almost nothing—$20,000–but Portugal is the end of a journey and the Portuguese psyche is death-orientated. To live there would be difficult.

Halsey preferred Monaco: "I used to like going to Monte Carlo. I had to dress in a tuxedo. I used to go often. I had a cousin in Monte Carlo. He ran a Rolls limo year round. I recall dressing for Grace's [Kelly] Red Cross Ball. Grace had elegance." Halsey recalls ruefully that he once fell down the stairs in his tuxedo at the swank Hotel de Paris in Monte Carlo. He was angry and bleeding, and then turned the corner and fell farther. He had to borrow a fresh shirt. On another occasion, he decided to swim across Monte Carlo harbor because it was the quickest way to get across to the other side, but ran into a big floating turd. At least he was able to borrow his wealthy cousin's Rolls whenever he wanted. Halsey also once nearly bought a farm in Tuscany to grow grapes, as he liked it there and found it an appealing notion to drink his own wine with a group of friends.

Amos Powell, Halsey, Helga and Bruce Balaban pose in Rome.

Stardom in Europe

Halsey's career took a fascinating turn when Egyptian-born Italian filmmaker Riccardo Freda approached him to play the lead in an adventure film. Halsey could not do the picture because of his commitment to *Follow the Sun* but was flattered by the offer. At the time, the summer of 1962, Halsey was a rising star, much in demand, but his personal life he deemed "a mess" with two divorces and "the potential of another bad marriage looming heavily on the horizon," a reference to his stormy relationship with Debbie Power Loew.

On the same day that Halsey learned the series *Follow the Sun* was being canceled, Freda renewed his offer and gave Halsey an escape route. Halsey was off to Rome within a few days for Paolo Moffa's Adelphia Films to make *Sette Spade per il Vendicatore,* a.k.a. *Seven Swords for the King.* It would be the start of a fantastic European career that would last nearly 10 years and then be revitalized again in the late 1980s.

Belgian poster for *Sette Spade per il Vendicatore*

Halsey does not know what Freda had seen to make the filmmaker so keen to bring him to Italy: "Whatever he had seen, he never told me." Sandy Lieberson, later a successful film producer and studio head, was Halsey's agent in Rome during the 1960s, while Dick Clayton remained his agent in Hollywood. Sandy had begun his career as an agent in Hollywood, and the Kaufman-Lerner Agency brought him to Rome when the Italian industry expanded. Sandy was responsible for getting Halsey to accept Freda's offer and had an idea of why Freda sought this particular Hollywood actor:

> He saw in him an actor that might help get us distribution for his film. He also saw in Brett an actor who was the perfect type for the Freda-type movies. Brett was incredibly handsome and had a real charm in his screen persona and in real life.

Halsey himself did not hesitate long about accepting Freda's offer. He had consciously been looking "to escape" but had not known where he could go: "Where do you run when you're a rising young Hollywood film actor? In those days, if you wanted to be in the movies, there was Hollywood, and that was that. Or so I thought."

Furthermore, the offer intrigued him:

> I was aware that something was going on over there. I remembered that my ex-wife, the sex kitten of Italian cinema, Luciana Paluzzi, had spoken about working in *Three Coins in the Fountain* and with Steve Reeves in his first international hit, *Hercules*. I had also talked with Stephen Boyd about his experiences on *Ben-Hur*.
>
> The more I thought about it, the more I was determined to go. I went through the motions of seriously discussing the advisability of leaving town at that point in my career, but when my agent Dick Clayton offered no firm resistance, I eagerly accepted the film.
>
> As I sat in the plane looking out over the endless clouds passing beneath us, I had no idea that I was about to become part of a time and place which would turn out to be as memorable as Paris in the 1920s, Hollywood in the 1930s, Paris again in the late 1940s, and Greenwich Village and North Beach in the 1950s. The intangible ingredients that made this epoch possible did not exist before the 1960s and certainly no longer exist today.
>
> The Italian post-war economic miracle created a favorable financial climate. Forces as diverse as the 1960 Olympic Games, Fellini's *La Dolce Vita*, and kindly Pope John XXIII caused public interest and curiosity to focus once again on the ancient world's capital. The international press kindled that interest with a daily log of the antics of Elizabeth Taylor and Richard Burton, while 20th Century-Fox muddled through their near-ruinous film *Cleopatra*.
>
> The spectacle films, which had become financially impossible to shoot in Hollywood, began to flourish. *War and Peace*, *Barabbas* and *Ulysses* became popular favorites with the world movie audience.
>
> But the force that probably had more influence than all the others was television. It wasn't long before the studio heads got wise and joined the TV bandwagon. They stopped making B movies for the theaters and, with some slight modifications,

began making them for television. The major difference was they now were called TV series.

What the wise men who ran the studios failed to realize was that television did not take over the rest of the world as fast as it did the U.S. There was still a tremendous world market for B adventure films and no one was providing the product for that market.

If there was one person who first recognized and exploited this situation, it had to be Joe Levine. He bought the rights to a film called *Hercules*, a relatively insignificant Italian imitation of the American spectacle, and ballyhooed it into a smash financial success. Levine started it, but it didn't take long for others to join the parade, and the Italians were only too happy to accommodate. They quickly developed a formula, which seemed to satisfy everyone. Hire an American actor whose salary could be covered by the American TV or theatrical sale; put him together with a well-known Italian, French, German or Spanish female—depending upon which country or countries made a European co-production agreement; and round out the cast with the best Italian actors available.

Before long, every American body-builder capable of tying his own shoes was in Rome making movies. Gordon Scott, who became famous as one of the most popular Tarzans, was brought over by Joe Levine to co-star with Steve Reeves in *Duel of the Titans*. This film led to a long string of heroic films for Gordon and established him as one of the most durable of the strongmen stars. Peter Lupus, who would later star in *Mission Impossible*, made a series of films under the name of Rock Stevens. There was also Richard Harrison, Mark Forrest and Burt Nelson, among the more notable.

The world market quickly became saturated with the muscleman films and, anyway, there weren't that many Hollywood stars with overdeveloped bodies who were available, so the next logical step was to the romantic costume adventures, *Scaramouche*, *The Three Musketeers*, *The Scarlet Pimpernel* and more. All of history's and fiction's noble swordsmen who fought against tyrannical oppression were about to become immortalized by Italian cinema; and that is where I came in.

Seven Swords for the King was the title of the script that lay in my lap as the 707 jet cleared the Alps on the last leg of my journey. The months of fencing lessons I had taken at the Hollywood YMCA were about to be put to use. Move over

Errol Flynn, Stewart Granger, Cornel Wilde and Burt Lancaster. Halsey's coming to town and his sword is hot.

Sandy Lieberson greeted Halsey upon his arrival in Rome:

On the drive into the city, Sandy tried to apprise me of the different methods and approaches I was about to encounter in Italian filmmaking, but I was more interested in the fascinating sights that were popping up one after another. I realized we were travelling on the renowned boulevard of *La Dolce Vita*, the Via Veneto. Like any other tourist, I searched the fleeting blur of figures seated at the sidewalk café tables on both sides of the street, looking for familiar faces. After a couple of short blocks, we drove through the Porta Pinciana gate of the medieval city wall and crossed the grand Villa Borghese into the fashionable Parioli section and the Residence Palace Hotel.

While signing the register, I couldn't help but notice two sinister-looking Italians across the lobby giving me a suspicious once-over. After a bit, they nodded satisfactorily to each other, assumed a much friendlier attitude and approached the reception desk. These were my producers. They greeted Sandy like a long-lost brother and vigorously pumped my hand, all the while peering intently into my eyes as though they were searching for some secret of life. After a final round of effusive hand-pumping, the portly pair turned and hurried out of the hotel.

"What was that all about?" I asked Sandy.

"It's typical," he laughed. "Italians don't trust agents any more than everybody else, and since we're foreigners, they trust us even less. They were here to reassure themselves that the actor they bought is really the actor they got."

As I stood digesting this dubious information, I noticed Stephen Boyd walking through the door. As we greeted each other, Gordon Scott sauntered out of the men's room, heading towards the bar. We agreed that I should send my luggage to my room and join the boys for a quick one.

Stepping into the bar, I immediately recognized Howard Duff and Ida Lupino, Lang Jeffries and Dick Haymes, among the other Americans seated around the modestly decorated room. "Good God," I said. "Aren't there any Italians in this country? We might as well be in the Polo Lounge at the Beverly Hills Hotel."

I soon discovered that the Residence Palace Hotel was the spot for visiting American show folk. It wasn't as luxurious as the Excelsior or the Grand. Its restaurant was a bleak disaster, its service was mediocre, and its location somewhat inconvenient, but its large, sparsely elegant suites were relatively inexpensive and the bar was the most show-biz chic of all the hotel bars in southern Europe.

That night, the famous old Hollywood director Irving Rapper was having a party in his apartment overlooking the Tiber. Although I was tired from the long journey, I was still too excited to think about going to bed. I put on a suit and tie and went to my first Roman party. Again my taste for a bit of exotica was frustrated. Sure, there were a few Italians in attendance, but there were also a few Italians at the parties back home. Even my sexual fantasies were frustrated. I ended the evening with an American actress whom I had previously dated in Hollywood.

I arrived in Rome only a week before the scheduled start date of the movie, so bright and early the next morning I was taken to the costumer to begin fitting my splendidly ornate costumes. I don't remember very much about the character or the plot of that first Italian film, but I do remember I was beautifully dressed.

Halsey wears an extravagant costume in Freda's *Seven Swords for the King* which weighed 70 pounds. His abiding impression is one of discomfort: "The thing I remember about that is it was so hot. There was a scene where we threw these chickens in the air; when they came down, they were dead."

Halsey has vivid memories of his first experiences on an Italian film:

After the costumer, on to the studio where I met the stunt master and his team. He got me started on the complicated routines. The stuntmen were all excellent fencers and I was grateful that my YMCA training had at least taught me the proper form. Fencing routines must be precisely choreographed and rehearsed. Contrary to popular belief, those swords are real and there are many actors with the scars to prove it.

The balance of the week was spent preparing for the picture and becoming acquainted with the more or less permanent resident American film colony.

The first day's shooting was soon upon us and, as we began rehearsing the opening scene, I knew I was in trouble. There was a Spaniard, a German, a Frenchman, an Italian, and me, each of us acting in his own language. I realized that I not only had to know my dialogue but, if I was going to make any sense of the scene, I would have to learn the other actors' lines as well. There wasn't time for that, so I counted: the Frenchman had a line, then my turn. The German had a line, the Spaniard had a line, then me again.

Another problem was the incredible noise. Because of sound recording, a Hollywood set is quiet as a tomb. The Italians didn't worry about sound. Their final version was dubbed into many different languages, so they concerned themselves with the sound later, after the film was finished. The film crews seldom interrupt their conversations just because a scene is being filmed. Often during a shooting they raise their voices so they can be heard over the din of the generators and the unmuffled chatter of the camera motors. There is no question that acting in Italian films is the ultimate test of an actor's concentration.

Another thing that took some getting used to was the pace of a day's work. The mornings would ordinarily start with a leisurely coffee well laced with brandy or grappa. We would usually get a master shot and maybe a couple of other angles before lunch, then take a comfortable break for a heavy midday meal, complete with wine. Then, in the middle of the afternoon, things would start jumping. The production manager would look at his schedule and find we were way behind, so he would start to yell. As the buck passed to the lower echelons, the yelling would become more intense and soon everyone would be racing like hell to finish the day's labor.

It was interesting that the Italians never yelled at Americans. Among themselves it was accepted as a natural, inoffensive means of communication; but a few quick-fisted Americans convinced the Italians early on that we didn't like it. One actor, who had a long career in Rome, silenced a vociferous director by breaking his jaw. The following day, the replacement director began loudly berating the American and he, too, got his jaw broken. The third director was more prudent.

Although he carried the title Count, Riccardo Freda was not above practical jokes. Early on in the film before Halsey had to perform a dueling scene, Freda got him drunk at lunchtime: "It could be dangerous. I never did it again." Still, Halsey found him "a charming old rogue" and they became "fast friends." During his years in Italy, Halsey had a lot of minor accidents. He explained to D. Hood (*Afternoon TV,* September 1977):

Halsey practices his swordplay.

Most of the films I made were action films. I usually did my own stunts. Actors aren't as protected there as in Hollywood. They don't know anything about the sophistication of the American stuntmen, the way they wear pads, the training, the

Art or Instinct in the Movies...

routine of physical training, just to keep yourself in shape. They get hurt all the time. Every picture I made there, someone was seriously injured.

Sette Spade per il Vendicatore

Halsey might have been injured on *Seven Swords for the King*. In a swordfight scene in a torture chamber, Halsey was underneath pots of burning oil and realized he was likely to be splashed, so he insisted on a live rehearsal, which cost Freda to lose half a day resetting the effect, but the rehearsal showed that Halsey was right and he would have been burnt the way it was originally set up.

In Italy, expatriate actors did not enjoy union safeguards the way they did in Hollywood:

> In the beginning, many foreigners complained about and sometimes derided the primitive, lackadaisical methods of Italian filmmaking. There are no effective actors' unions in Italy, so some of the working conditions were like those of pre-Screen Actors' Guild Hollywood. The hours were long, the rest breaks few, the sanitary facilities on location non-existent, and the emergency first aid supplies usually consisted of a bottle of iodine and a roll of gauze somewhere in the bottom of the makeup man's case. And everyone has heard stories of the difficulties many actors had getting paid.

Halsey had to look out for himself, he explained:

> For example, all my contracts in Italy, I had 12-hour turnaround time. In other words, they could only work me 12 hours, and I had to have 12 hours free between calls. And I would enforce it and finally what I learned to do was I would tell the producer, "Look, I know you run into problems. And one time if you have a problem, I'll give you that 12-hour period but I'm telling you now before we start the picture, I'll give you that 12 hours but you must promise me now you'll never ask me again. Just once." He never used it. He was saving it. So I always had my 12 hours.

Halsey has been on both sides of the fence in picture making:

> I'm ambivalent about it, because the unions for actors are really important mainly to protect actors. Actors were badly abused in the early part of the business. And then I get my pension from the Screen Actors Guild, so that is important to me, of course.
>
> But unions can get in the way. My feelings about unions is, especially the craft unions like the Screen Actors Guild, we should also protect the producers. If you hire a union actor, you should know you're getting a journeyman actor who will do the job as expected, and if he doesn't do the job properly, I believe the union should punish him. We don't have that.

In any case, the unions in Italy were powerless:

> One of my first films in Italy, the driver was taking me to the studio and outside the studio were some pickets. I said, "Who's that?" He said, "Actors." I said, "Oh, I can't cross the picket line." They said, "No, the only people who strike are people who don't have a job, and every political party has its own unions, so there's like six actors' unions, none of which have any power to do anything anyway." So I went to do it.

Halsey's leading lady on *Seven Swords for the King* was Beatrice Altariba, described by him as "a delight." "We did have a rapport during the filming but, afterward, I don't know what happened to her. Because, after *Seven Swords for the King,* I went back to the States. I don't think I ever saw her again. She was very nice. We got along very well." On this film, Halsey first encountered Mario Bava, who was a consultant to his friend Riccardo Freda on the picture. Bava would later make two fine films with Halsey.

Halsey had initially been lured to Rome with the offer of one picture:

> As much as I enjoyed the experience, I hadn't entertained the idea of remaining in Rome after the film was finished. I had another picture to do in Hollywood with Vincent Price, my old co-star in *Return of the Fly*. My family, my friends and my home were in Southern California. Why shouldn't I go back? So I did, but only briefly.

Around this time, there was a press announcement for a Fox film called *The Amazing Miss Bartlett* starring Brett Halsey and Diana Darrin. Halsey had no knowledge of this mysterious picture that never came about. Then the Italians offered four films to be made in the course of a year, then five and then six. The temptation to return to Rome was great. Halsey said, "My decision was made the morning my lawyer called to tell me one of my ex-wives was hassling me. Within the week, I was winging my way back to *bella* Roma." Before he knew it, Halsey had become an Italian actor.

Once he had decided to stay in Rome, Halsey soon found his niche in the local society:

> Charlie Fawcett, the most incredible actor, writer, soldier of fortune, and the unofficial American mayor of the Via Veneto, went out of his way to help me get established. He also introduced me to the international party set. I was truly impressed by this group whom I had first seen as fictional characters in the film *La Dolce Vita*. Their sophisticated decadence was real, their talk, their dress, their whole way of life oozed with worldly *savoir-faire*. Sexual appetites were freely and openly satisfied, but always with a little something extra—something special.
>
> Those of us devoted to life, liberty and the pursuit of happy times took full advantage of the marvelously unique opportunities available to us. When the parties in Rome became tiresome, there were always invitations from Monte Carlo, Gstaad, Malta and Beirut. There was hunting in Kenya, Scotland and Bavaria; restaurant excursions to Paris, London and Amsterdam; film festivals in Venice, Berlin, Cannes and San Sebastian; sailing to the mythical islands in the Mediterranean; and then, of course, there was work to pay for all this frivolity.

Halsey happily worked in *Seven Swords for the King* and subsequent costume pictures *The Avenger of Venice* and *The Magnificent Adventurer*, because, "I wanted to do swashbucklers. It was Errol Flynn, Tyrone Power, *The Black Swan*. I studied fencing at Talent School."

Halsey wrote:

> I was eventually to make so many of what the Italians call the "cape and sword" films that the stories tend to run together in my mind. During one film, the director and I had a terrific argument over whether or not we had shot a scene that he was setting up. It turned out we were both right. We had shot the scene, but in a picture we had already finished.

The movies were well received in Europe, and Halsey recalled the Italians made *fumetti* (still photo comic books) out of them. Halsey recalled that *The Magnificent Adventurer*, in which he played Benvenuto Cellini, was "pretty successful" in Rome and made him a big star in Italy. In fact, Halsey once told his fan club that Cellini was his favorite role: "I've thought about this…it was a nice combination of a character who was an artist and a warrior." French actress Francoise Fabian was his co-star in *The Magnificent Adventurer,* and he said of her, "We were very close."

Halsey singled out one particular memory of the shooting:

> I was in my hotel room in Madrid, Spain, enjoying the luxury of a late call to work as the star of *The Magnificent Adventurer*, when I received a call from the hotel manager. He was apologetic about disturbing me, but he said he felt obligated to tell me that the president had been shot.
>
> I thought he had confused me with someone else and believed I might be interested in knowing that the President of the hotel company, or some other local business, had been involved in some sort of a shoot-out. I thanked him as politely as possible, hung up and returned my interest to studying my scenes for the day's filming.
>
> After a few moments, he called again, repeating his message. Again I was as polite as possible in my thanks for the information. The third time he called, I was beginning to get annoyed by his interruptions, but he was more forceful. "You don't understand," he insisted. "*Your* President has been shot. Your President Kennedy may be dead."
>
> This time, he had my full attention. "Where did you hear this? How do you know?" I demanded. "It is on the radio," he responded, obviously upset with the news.
>
> At that time I had been dating a girl, Kit, whose father was the Naval attaché at the American Embassy. I immediately called her and asked for the latest news. She said that she hadn't heard anything about it, but would call her father at the Embassy and call me back.
>
> The irony of this story is that Kit's call to her father was the first news he heard about the shooting. The people at the American Embassy first heard of the President's assassination from the daughter of the Naval attaché, who heard it from a visiting actor, who heard it from the manager of his hotel, who had heard it on a Spanish radio news broadcast.

Freda and Halsey fell out when Freda saw him as the perfect Romeo in a new film he was planning of *Romeo and Juliet*, to be shot in English. Halsey was not trained in Shakespearean speech and declined the offer when Freda revealed there would be no rehearsal, as he was afraid he would embarrass himself. A disappointed Freda cast actor Geronimo Meynier instead and did not speak to Halsey for a long time. Halsey was right to turn it down. Freda's version (1964) was a flop and has been eclipsed by the 1968 Zeffirelli version.

Of the films made in Italy, Halsey observed:

> The Italian pictures were rewarding in the sense that they were fun. I always wanted to do action-adventure. I love the sword and all that, so it was rewarding in most ways. Certainly not in artistic ways, but I always said I'm an entertainer. I'm not

necessarily an actor in the sense of the classic actor, and I enjoy entertaining. That's my job. And I'm treated as a star.

Halsey respected the inventiveness of Italian filmmaking:

As the weeks rolled by, I became more appreciative of the freedom to experiment. I marvelled at the artistic effects the lighting director would achieve with less than a third of the equipment available to his Hollywood counterpart, and at the ingenious way the director would cheat with his camera to make small groups of extras look like multitudinous throngs. Even with the different languages, the unit functioned almost like a family.

In sequence, Halsey made costume pictures for Freda and then pseudo-James Bond espionage films, which are, arguably, his finest work. Both *Espionage in Lisbon* and *Spy in Your Eye* are very good films. Then he made five spaghetti Westerns, which he became best known for in Britain and the U.S.

Halsey was not confined to Italy during these years. The productions were shot in various European countries, and his popularity in Europe increased when the films were released, which led to offers from local producers. Dorris Halsey remembered, for instance, that Halsey was "very big in Spain, too, not just Italy."

Halsey went to Berlin to make a picture with Senta Berger, *Jack and Jenny* (1963). The picture would be memorable for a variety of reasons, particularly since he would meet his future wife Heidi on the set. Halsey was inspired by one of the incidents that occurred when writing his novel *The Magnificent Strangers*:

Funny story about that picture, the book was found by a director, Steve Previn. Steve Previn had directed some Disney pictures in Austria and Germany, and he was president of American-International in Europe. Anyway, he found it and he had done a picture with Senta and he was in love with Europe, so they hired me to play the male lead. So what happened was, Senta decided she wanted her makeup person to be flown out from Vienna, and the producer said, "No. Are you crazy? We have plenty of makeup people in Berlin." So, she stood her ground: "I'm not going to do the picture unless I have my favorite person." The producer said, as reported to me, "You're not doing the picture." Steve said, "I conceived the picture for her, and if she doesn't do the picture, I'm not doing the picture either."

They were at an impasse and I was already in Berlin, and they had to pay me if they did the picture or not, so they couldn't fire me. So they went back to Senta and said, "Okay, we forgive you, we'll take you back…but we don't need Steve." And she said, "Okay." So poor Steve was left high and dry. Then they found Victor Vicas, who I think had been working for CBS News or something. He was a good director, but Steve Previn was destroyed. He'd bit for her and she wouldn't [for him]…

Last time I saw her was really kind of sad. There was this RAI trilogy of women's pictures called *Rose*. I did one with Valerie Perrine. Anyway, they had a screening in Rome. Her story was an older woman and a younger man and, what Senta didn't understand, I think, was when they photographed her, she looked like hell, but deliberately. I don't think she realized

Senta Berger and Halsey in *Jack and Jenny*

it until she saw the picture and she was really disappointed. She was good. I liked Senta, but it was really kind of difficult, because Steve was a friend of mine and the first scene we have in the picture was Senta and I half-naked in bed, and I was a little resentful because of what had happened to my friend.

Performing in a minor role in *Jack and Jenny* was Michael Verhoeven, who later became a world-acclaimed director of films detailing the tragedies of the Nazi era (*The White Rose*, *The Nasty Girl*). He also married Senta Berger. Halsey could remember him being there, though not his acting in the film.

Halsey returned to swashbuckling with Piero Pierotti's *The Avenger of Venice* (1964), which was "fun." Well-known director Duccio Tessari co-wrote and some have credited him with co-direction. Halsey commented, "I think he did co-direct some of it, but I don't know what he did, and it is Piero Pierotti's film." Tessari directed Halsey on Italian television many years later. The film is handsome but not as good as Freda's swashbucklers. It contains too much dialogue between the action sequences, and Pierotti lacks Freda's keen eye for composition. For Halsey, Freda was "a better director." The film ends with a magnificent swordfight in St. Mark's Square, as good as anything Tyrone Power had ever done. The Square was quite wet because there had been recent flooding. Halsey recalls that they spent two weeks rehearsing the swordfights. Sometimes a stuntman was used, but most of it is Halsey.

One day during the filming in Spain, Halsey, in rags and false beard, and co-star Burt Nelson, similarly in costume, decided to go to a restaurant without changing. Halsey recalled with amusement that "the maitre d' and the waiters swooped down on us, until they recognized us."

Halsey recalls that Burt had a scene where he had

The Avenger of Venice

Hour of Truth

to fall into the canal, which was cold and filthy, and Halsey teased him that he should have been a star, not a character actor, then he would not have to go into the water. As it turned out, Burt had to do the fall twice, as he was out of the camera shot the first time. Even the stuntmen balked at jumping into the dirty canal water in another scene and a couple of gondoliers offered to do it. Bizarrely, *The Avenger of Venice* was once released on video in France as a pirate movie (which it isn't) called *Le Seigneur des Mers* and with Halsey credited as "Steve Johnson."

Hour of Truth (1965), another obscure film in Halsey's resume, showed what a dedicated actor he really was. Henry Silva was very impressed: "Once in Paris they offered Halsey a movie where he was supposed to speak French. They asked, 'Do you speak French?' 'No.' They said, 'Sorry.' Brett said, 'I'll get a translator. I'll learn it word perfect.' I thought, 'My God...this guy.'"

Halsey agreed it was difficult to perform in French when he did not speak the language: "But I had plenty of preparation time. I didn't have a problem. And I did my own voice in the dubbing, in French."

This movie could have really had potential, but there were problems. Director Henri Calef decided to shoot the picture in Israel. The theme of the picture was "Can a man ever be redeemed?" The plot concerned a former Nazi who went to Israel and became a productive member of society, but then he was discovered and faced a trial: "The dilemma was—do you kill him?" The Israeli Government had approved the script but, when filming began, they decided it was anti-Israeli. The delivery of raw stock was blocked. The first cameraman got fired and Claude Renoir finished shooting the picture. Halsey was disappointed that the makers compromised the ending, which weakened the point of the picture:

If we had let this man go free, it would be seen as anti-Israel. If we had killed him, it would be seen as anti-humanity. So they compromised. He died when his Jeep turned over in the desert, which meant nothing.

This was another low-budget picture:

> The producer came to me and said, "I can't pay you. I don't have any money." I said, "I love this picture, but I can't do it if you don't pay me." The producer said he had an interest in a jewelry concession and I could take something for my wife in lieu of salary. [He chose a pair of silver cups.] I had the choice. I could have quit. But I wanted to finish the picture. I liked the picture. But I could have walked. I never thought it would ruin my career.

Although it was not widely seen, the film brought Halsey some recognition. He recalled, "Vincente Minnelli told me it was shown at the Buenos Aires Film Festival, and I was nominated for Best Actor."

In 1965 Halsey made one of the worst pictures of his career. It was a feeble historical comedy called *Lovers and Kings*, and was directed by Geza Radvanyi, who was famous for pictures like *Maedchen in Uniform* (1958). Halsey identified the main reason for its failure:

> I couldn't understand from the script and from the tone of the first shooting—is this a comedy? Or is it serious? What is it? One day the director was sitting in his chair and I came over and said, "Geza, I'm having a little problem with this script. I can't figure out, how am I supposed to play this? Is he funny? Is it this? Is it that?"
>
> He said, "Brett, I hate this fucking business. The directors get screwed. The only people who make any money in this business are the producers. I'm not going to direct any more. I'm going to produce." And he's going on and on and ranting about how he hates this fucking business…After a while, I said, "Thanks, Geza, that helps me a lot." That was the extent of the conversation.
>
> I never saw the film. I was on it about six weeks. Well, it was a disaster. It was a million dollar production when a million dollars *was* a million dollars. It was booked to premiere in Munich, and they booked the theater for six weeks or something, and it closed in a week and a half. Wonderful

cast, such fun to work with, but as an actor, I wanted to know if it was a comedy.

The failure of *Lovers and Kings* effectively ended Radvanyi's directing career. Halsey was rescued from misfires like this with the advent of the spaghetti Western.

Rome in the 1960s was also the epicenter of art cinema with Antonioni and Fellini at their peak. Halsey crossed paths, as he put it, with Antonioni's muse Monica Vitti, but he never appeared in any art movies because, "the art crowd looked down on the adventure films crowd." The closest Halsey came was appearing in a film by Antonio Pietrangeli, a director who had something of Antonioni's stylishness in films like *I Knew Her Well* (1965) but was clearly more inclined to comedy. Halsey's *The Magnificent Cuckold* (1964) is a Claudia Cardinale comedy. He remembers little of the film or cast and director: "I worked only two or three days on the film, mostly with Claudia Cardinale. I had very little contact with either of them apart from the actual filming. I still haven't seen the film."

Producer Gene Corman remembers when Halsey was working in Italy:

Lovers and Kings

I think he captured a moment when Italian filmmaking was at its zenith. And there were a lot of other actors there too, probably enjoying the good life. My wife and I were there in Italy and by accident we saw Brett and met him in the Via Veneto for coffee that evening. Brett *was* enjoying the good life.

Halsey invited screenwriter Amos Powell to come to Rome to help him write his Western script *West of Hell*. It was Halsey who introduced Powell to the talented young British director Michael Reeves. Powell wrote the treatment of Reeves' first movie, *Revenge of the Blood Beast*.

Halsey had some dinners with Reeves in Rome and described him as "a film buff, friendly and open." Reeves hoped to direct one of Halsey's epics and mentioned it in his diary; it was a shame that it never came about. Reeves, very astute at recognising talent, clearly understood that Halsey was a talented actor. They first met at the American Palace Hotel, an apartment hotel popular with American and British visitors. Reeves had an apartment there with his girlfriend Annabelle Webb. Halsey was friendly with Annabelle before and especially after Reeves' unfortunate death, meeting her at parties and social occasions.

Powell got on well with Reeves and moved to Roundhurst in Surrey to continue working with him. When Reeves died, Powell returned to California.

Secret Agent Man

Brett Halsey's height, looks and charm made him the perfect candidate for the immensely popular Eurospy pictures. Halsey was offered the Bond-like role of George Farrel, agent 077, in *Espionage in Lisbon*: "My wife was doing *My Fair Lady* in Hamburg. I went there and read six James Bond novels in a week. I did it to get a flavor for the character." This author feels he could have easily stepped into the 007 role when Connery left it the first time. Of course, with the backlash actor George Lazenby suffered from *On Her Majesty's Secret Service*, Halsey's subsequent career would have suffered.

Espionage in Lisbon (1965), directed by Tulio Demicheli, is one of Halsey's most enjoyable films, but, unfortunately, it is difficult to find in any format. Halsey never saw the completed film. He commented, when first approached for this book: "I really enjoyed making *Espionage in Lisbon* but, unfortunately, for one reason or another, I've never seen it. I have always considered Tulio Demicheli to be one of the most talented Italian directors with whom I had the pleasure of working." Halsey later saw the video and felt that the story meandered a little, something this author regards as part of its charm.

Tulio Demicheli was based in Madrid, where he ran his own film production company as well as writing scripts for other filmmakers. He commuted to Rome for work, and was, in fact, an Argentinean expatriate who had to flee for political reasons, leaving behind an extensive film career. He was born Armando Bartolome Demicheli in Buenos Aires in 1914 and died of cancer in Madrid in 1992. Most of his Argentine films have never been seen outside that country. He is known for a handful of lackluster Italian films (*Ricco*, *Dracula vs. Frankenstein*, *Gunmen of the Rio Grande*, *Son of Captain Blood*). One of his final films, a documentary about Eva Peron, did get shown at the National Film Theatre in London.

It was Demicheli, rather than producer Frederic Aycard, who sought out Halsey for the film. Sandy Lieberson remembered a phone call from Demicheli concerning Halsey's availability. Sandy recalled that Demicheli spoke Italian.

What makes *Espionage in Lisbon* a cult film is the involvement of director Jess Franco. Franco wrote the original story and uses one of his jazz musician pseudonyms, David Khunne, in the credits. But Jose Bayonas, Juan Cobos and Monica Felt wrote the script. Bayones, a playboy–type, is profiled in producer Sidney Pink's memoirs, *So You Want to Make Movies*. Monica Felt was later an assistant director in the Italian film industry and scripted thrillers and spaghetti Westerns such as Pasquale Squitieri's *Vengeance Trail* (1971).

Jess Franco, when asked why he did not direct the film, explained that he was intending to direct, but the production company, Hesperia Films, kept delaying the film, and by the time they wanted him to go ahead, he was already commit-

ted to his next film, *Miss Muerte* (1966). So the job went to Tulio Demicheli. Franco thought the finished film was "funny."

He also claimed to have written the music with Daniel White, but is not listed in the credits. Halsey could not recall Jess having any involvement in the film.

For a number of reasons, *Espionage in Lisbon* is possibly Halsey's most interesting performance. One is his extraordinary screen chemistry with actress Marilu Tolo. Marilu, born Maria Luisa in Rome, was a former model who was discovered by Carlo Ponti. She had an extensive career in Italian cinema—sword and sandal, spy movies, and gialli—although her earliest ambition was to be an architect. Later, she lived with director Dario Argento, after working for him on Italian television in *Doors Into Darkness*. At that point in her career, the role of spy Terry Brown was her most intriguing. So effective was her pairing with Halsey that producers cast them together two more times, in *Perversion Story* and *Roy Colt and Winchester Jack*.

Sandy Lieberson confirmed that the pairing was deliberate: "I think Brett had a thing going with Ms. Tolo. She was something else at that time. All the films were successful, so a re-team was a good thing." However, Halsey told Steve Fentone in *European Trash Cinema*:

> We didn't get along too well. On the first picture we were shooting a scene in a taxicab with the director and cameraman in the front seat, and Marilu and I were in the back. I didn't know what she was saying to me. The camera was rolling and I turned to her and said, "Marilu, why don't you go fuck yourself?" She gave this big reaction and the director said, "Cut. What did you say to her? That was great. I've never seen her give such a good reaction."

When queried, Halsey said, "I never understood it, but I believe it's true that Marilu Tolo and I appeared together three times because of the chemistry we seemed to have onscreen. It isn't fair to say that we didn't get along. I would prefer to say that our offscreen personalities were not so much in synch as our onscreen ones."

Halsey characterizes Marilu as "amusing," but they were "not particular friends":

> She would do anything for publicity. She wanted me to be seen leaving her apartment in the morning for the paparazzi. I said, "But I'm married, Marilu." She said, "It's publicity. Your wife should understand." I replied, "No, Marilu, my wife *won't* understand."

Halsey was surprised to learn that Marilu had posed nude in *Penthouse*: "She didn't have that good a body." Today, she is retired from the screen and lives a very private life in Switzerland and refused an invitation to comment in this book. She was an excellent screen actress and absolutely sensational in *Espionage in Lisbon*.

The spikiness in their relationship bears interesting comparison with the more comfortable relationship in their later film, *Perversion Story*. This is due in part, to the scripts. In *Espionage in Lisbon*, Terry Brown (Marilu) has cause to be suspicious of Halsey's George Farrel and wary of his flirtatiousness. In *Perversion Story*, there is no scripted reason for her to be anything other than supportive to Halsey's Richard, who is not flirtatious, in his sad quest to find out why his sister died. However, the two performers were more comfortable with each other in their second film and felt at greater ease onscreen. Their relationship was not as edgy as on the first picture, even though Halsey has said that the shoot was difficult.

Espionage in Lisbon wastes no time in depicting George Farrel as a ladies' man. As in many Bond openings, a call to work in-

terrupts Farrel's bedroom Olympics with a nubile creature we never see again. Halsey plays this matter-of-factly, without the knowing innuendo of a Sean Connery. And, as the *Monthly Film Bulletin* noted, the film was "unabashedly manufactured to order." Indeed, it met the criteria of the current craze for spies like James Bond, *The Man from U.N.C.L.E.* and others. From that point, the film, which garnered a U certificate in Britain, making it suitable for children, becomes rather chaste, limiting itself to Halsey's flirtatiousness, unlike more sexually explicit espionage films such as Maurice Labro's *The Spy Who Went Into Hell,* which came out around the same time and where full frontal nudity occurred in a scene with actor Ray Danton and Pascale Petit. Pascale later worked with Halsey in Mario Bava's rather more lurid *Four Times That Night*.

The chaste quality is rather surprising given the pedigree of the filmmakers. Jess Franco would make notorious soft and hardcore pornography in addition to mainstream thrillers. Tulio Demicheli would feature sleazy scenes in films like *Ricco*. Halsey had no qualms about appearing nude in films like Lucio Fulci's *The Devil's Honey* (1986). The decision seems to have been made at the script stage to concentrate on the intrigue element (one foreign title for the film is *Intrigue in Lisbon*) rather than bedroom shenanigans. This is noticeable in the opening scene when George Farrel, after accepting the mission, returns to his bedroom with a weariness that speaks of resignation (perhaps of having to go through the Bond clichés?).

Although he spoke no English, Demicheli managed to get good performances from his cast. Halsey explained how Demicheli directed, even though he could not communicate with them verbally:

> You get a feeling. He would talk to me in Italian, and I understood enough Italian, and you get this connection. You put your hands on somebody and you talk to them, it happens. I never had any trouble with directors understanding language. But he was a good director. I really enjoyed working with him.

Among the fine performances by Halsey, Marilu and Fernando Rey was a memorable one given by French actress Jeanne Valerie. Halsey commented, "She was good and I did like her, but I didn't have any real contact with her. I didn't socialize with many of the people on that picture, because Heidi was there for a good part of it in Lisbon, and so we were with each other." Heidi can be glimpsed around the gaming table in the early casino scene. Another in-joke features an unbilled cameo appearance by Hollywood star George Nader, which was specially written for him because he happened to be in the city when they were filming.

During shooting Halsey and Heidi actually stayed in the Estoril-Sol hotel, which is prominent in the film: "One thing that was nice is I'd go down and get my makeup and then I'd go back up to my room and lie down on my back very carefully and go back to sleep until we were ready to shoot."

Producer Frederic Aycard met Halsey at the Lisbon airport when he arrived. He recalled, "I think I did a couple of pictures with him. He was a very nice man. I liked him. We got along well." Producers "always" met Halsey when he arrived at a new location.

Spy mania was at its height, making *Espionage in Lisbon* internationally successful, which led Halsey to be hired for a similar role in another Italian film, *Spy in Your Eye* (1965), which was sold to AIP in the U.S., exposing it to a much larger audience than *Espionage in Lisbon*. It went into production as *Epitaph for a Spy* and has been screened under a bewildering variety of titles, including *Bang You're Dead*, *Cult of Violence*, *Berlin Operation Laser*, *Berlino-Appuntamento Per le Spie*, *Berlin, Cita Con Los Espias*, *Operacion Polifemo*, and so on. *Spy in Your Eye*, like other espionage films and TV shows of the time, used emerging technology of the 1960s to move the plot along and to provide the spies with showy gimmicks and exploding toys. An outrageous spy fantasy inspired by advances in microelectronics, *Spy in Your Eye* explores the espionage implications of inserting a tiny camera into the eyeball. This sets *Spy in Your*

Brett Halsey does the secret agent bit in *Spy in Your Eye*.

Eye in a more fantastic realm than *Espionage in Lisbon,* where the electronic waves invention is barely dwelt on and is just a McGuffin. Director Vittorio Sala uses complicated events that were common in 1960s' Italian spy fare to divert attention from this ludicrous premise. Albeit lacking in narrative logic, many of the scenes are agreeable fun, especially when they exploit Halsey's heroic capabilities, such as an athletic parachute jump. Halsey's terse scenes with Pier Angeli (in one of her final films) also play well. Angeli received the Golden Globe for Most Promising Newcomer in 1951, but her career floundered as she aged. She fell into a depression and committed suicide not long after the film was completed.

Halsey's characterization of spy Bert Morris is slightly harder-edged than his George Farrel, partly because the script lacks the humor of *Espionage in Lisbon.*

Halsey remembered director Vittorio Sala favorably:

> He was competent. Stayed in good spirits. He knew what he wanted. We shot that picture all over…Berlin, Beirut, Jordan… I think he was well connected in RAI (Italian State television). He was more interested in producing than directing.

One of his strongest memories is of his co-star Dana Andrews' alcoholism:

> We were filming in Rome before we went abroad. Dana's wife had not joined him yet. She was going to join him to go abroad. I was walking down the street with him and he was slightly veering to the side. His drinking killed him.

Assistant director on the film was 28-year-old Stefano Rolla. Halsey remarked, "In spite of the fact that he was a lousy sailor, I knew and liked him very much. I left my catamaran in his care, and he was embarrassed to see me after he sank it by running it onto the rocks near Anzio. He avoided me." Stefano went on to work on other Italian movies (including the spaghetti Western *My Name Is Nobody*, Argento's *Deep Red,* and Halsey's thriller *Web of Violence*). He later became a director. In November 2003, he was one of 27 people killed in a car bomb attack on the Italian military headquarters in Nassiriya, Iraq, while preparing a documentary about Italian peacekeeping forces.

Halsey had never met Pier during her time in Hollywood, even though she was briefly engaged to his friend James Dean. During the filming, they were friendly but did not talk about Dean. Mostly, they talked about their children. While filming *Spy in Your Eye* in Jordan, Halsey traveled with King Hussein's

Arab patrol, eating and sleeping in the desert. He was prepared for this harsh trip after spending nine weeks in Israel's Negev Desert when making *Hour of Truth*.

Halsey's excellence at imitation of James Bond roles did not go unnoticed in the 007 camp. The course of Halsey's career and, indeed, of film history was nearly altered when Halsey actually *was* considered for the role of James Bond when Sean Connery quit after *Diamonds are Forever*. Bond producer Cubby Broccoli wanted to cast him. Halsey said:

> Cubby Broccoli approached my manager Cal Ross when Sean was going out of the picture. Cubby and I had become friends before I was at 20th Century-Fox, and he had offered me a contract to go to the U.K. to play in British films, but I chose Fox instead. The trouble was, I couldn't see myself as Bond. I couldn't convince myself I could be Bond. Cubby set up a meeting with Guy Hamilton at a private house. I went to the meeting and I was so low-key, I virtually talked myself out of the role. I couldn't see me replacing Sean. Johnny Weissmuller *is* Tarzan. Sean Connery *is* James Bond. It was the end of my relationship with Cubby, because I'd turned him down.

This rare example of an actor's integrity cost Halsey millions of dollars and worldwide fame. Dorris Halsey agreed:

> The biggest mistake in my opinion—he doesn't think so—was when he turned down the possibility of being James Bond. I can confirm it, because Cal Ross, who offered it to him, had offices at 8721 Wilshire Boulevard. I also knew Cubby Broccoli and Dana, and I think Cubby was very angry at Brett at the time, but Brett felt it should be an Englishman and, at the same time, was offered a contract at CBS and he chose the CBS contract, which would have made him a much richer man now if he hadn't. They talked about it with Cal Ross.

Halsey confirmed, "Cal put that deal together." It seems incredible that any actor would turn down such an opportunity of guaranteed fame and fortune.

It was even more extraordinary for Halsey to turn down the offer during a slow period in his film career. Most of his work was for TV. When asked if he had any regrets in turning down Bond, Halsey replied:

> No, I never regretted it. As a career move, it probably was a mistake…It *was* a mistake. But, personally, I just didn't *believe*

it. But I never believed that James Bond could be an American. It just didn't make any sense to me.

Spy in Your Eye

Roger Moore should be eternally grateful.

According to Cubby Broccoli's memoirs, United Artists even approached Clint Eastwood to play 007, without Broccoli's knowledge. The reasons he cited for Clint's refusal were the same as Halsey's—that Bond should be played by an Englishman and that he could not follow Sean Connery, no matter how much money was offered. Halsey feels that Clint was right to turn it down: "Clint Eastwood couldn't play James Bond, just as Sean Connery couldn't play Dirty Harry." Other names proposed were Burt Reynolds and Steve McQueen. Broccoli was opposed to all these names and supported Roger Moore, who, of course, got the role.

Guy Hamilton tested many actors for the role of Bond after George Lazenby's go at the master spy. Connery filled in for one more movie until Roger Moore was cast. Hamilton unfortunately cannot recall his interview with Halsey:

> The pre-production of *Diamonds Are Forever* took place in Hollywood and I tested John Saxon [among many, many others], who was signed to play Bond 'til Sean stepped up to the plate again. After six weeks' filming, we moved back to Pinewood to complete the shooting. It was a given that this was Sean's last appearance and I'm pretty certain that Roger Moore was already the chosen successor. I think it is unlikely that Cubby would have offered the part to Halsey, as he took the 007 trademark very seriously and I'm sure would not have

tolerated anyone who, in his opinion, defiled it. Harry Saltzman, too, would have insisted on a test.

Guy Hamilton's reasoning is sound, but Halsey had not really defiled the Bond trademark. *Spy in Your Eye* is a typical spy movie in which his character, Bert Morris, makes no reference to Bond or 007. As for Halsey's character in *Espionage in Lisbon* (although in the Italian and a few other European prints there is reference to 077 in the title) there is no overt Bond connection. But it is pointless to ponder what might have been had Halsey appeared as 007. It's better to look at what he achieved in future years without the license to kill.

Contemporary Thrillers

Although Halsey does fine work in costume pictures and Westerns, he seems most at ease in contemporary films. In *Web of Violence* (1966), he starred opposite English actress Margaret Lee, who, like Halsey, was an expatriate in Rome. Halsey said Margaret was really a lot of fun:

> I liked working with Margaret Lee. She was a good actress and smart girl. We got along really well, worked well. It's nice when it just kind of comes together.

The major movie career anticipated for Lee early on did not materialize and, later, an attempted comeback failed, but she made many excellent minor movies. She has an onscreen chemistry with Halsey and comes close to rivaling the rapport he had with Marilu Tolo. It is a pity they only appeared together in this one film. Halsey's character is searching for the man who killed his wife. Halsey was unsurprised that the film never found an audience: "It wasn't very good. It made no sense."

Contrary to Halsey's opinion, the film is quite good. Halsey's performance is strong and the story is fast-paced and exciting. Halsey's character is involved in nasty fights and alternates between melancholia and good humor. The story is convoluted but holds your attention. *Web of Violence* was another Hesperia production and a repeat performance for *Espionage in Lisbon* scriptwriter Juan Cobos.

Web of Violence

Sheila and Halsey in *Bang Bang*

Ottavio Poggi produced the movie. Halsey commented, "Poggi was a good producer and he had a real eye for the photography, for the picture. He had a primary interest in art, in buying and selling." The film was released in the states because it had some U.S. financing and Poggi had a relationship with a U.S. distributor.

Director Nick Nostro was a minor talent whom Halsey found "a nice little guy" but incompetent: "He couldn't direct. It was unfortunate. He didn't like to go to work. No talent. I don't know how he ever got the job. It was a fight from start to finish with him, because he just didn't *know* how to do it." Of the dangerous car chase where it appears to be Halsey behind the wheel rather than a stuntman, Halsey said, "I probably did it. He was dumb enough, he would let me do it, and I was dumb enough to do it."

In a complete change of pace, Halsey appeared with pop star Sheila in *Bang Bang* (1967). The film resembled a French version of Cliff Richard's British musicals (*Wonderful to be Young, Summer Holiday*). Halsey remembered:

> It was all right. It was kind of fluff. It was a tremendous hit in France. It was fun to make. I think that was Sheila's only film. It's a modern musical comedy. The director was Serge Piolet. I think it was his first film and, with what they gave him, I thought he did a good job. She had a big, big record called "Bang Bang," the Sonny and Cher hit—she covered it in France.

Art or Instinct in the Movies...

Halsey portrays Englishman Dan Smith, a Scotland Yard inspector. His Englishness is suggested more through wardrobe (three-piece suit) than accent; even the script acknowledged that he looked like an American.

When the story moves to the South of France, Halsey, wearing a white suit similar to the beige one he wore in *Spy in Your Eye,* seems more comfortable in the action scenes with actor Jean Yanne. Yanne progressed to more prominent films for Godard and Chabrol, and eventually became a director. A library fight scene depicts Sheila throwing books at her attackers. The scene at first seems silly but, as it goes on, it actually starts to become amusing. Although the film has little plot, some scenes are stylishly directed (the first musical routine) and the lovely Cote d'Azur backgrounds are pleasant viewing. Halsey again took on some potentially hazardous stunts such as a headlong dive into the sea, swimming to Sheila's rescue. The film did not have much of an impact, but it did make Halsey a well-known face in France.

Halsey saw the film for the first time in May 2007 on video. He recalled that the scenes on the boat were shot in the studio in Paris because the actors all got seasick.

When the producers hinted to the press of a romance between him and Sheila to stimulate interest in the movie, Halsey wasn't amused. He was concerned over what his wife Heidi would think. He remembers that Sheila was "very disappointed" that he was not interested in having an affair. In any case, Halsey recalls that he was not attracted to her because she was too shy. He did have a brief liaison with one of the dancers from the dance sequence, visiting her in her hotel room. Heidi never heard about that.

The comedy *Anyone Can Play* (1967), directed by Luigi Zampa and starring Ursula Andress and Claudia Cardinale, features Halsey in a minor role. He

Halsey and Ursula Andress in *Anyone Can Play*

was very friendly with Ursula, whom he found "very feminine," and through her met her partner Jean-Paul Belmondo. Also in the cast are Mario Adorf and Claudine Auger, who played the fabulous Domino in *Thunderball*, but Halsey recalled he "didn't do much with her." He remembers, "My best pal was Mario Adorf."

Halsey became very popular in Spain, making movies like *One Day After August*. Although still photographs of the film exist, the film seems to have disappeared. Halsey joked to the producers, "Why don't you call it *The First of September*…that's one day after August."

Halsey recalled an amusing memory of the shoot, which connected many relationships and periods of his career:

> It was around 1967 when I was in Marbella, shooting *Un Dia despues Augusto*. At the same time, Leslie Martinson, director of *Hot Rod Rumble*, was there shooting *Fathom*, starring Raquel Welch. His production assistant was Michael Reeves' partner, Annabelle Webb. I don't remember exactly how but somehow Annabelle and I made contact and made a date to go to the bullfights on the following Sunday. We ran into Martinson at the bullfights, exchanged a few words of greeting, and thought no more about it.
>
> A couple of weeks later, I was in Madrid, where I ran into a friend from Rome. My friend said, "I didn't know you and Heidi were getting a divorce." I replied that we were not getting a divorce and where did he hear such a ridiculous thing? He said that he had seen Martinson, who told him he saw me at the bullfights with my ex-wife Luciana and that we were back together. I was amazed. How he could confuse his own production assistant with Luciana was beyond my comprehension. I figured it must have been a combination of the hot sun and the Spanish wine.
>
> Anyway, I didn't want Heidi to hear this story through the gossip grapevine, which is faster than a speeding bullet, so I immediately called her and explained the situation. Annabelle was confused, and a little hurt that the man she had been working with every day could confuse her with Luciana. Heidi was amused by the idea I might be back with Luciana…but wondered what I was doing with Annabelle.

All on the Red (1968) is a caper film about robbing a casino, which was shot partly in Zagreb, Yugoslavia. Halsey did not get on with the director Aldo Florio,

Barbara Zimmerman and Halsey in *All on the Red*

who had hired the leading lady, hoping he could seduce her. Florio was exasperated when she refused him. Halsey told Steve Fentone (*Giallo Pages*):

> So he cornered her one day and said, "I know why you don't want to sleep with me, because you're sleeping with Brett." She said, "Yeah, I am sleeping with Brett. But I'm also sleeping with John, Pete, Joe, this one and that one...I'm sleeping with everyone on this film except you, you sonofabitch, because you're a pig."...When you say it's hot in Italian, the expression is *fa caldo*. We were shooting the film in the dead of winter, and used to walk around saying *fa caldo* (fuck Aldo), and the crew never did figure it out.

Halsey found Florio "adequate" as a director. "He'd get the job done." The movie was shown in Rome but did not get a good release. Halsey remembered the difficulties involved in shooting a low-budget caper in Zagreb in the winter:

> There were no good restaurants. The only place we could eat that was even halfway decent was in the hotel *until* a couple of the crew came back and they were very happy with their

meal the night before. We said, "Where did you eat?" "This whorehouse." So, it got to where most of the crew would go to this whorehouse—for *meals*. Not to have anything to do with the girls. We'd just go there for meals—and ate very well.

But it was another cheapy production. I remember once we were shooting this scene, planning the caper, and in the script I have a drink of whisky, and I said, "At this point he wouldn't be drinking whisky, he'd probably be drinking coffee, because he'd have to keep sharp." The director says, "Okay, let's have a cup of coffee." We were shooting in the hotel. Well, we're waiting for it. The coffee doesn't come. Finally, the director says, "Where's the coffee?" And the production manager says, "Who's going to pay for it?"

Gordon Mitchell, another expatriate American actor living in Italy, was also in the film. Halsey remembered him as "a very nice man." Mitchell built his own studios in Rome. Halsey never worked there: "I heard about it. He built a Western street."

Halsey continued to take risks on low-budget films by doing dangerous stunts to enhance the quality of the movie. He now puts it down to "the folly of youth":

I would do things like that. I remember once we were shooting in Yugoslavia and there was this scene where there is this train coming and I was being chased by the bad guys and I had to run across this trainyard and jump in front of the train to get to the other side so the train would block their path. I did it myself and I should never have done it. There was gravel and I could have tripped. And then I realized later how really stupid it was because it was all filmed in long-shot. It could have been anyone.

In 1969, Halsey was reteamed with Marilu Tolo for the film *Perversion Story*, a film that is endlessly fascinating. The title of the film is misleading and the film often finds its way into the porn section of video shops. In England, it had the rather enigmatic title *Again*, possibly a reference to the reteaming of Halsey and Tolo. The original Italian title was the more meaningful *I Caldi Amori di Una Minorenne*. Halsey's character had several seduction scenes with Romina Power, daughter of his old friend, Tyrone Power, and Linda Christian. Romina also starred for Jess Franco in *Sade* before retiring from the screen.

Perversion Story was shot in Madrid for Spanish director Julio Buchs, who is best known for the Ernest Borgnine spaghetti Western *Vengeance is Mine*.

Perversion Story

Scenes in London were shot on the actual locations and in a hilarious studio recreation of Soho. The film is located somewhere in between the 1960s psychedelia of swinging London movies like Michael Reeves' *The Sorcerers*, Barry Shear's *The Karate Killers* and Antonioni's *Blow-Up*, and the lurid Gothic romanticism of movies like the various retellings of the Jack the Ripper story, including Tony Tenser's production *A Study in Terror* (which was brilliantly directed by James Hill), the Hughes Brothers' *From Hell* and Jess Franco's *Jack the Ripper*. In terms of sheer weirdness, Franco's *Jack the Ripper* comes closest to *Perversion Story*'s crazy recreation of London. (The Soho set piece is an absolute delight that elevates *Perversion Story* to a cult classic.) Franco clearly hasn't a clue about London's topography. He has Lina Romay enter a horse-drawn cab in London and wonder if she is being taken to Sherwood Forest. *Perversion Story*, despite its strangeness, includes Halsey's character's grief at his sister's death, giving him the dramatic material for some powerful scenes.

Marilu Tolo's very cool performance is another great asset, providing an emotional counterweight to Halsey, helping their partnership frame the film's psychedelic excesses. Director Julio Buchs—to whom all praise for this strange gem belongs—clearly had no idea of London, either, as Halsey and Marilu walk from the Albert Hall to the Tower of London in the course of a sentence. He also populates the streets with helmet-clad, whistle-blowing bobbies and drenches

Soho in thick fog. Another amusing bit includes the dancing in a nightclub stop while the disc jockey turns over the record. These silly factual errors actually contribute to the film's dream-like atmosphere. The pervasive, excellently photographed night scenes further suggest a dream. Halsey would never have starred in something this unusual if he had stayed in Hollywood.

Halsey reacted to the suggestion that *Perversion Story* is weird:

> I wonder if it's weird because that's the Spanish idea of London. It was all shot in Madrid. We had a good director. I don't think he spoke English. He was older, so maybe he didn't know; he thought they did still change the records in discos. The main thing I remember about the picture is this fight sequence in this car junkyard. That was difficult—night shooting—and dangerous. The car wrecks had a lot of exposed metal.

Halsey remembered Romina Power fondly: "She married Italian singer Albano and I think she just retired. Her mother is a friend of mine." When discussing her performance in the film he said, "It was more instinctive. She had no training. She was very young. She was 17."

Seen in the film in the Soho disco is a poster of Heidi Bruhl. Halsey confessed it was a private joke: "I brought it from Rome."

In Halsey's Eurofilm phase, and even in his Costa Rican work, we see the transformation of his all-American persona into a convincingly Latin movie star, one who fits as comfortably into the worlds of Gianfranco Baldanello and Antonio Pietrangeli as any Franco Nero or Fabio Testi. Halsey arrived in Italy in 1961, and spoke no Italian. He ended up fluent in Italian as well as Spanish. He is very adaptable to his surroundings, whether Hollywood or Canada or Italy or Costa Rica. Halsey, when asked if he was so often sought for Italian pictures because he looked Italian, replied:

Italian poster for *Perversion Story*

Art or Instinct in the Movies...

Four Times That Night

It could be. It has happened—not often, but it has happened—that people say, "You're not an American, you're a European." I say, "No, I'm not." "No, you're European." I say, "Try me in one of your languages. No, I'm not." A friend of mine, a columnist in Germany, Hans Obermeyer, said, "I don't care where you're born. You're not an American. You're a European."

Four Times That Night (1968), Mario Bava's first film starring Halsey, was a comic take on *Rashomon*, which was a recounting of an incident from different points of view. The film, which was shot from October to December 1968, has been described by Bava's biographer Tim Lucas as his "least interesting and most disappointing" film. But the film is chockful of period charm and excellent performances by Halsey, Daniela Giordano and Pascale Petit. It admittedly is not typical of Bava's other work, but in this writer's opinion it is one of his most entertaining films.

Halsey is reveling in his Italian leading-man status at this point and exudes confidence and ease in the role of a wealthy playboy seducer. The seduction scenes with Daniela Giordano are quite convincing and it is difficult to believe that Halsey did not find her attractive, but apparently so. Daniela related a story to Tim Lucas that might have been the cause of this, although Halsey denies it ever happened:

> I had a scene where I had to kiss Brett Halsey, and the kiss had to be full of passion. I was almost blind without my glasses, so I had to measure the distance between him and me. I got the right position, I got the right place for his mouth, but I did not get the right distance. And I gave his teeth a good hit with my teeth, and he lost three caps in front.

Halsey had no knowledge of any of this and pointed out he has never worn caps. Tim Lucas also commented that there is no such scene in the film, so Daniela's memory seems to be at fault.

Although the offscreen rapport between Halsey and Daniela was negative, their onscreen chemistry is as strong as it was between Halsey and Margaret Lee, and second only to the compatibility with Marilu Tolo. Sadly, the film was a box-office disaster after it was rejected by the Italian censor board, which was ironically chaired by Halsey's sponsor Riccardo Freda. Freda said he thought the film was "terrible" and that he was doing his old friend Mario "a tremendous favor" by not allowing it to be seen in Italy. Was he perhaps influenced by Halsey's refusal to play Romeo for him and annoyed by Mario's usage of a star that he had brought to Italy? Or again, maybe he just thought the film was bad. Bava certainly did not find the ban a favor and was later caustic about the decision. The film's worldwide release was not to happen, only a few scant showings were held in the U.S. and Canada in 1973. Bava claimed in 1971 that he only directed the film because at the time, in Italy, "if you refused to direct an erotic film, people took you for a homosexual." Halsey never knew that Freda was responsible for banning the film.

Halsey's international profile was always much lower than the number and variety of his movies might lead one to expect. This was not entirely due to patchy distribution. Jay Bernstein pointed out that Halsey never employed a PR agent to raise his profile, and Halsey admitted: "I avoided the Press. I was married to Heidi, and in Germany there was terrible Press."

Looking back on his career, Halsey thought he probably should have employed a PR agent:

> I wasn't interested. Should have been. If I were doing one thing over again, that's probably what I would do, pay more attention to the business of the business…I can remember once, it was a German called to ask for an interview. He wrote for some paper I didn't like. I said, "You don't have to talk to me. Just go ahead and write it, you can write whatever you want."

Spaghetti Westerns

Halsey's abilities would fit nicely into spaghetti Westerns—the next commercial fad of the Italian film industry. Halsey's easygoing nature from earlier films was now eclipsed by an intense and brooding quality that was dramatically effective in darker material like *Perversion Story*.

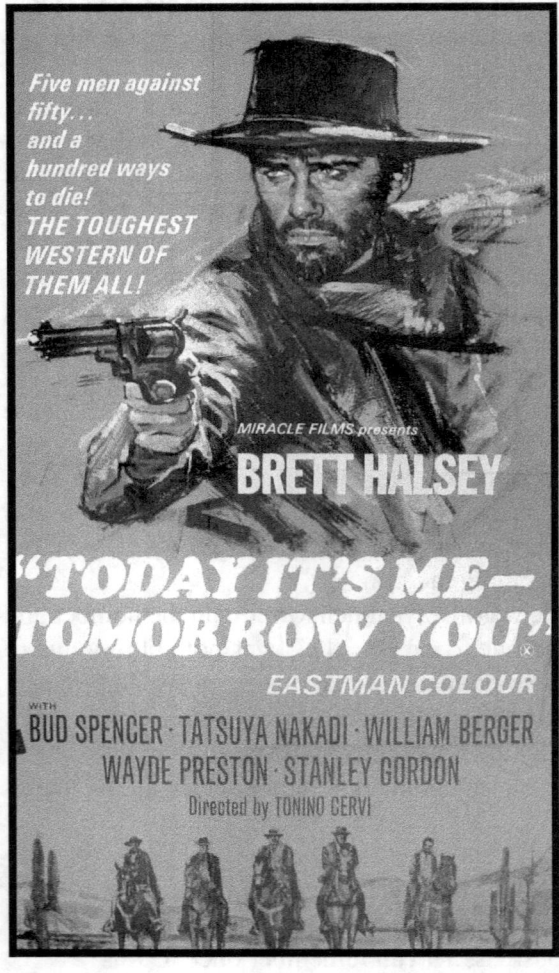

Some regard Halsey's work in the spaghetti Westerns as his finest screen achievement. Halsey's career included some traditional Hollywood and TV Westerns like *Four Fast Guns, Gunman's Walk, Gunsmoke, Brave Eagle* and *Alias Smith and Jones*, but he enjoyed some of his greatest critical successes with the Italian Westerns.

While Halsey only portrayed secret agents twice, he strapped on his spurs five times in the Italian Westerns. His work as the vengeful loner deserves closer inspection. Certainly his performance in *Today We Kill...Tomorrow We Die* is an absolute knock-out, and it is his favorite performance.

Kill Johnny Ringo (1966) was the first of his spaghetti Westerns. The success of the *Dollars* Westerns had given the Italian film industry a boost and created new opportunities for American actors overseas. Unfortunately, Halsey's involvement with *Kill Johnny Ringo* proved expensive:

> That cost me money. I was co-producing that picture and investing in the picture. I had the English-speaking world [rights]. I hired a couple of people. I rewrote the script. The

picture went bankrupt. I got no salary. I got no money. My investment was lost.

Adding injury to insult, he was hurt while filming the scene where Ringo lets a young man out of a cell. Halsey was acting with "a nervous kid," who had to hit Halsey on the head with his pistol. The kid was a student from the National Acting School. Halsey realized the kid was going to hit him for real and grabbed him and warned him that if he actually brought the gun down on his head, "Really, I am going to kill you." Then the kid hit Halsey for real. He opened up the back of Halsey's head and Halsey went down. The kid shouted, "Don't hurt me," and broke down on film. Halsey said:

> We had to reshoot it. They had to shave the back of my head. I had 15 stitches in hospital, so I had to wear the hat for the rest of the film. Poor Heidi. She screamed when she saw me. I was covered in blood and I had to work on the next day's script.

Halsey also suffered for his art through minor injuries acquired from falling off horses:

> Many times the horses weren't what we would call gun-broken, which means if you're riding along with shooting, the guns went off right against the horse's ear and, if he's not used to it, he'd *go*. I was quite an expert horseman, so, first of all, before we started shooting, I'd speak to the head wrangler. I would insist that they take the horse out and ride it, so he's calmed a little bit. So often they would just say, "Yeh, yeh, yeh" but the horse *wasn't* calmed, so then I tricked them. I'd get the horse to start bucking, but I'd *made* them buck, just to make the point....I avoided injury because I was afraid of getting hurt, so I was extremely careful.

Kill Johnny Ringo is a more conventional Western than its successors, showing less influence of Sergio Leone and more inspiration from Burt Kennedy or Henry Hathaway. Halsey's performance as Texas Ranger Johnny Ringo is more like the Hollywood cowboy than the Italian version. The plot is simple enough. In a town along the Mexican border, Johnny Ringo goes undercover to infiltrate a gang of counterfeiters. When the leader of the gang is arrested, there is a violent showdown.

Johnny Ringo was a true-life character (c. 1850s-1882, described by Steve Fentone and Michael Ferguson in an unpublished encyclopedia of spaghetti Westerns as "a mysterious troublemaker, frequent jailbird and former deputy

Kill Johnny Ringo

sheriff"). Ringo was featured in several other spaghetti Westerns, including Lex Barker playing Ringo in *Who Killed Johnny R* (Jose Luis Madrid) and *Kill or Be Killed* (Amerigo Anton), where Robert Mark took on the role of the outlaw. Halsey did no research into the history of the character because the film was not really about the real Ringo: "It was just a made-up name for the film." (Fentone and Ferguson suggest the project began life under the title *Saludos Gringo*.)

Regrettably there is none of the crazed vengefulness of the subsequent Westerns *Today We Kill...Tomorrow We Die* or *The Wrath of God*. *Kill Johnny Ringo* is closer to an episode of TV's *Gunsmoke* than a Sergio Leone oater.

The director of *Kill Johnny Ringo,* Gianfranco Baldanello, wrote, edited and directed the minor Italian Western *Gold Train/30 Winchesters for El Diablo* (1965) after a long career as an assistant director. Although the film was not successful, Baldanello managed to go on to a passable commercial career including a Gordon Scott spy movie *Il Raggio infernale* (*Nest of Spies*, 1967). *Kill Johnny Ringo* is not especially distinctive or original and continually promises to be better than it is. Of Baldanello, Halsey commented to Steve Fentone in *Giallo Pages*: "Nice person, but I just didn't feel that he had any original ideas...he'd come to work empty handed."

The film does feature some exciting gunplay toward the end and captures a superb fast draw by Halsey when he stands up from a poker game. Halsey would practice his draw in between scenes and became quite fast. This once led to an incident with German singer-actor Freddy Quinn, Halsey recalled:

> It was a joke. What happened was, there was a fan magazine called *Bravo* and there was a photo of Freddy Quinn showing how to fast draw. I was at a party and I don't know why

I said this, because I always liked Freddy Quinn, but I said, "I'll bet Freddy Quinn $100 that I can draw and fire before he shoots himself in the foot." Well, they printed it and it really embarrassed me. I was so afraid of what Freddy Quinn was going to say next time I saw him. The next time I saw him, he said, "Brett, I saw what you said. Would you give me a hand? Would you teach me how to fast draw?" and I was so embarrassed, I said ,"Yeah."

Then, later, he came to L.A. He was playing the Wilshire Ebell Theatre. It's a rather important theater. I guess I was the only one from those days who went to see him. It was a stupid thing that I said. I should never have said that in front of a journalist.

Kill Johnny Ringo is not a top shelf spaghetti Western, and does not have the sly humor of *Death Rides A Horse* (Giulio Petroni), the tragedy of *Man, Pride and Vengeance* (Luigi Bazzoni) or the weirdness of *Cut Throats Nine* (J.L. Merchant), but is superior to the movies of Gianfranco Parolini, which have received more U.S. and U.K. distribution First-time viewers of Halsey's spaghetti Westerns would be better advised to begin with *Today We Kill...Tomorrow We Die* and *Roy Colt and Winchester Jack*.

Today We Kill...Tomorrow We Die

Halsey also made Westerns for the Leone Film company, including Tonino Cervi's *Today it's Me...Tomorrow You*—a cumbersome title which has been translated from Italian. The film was retitled *Today We Kill...Tomorrow We Die* in the U.S., which is no less cumbersome but perhaps more meaningful. The script by Dario Argento is a blatant retread of *The Magnificent Seven* and, as such, inevitably suffers from the comparison. *Today*'s worth lies in its differences from *Seven*, and it is therefore best appreciated not as a remake of *Seven* but as an Italian view of Western clichés.

The casting of American Brett Halsey, within a specifically Italianate interpretation of Western myth, grounds the surrealism of the film. Halsey brings an air of authority to his character of the vengeful Bill Kiowa, combating the overblown anti-realism of most Leone-influenced spaghettis. Halsey's authentic Western performance causes *Today* to be too realistic to be one of the great over-the-top spaghettis, and yet the film contains too much strangeness (notably the Samurai element) to work as a conventional Hollywood Western.

Sadly *Today We Kill...Tomorrow We Die*'s parts are greater than its whole, although it does include some fine performances from Brett Halsey and the late William Berger, as well as an interesting script and impressive directorial sequences. Nevertheless, in *Today,* Halsey's character provides enough brooding menace for any spaghetti Western—the quality even comes across on posters for the film. Halsey commented, "That's what they were looking for." When speaking of Cervi the director, Halsey has this praise:

> First of all, the underplaying and minimal dialogue was part of the director Tonino Cervi's vision from the beginning. Cervi was very good about consulting and collaborating with his actors about how each of the scenes were to be played. I'm pleased that you found Kiowa's stunned reaction to the rape and murder of his wife to be genuine and very effective. Even after all these years, I can still remember the emotion of playing that sequence...While it wasn't spelled out, Kiowa had a close friendship with the renegade character played by Tatsuya Nakadai, prior to his wife's murder. Nakadai's character was originally written as a Mexican. I thought it was very interesting how Nakadai brought his Samurai training to what could have been a stereotypical Western villain. I was fascinated by the character he created and was extremely pleased at having the opportunity to work with him.

The film was shot in the forest of Manciano, north of Rome, which was also a location in *The Magnificent Adventurer.* Cervi had been a producer, most notably of Antonioni's *The Red Desert.*

Halsey looked back on *Today We Kill...Tomorrow We Die*: "I liked that picture. The director Cervi was good. I liked him. He was a friend of Dario Argento. The oddest thing is that Argento wrote it." Horror director Argento was a Western fan and co-wrote Leone's *Once Upon a Time in the West*.

Halsey retained warm memories of co-star William Berger, who was a top spaghetti Western star. Halsey deemed him a fine actor who would have become a big star but for a drug problem. Berger was a former track star who was part of a commune of actors who traveled around Europe. Berger was a pot-smoking hippie, Halsey recalled:

> William Berger rode into the lights. He turned the wrong way on his horse. We all went left, he went right.
>
> He was an intellectual. One time he went out into the woods with a book. I went out to find him. He was sitting there with the book. I picked it up. It was upside-down. He was stoned.

Halsey himself did not have much to do with recreational drugs after the LSD experiment. He once tried smoking banana skins, a common activity in the 1960s, to no effect. He also recalled someone once brought some morning glory seeds back from London: "We didn't know what to do with them. We made a tea and drank it. It was disgusting. I threw it away."

Also in the cast of *Today* was Wayde Preston. Halsey said of him:

> He was difficult to get along with. He had a lot of problems. He was a prisoner of war during the Korean War, but he did a series of Warners' called *Colt 45*. He got into some trouble with Jack Warner. They got into an argument over money and Wayde walked. Warner had him banned from the lot and blackballed throughout the industry. From that time, Wayde never worked again in Hollywood, in all the studios. In those days, studios had that power.

In the film, Halsey makes a reference to the Getty band, which was an in-joke about the high society Roman elite. Gail Getty was married to actor Lang Jeffries, and actor Edmund Purdom worked with Paul Getty, Jr., who went to Lily Gerini's parties.

In a strange move, Halsey is not credited as Brett Halsey but as Montgomery Ford. Halsey soon realized this was a big mistake when the film was one of the highest-grossing films of that year in Italy.

Halsey explained that the pseudonym was not a tribute to Montgomery Clift and John Ford, as one might imagine: "No. Just a meaningless name

that sounded American to the Italians." Halsey explained that the reason for the change was due to being tired, and when offered *Today*, he didn't want to do it. He could not have predicted it would be Italy's fourth-biggest grosser of the year. Halsey agreed to do the film when the Leone company said they would use a pseudonym and, due to the film's extraordinary success, the company used the name again on the next two pictures, Alberto Cardone's *The Wrath of God* (1968) and *Kidnapping* (1969). Halsey always rued the fact that one of the biggest films he made in Europe did not even have his name on it. Although through some anomaly the contract specified the British release would credit the name Brett Halsey.

While Halsey's performance in *Today* betrays the influence of Clint Eastwood's spaghetti Westerns, his character in *Roy Colt and Winchester Jack* (1970) is entirely different and has little in common with Eastwood's approach, offering a wry humor instead of dry cynicism.

Next came two fine pictures directed by Alberto Cardone (credited as Albert Cardiff on English language prints). He had been an assistant director on Italian movies like Steve Reeves' *Morgan the Pirate*. He was a commercial director who turned from a spy movie, *Agent S3S: Operazione Uranio* (1965), to Westerns. He had made a couple of Anthony Steffen Westerns in 1966, including one in the Sartana series, *Mille Dollari Sul Nero*, and is perhaps best known for a Margaret Lee episodic film *Le Carnaval des Barbouzes* (also 1966).

Halsey respects inventiveness in a director and, although some of Cardone's films have been criticized for flat direction in places, Halsey ranked him a lot higher than Gianfranco Baldanello, because Cardone found original and inventive solutions to problems. Halsey was particularly impressed how, on their first picture together, Cardone achieved a crane shot on the location in Almeria in Spain, when no crane was available. He rented a truck from the local fire department, ran the ladder into the air and filmed from the top of it. The shot is extremely impressive, revealing Halsey struggling on a sand dune in the desert with an actor who was actually a top stuntman. Halsey recalled that during the struggle on the hot sand, the stuntman said to him, "I can't, I can't any more." Cardone also uses unusual tricks such as pink clouds of smoke to make the visuals interesting. There are some classic visuals of Halsey riding through impressive landscapes to stirring music.

The first Cardone picture was shot as *To the Last Drop of Blood* but released as *The Wrath of God*, which has sometimes been confused with a better-known Robert Mitchum Western

Thai poster for *The Wrath of God*, released as *The Rage of God*

of that name. The synopsis runs: "A bitter widower, Mike, revenges himself upon the murderers of his dear wife, a gang led by his own friend David." The film paired Halsey once more with Wayde Preston. Steve Fentone has written that Horst Frank was originally announced in the cast but did not appear. Prolific producer Elio Scardamaglia (who directed an interesting William Berger movie *The Murder Clinic*) was involved in this one, but Halsey does not recall him ever being on location. An above-average spaghetti Western because of Cardone's visual approach, *The Wrath of God* is not as original as *Today We Kill* on a script level.

Kidnapping (1969) was another Cardone picture, with Halsey credited as Montgomery Ford in Italy and Brett Halsey in Spain. The plot synopsis reads: "A child is kidnapped in a town in the West; he is the son of a widow whose officer husband was killed in the War of Independence. The Sheriff is convinced that the author of the kidnapping is an outlaw, so he starts off to search for him. But the outlaw's wife and son had been killed by a group of bandits, and he too sets out to hunt down the real kidnappers." Halsey recalled, "I think it was a good picture. I don't remember having seen it, but it felt good while we were

Kidnapping

doing it. Cardone was a good director." The film's visuals are similar to *The Wrath of God* but Cardone really overdoes the trick of reddish-pink smoke in the forest (Manciano again). When the boy is kidnapped, the screen is smothered in red smoke. However, the film benefits throughout from Cardone's interesting imagery, which is even more pronounced than in *The Wrath of God*. There are frequent zooms (á la Jess Franco) and stunning compositions such as one involving Halsey, who has been shot off his horse, climbing a desert slope. Halsey's character is called upon to express a greater range of emotions and reactions than were called for in the earlier film: there is an excellent flashback showing him grieving for his dead wife and son, and scenes that show him drunk, defeated, defiant and tender with the boy. Halsey is admirably effective in these scenes. In his first scene, at the saloon bar, Halsey simply uses his eyes to convey emotion. His rather rough look, a million miles from his espionage pictures, looks very authentic. Both Cardone pictures stand up well alongside the best spaghetti Westerns.

As in Hollywood, Italian filmmaking also had its problems. Halsey recalled:

> On one picture, I didn't get paid, so I sued. They never made the picture, a Western, but they had to pay me anyway. Somehow my suit went to court in Naples. The producer, who didn't have his name on the project officially, was Mussolini's son, Romano Mussolini. The judge said, "They can't pay you. The company is bankrupt." So my solicitor said, "Well, if the company is bankrupt, distribute the assets." They said, "They can't, because they have *too many* assets to distribute." My solicitor said, "Well, is the company bankrupt or not bankrupt?" We played this game back and forth for about a year. My agent said to me, "Look, we're dealing with the Mafia here. They're just not going to give you the money. Let's just walk away." So we did.

While living in Italy, Halsey had difficulty being paid a few times and found the legal system difficult:

You can go to the courts, but the courts over there are corrupt. And I'm a foreigner. The foreigner is at a disadvantage. One of the first things I was told in Italy was the best thing that any foreigner can do here is don't make waves, don't draw attention to yourself. I'm not talking about as an actor, just as a foreigner: don't make trouble, because they'll get you.

In Italy it happened once, with my BMW 507. I'm driving along the street and this guy in a little Fiat makes a right turn in front of me. Well, I hit him. So we wait for the police. Police came. Anywhere in the world, the car on the right has the right of way, you don't make turns. So the cop says, "Well..." I said, "Well, what are you going to do about this?" He said, "Oh well, obviously you're rich and he's poor...look at his Fiat." It wasn't even over then. I got a call from my insurance. The guy had put in a claim and my insurance company *paid him.* They said it's cheaper than fighting.

Halsey had a good relationship with Mario Bava after working with him on the 1968 sex comedy *Four Times That Night,* so it was no surprise when Bava cast him in the comedy-Western *Roy Colt and Winchester Jack* (1970). Marilu Tolo is excellent in a comic role very different from her characters in *Espionage in Lisbon* and *Perversion Story*. Halsey commented, "That's her natural side. She's naturally comedic in life." The shoot went well. "Bava loved the picture while we were shooting it. He had such fun." A long slapstick scene in a bordello slows the film. Halsey agreed: "I saw the picture recently. It doesn't work. Nice to be able to do your own edit."

Roy Colt and Winchester Jack failed to find an audience, much like most other

Roy Colt and Winchester Jack

Art or Instinct in the Movies...

Halsey and Mario Bava

comedy Westerns. *Alias Smith and Jones* was one of the few attempts to fuse comedy and the Western that worked. Halsey, fresh from his spaghetti Westerns, appeared twice on the U.S. TV series. The comedy was subtle and could accommodate authentic Western elements like his characteristic tough, bearded hombres. Even so, *Alias Smith and Jones* is only incidentally a Western and really a fine buddy series that could easily be transferred to any genre.

Halsey's productive Italian career came to an end in 1970, though it would be revived in the late 1980s. The reasons for its end were purely economic, as the bottom fell out of the Italian B-movie industry. Halsey explained:

> If any of us had bothered to look, we might have recognized that the insidious monster that killed B movies in the U.S. was now eating away at the world market. Television antennas were popping up everywhere and box-office receipts were beginning to slide disastrously. In West Germany, their gross income was cut by 50% in only one year.
>
> The unprecedented success of Clint Eastwood's Westerns provided a reprieve for all of us. The expatriate colony was joined by Burt Reynolds, Charles Bronson, Lee Van Cleef and a host of others, and, for a few more years, there was plenty of work. But the enemy was becoming more clearly visible every day.
>
> As the producers' revenue decreased, investors started looking elsewhere to put their money. Budgets were slashed. Producers began asking actors to take a participation in nonexistent profits in lieu of regular salaries. The conversation

on the Veneto turned to speculating about going home—but to what? By now, I'd been away nearly 10 years. God, if they forgot you after 18 months, what was it going to be like after 10 years? Anyway, I didn't want to go. I had a well-staffed penthouse apartment, a Ferrari, my BMW, my art collection, my sailboat docked in Porto Santo Stefano. Why the hell should I go? The answer was cruelly apparent: this kind of life was expensive and, if there wasn't any work, it wouldn't last very long. Once I made the decision, I moved very quickly. I'd seen too many others hold on until they dissipated the last of their emotional and financial resources.

And, anyway, I never liked being the last to leave a party.

A more minor reason for returning was advanced by Halsey in the September 1977 issue of *Afternoon TV*: "One of the reasons I came home is that I said to myself, 'You're too old to keep falling off horses.' I just got hurt too many times. I was becoming afraid of it. You know, when you're real young, you bend a lot."

In Italy, B movies moved to urban cop dramas and Mafia stories and the giallo film was just beginning to emerge, but Halsey was back in Hollywood by then.

Lost Opportunities

Halsey was nearly in the classic John Ford film *The Searchers* (1956) starring John Wayne. The very mention of John Ford made Halsey uncharacteristically vehement: "One son of a bitch. I was up for the part Jeffrey Hunter played. The writer [Frank S. Nugent] said to me, 'I wrote it for you.' Ford said, 'It's yours.' It turned out they had been negotiating with Fox for Jeffrey Hunter and they wouldn't release him. Then Fox let him go, so they didn't use me. That would have started a career."

In the 1961 Fox profile, Halsey spoke of the missed opportunity: "My greatest disappointment was when I tested for *The Searchers* for John Ford. Jeff Hunter played the part I tested for. I wanted the part, and right up to the time the picture started I was led to believe—at least I thought—I had it. I wanted so much to work with director Ford and still do."

Like all professional actors, Halsey has sometimes wound up on the cutting room floor. He was hired to appear opposite Diane Keaton in Francis Ford Coppola's *The Godfather: Part III* (1990), which would have brought him major attention. The offer came before he went to Sicily for *Demonia*. Halsey finished scenes in Sicily and then went to Rome for some final scenes,

Halsey and Keaton in a scene from *The Godfather Part III*

where he contacted the Rome production office of *The Godfather*. They did not give him a start date, so he prepared to go back to Toronto where he was then living. Suddenly the producer called him and confirmed he would be in Rome for the next three months, and Halsey asked his then-wife Firouzeh to come over to join him.

Making the film was a happy experience for Halsey, despite an unfortunate introduction to Al Pacino, when Coppola praised Halsey for being tall. Halsey felt bad about it, but Pacino did not mind, and they got on well.

Halsey became quite close to some of the actors, like George Hamilton:

> This happens often in films, people working together in a film become close because of the characters and stuff, and then, when the film's over, the reason for that closeness/intimacy is gone and everyone goes home. That happened in *Godfather: Part III*. We were a group together for months, and we did try to keep it together afterwards but didn't.

When dining with Hamilton and other actors, Halsey recalled they talked about anything but the movie business.

Halsey spent five weeks in Rome and stayed in his apartment. He told journalist Sylvia Train of *The Toronto-Sun*:

> As usual, the studio sent limos for everybody. But the studio is so far from the city, and the traffic so bad, it took hours of travel. So I canceled the limo and took my car to the subway instead—and got to the set in half the time. Pretty soon Eli Wallach, George Hamilton and everyone else were doing the same thing. You'd literally see more stars in the subway than anywhere else.

Halsey went to New York in April to record additional dialogue and then returned to Toronto. It was only at the premiere in Toronto that Halsey learned that most of his role of a New Hampshire judge involved with a mobster had been cut because the film was five and one-half hours long. Halsey was embarrassed because he was the only actor invited to the screening, although all his dialogue had been cut.

Halsey was philosophical, looking back in 2004:

> Yeah, I was really disappointed. The only thing I can say about that—I am still getting checks from that. I just got a check for $2,000. Residuals, like all actors get. That's 14 years ago.

Unfortunately, Halsey gets no residuals from his Italian movies when they are shown on U.S. TV, because different rules apply: "It's a damn shame."

Jay Bernstein remarked, "He never even told *me* he was in *The Godfather: Part III* and Gray Frederickson, one of the producers, was the producer on *Mike Hammer*."

Halsey's friend Stanley Winston, who is not an actor, was offered a role as a don in the picture, because the producers thought he looked the part. When he was told he was not needed any longer, he flew back to L.A., only to be contacted by the production when they required him back for more shooting. Stanley's response when refusing to return to Rome is one of Halsey's favorite movie stories: "It's only a fucking movie."

Producing

Halsey could see that the greatest financial rewards came—not from starring in—but from producing movies. After losing his investment in one of his spaghetti Westerns, he cautiously sought partners to share the risk when considering further ventures in producing.

In Rome, Halsey's friend Edward Palmer tried to help him realize his aspirations of producing. Palmer's company, St. Regis International, was into movie acquisition, distribution and co-financing. He and his partner Jay Cipes got to know Halsey when they bought the U.S. distribution rights to *The Avenger of Venice*. Palmer explained:

> I was part of the expatriate American colony in Rome. My partner Jay and I were the biggest importers of foreign films to America. We bought classic pictures, James Bond rip-offs, Hercules rip-offs. We were the biggest rival to AIP. Several pictures were shown theatrically. Most were on TV. Sometimes we'd get short theatrical runs on them and that added value to the TV price. We mostly bought only U.S. and Canada rights, sometimes only theatrical. Sometimes we traded dollars for extra territories, even Trinidad.

Palmer got involved in a project that Halsey was particularly excited about:

> We became socially involved with a Monsignor from Mexico, Pedro Lopez, who knew Amos Powell. At the time, Jack Haley, Jr. was doing successful documentaries—*Elizabeth Taylor's London*, *Sophia Loren's Rome,* and so on. Over a couple of drinks at Brett's in Rome, I said, "Pedro, why don't we do a documentary? We could get Bing Crosby or Perry Como to host *The Pope's Vatican*—a look at the private residences and various places the Pope inhabits." I said it would be great publicity, a very personal look at the Church hierarchy and a great personality everybody loves. We approached Jack Haley who was with Four-Star at MGM. I was doing a pilot and headquartered there. I went back to the States and was busy doing the pilot.
>
> Meanwhile, Pedro Lopez was secretly in L.A., staying with lay people in Westwood. I got a call to meet him. He'd gotten the okay from the Pope to do this special for TV. Everybody

said we were going to make a fortune; the Catholic audience worldwide was so large.

We asked Pedro to get us a letter on Vatican stationery to say it was a *fait accompli*. An executive at Four-Star was a top U.S. Catholic, the head of NBC one time, Alan Courtney. He was the best salesman for the networks to sell the package. He said, "This is wonderful. I'll have a deal with you in 48 hours." Forty-eight hours later he'd got contacted by all three networks. They all turned us down. One said it was a news special, another said it was paying homage to one religion only to the exclusion of others...the other network, I don't remember the reason.

But it was Brett that opened the door.

Halsey had also involved his friend Julian Ludwig, who thought it was a terrific property:

> He gave it to me. I tried to get it done in the U.S. but they thought it was too religious. Finally, someone else did it. We were too early and did not have the power to get it made. But it was Brett Halsey's personality that got us the permission to go into the vaults, see the paintings and the various rooms. It was Brett's charm, his personality.

Halsey had planned to have Prince Rainier and Princess Grace of Monaco co-host the show. He was mortified to have to go back to the Pope and tell him that all three networks had turned it down. The reason, the networks explained, was that it was a news special and could not be made by outside producers — news specials were all produced in-house. His biggest regret was on the financial front: "I would have had Latin America and made a fortune."

Palmer tried to produce other projects with Halsey. One was *Beautiful Person*, to be made as an independent feature from a screenplay by Gabriel Gladstone, whom they met through financier Bernie Cornfeld. Palmer remembered it as a hard-edged comedy about the Mai-Lai massacre:

> Lt. Calley becomes the President of the U.S. with right-wing support. It was a black comedy, a satire. We were a small setup and the big studios wouldn't do it. We hired a director called Charles Rondeau, who knew Brett. Some doctors needed a tax shelter. The budget was under $500,000 and they put up the development money. We hired Raleigh Studios and assembled the cast and crew.

Then, the night before shooting, the doctors had an argument, and withdrew the financing. So we had to tell the cast and crew it was no go on the day of shooting.

Palmer was also involved in trying to get financing for Amos Powell's script of *The Cottage*: "I tried to do something with that. I couldn't get any interest." Palmer thought that Halsey could have been a much bigger star than he was:

> Like any other actor that's good looking with female appeal, Brett could have been a personality actor rather than a classical actor. I don't feel his manager or agent handled him right. I don't know, maybe he was not in the right place at the right time.

Halsey formed a production company, Heidi-Ho Productions, Inc., to develop film projects. On October 3, 1973, he bought the worldwide rights to the life story of Bernhard August Ferdinand Sauvant, a WWII German commander of a tank division, the First Royal King Panzers. Eight days after the end of the war, the Panzers eluded the Russians by going around them and then they fought their way to the sea to surrender the entire division to the British. Sauvant desperately wanted to avoid the Russians because the German tank crew uniforms resembled the dreaded S.S. and the men would have been shown no mercy from the Russians. The rights were bought from Sauvant's widow but the film was never made. Heidi-Ho mainly operated as a tax shelter, though: "It was mainly for taxes, because we both were working. If I worked at Universal or someplace, they would borrow me from Heidi-Ho Productions. It was a tax thing."

On Teaching

Halsey's acting skills increased with his work experience: "I told my students [when teaching recently in Costa Rica], I harped on them to learn how to really get involved in the scene. I said, 'I can fake it. You'll never know it. All these things that I'm teaching you, I can fake it, but that's 50 years' experience. *You* can't do it'."

Halsey's teaching acting for the camera began at Warner Bros. in 1985:

> I was teaching at Warners, because I was working on *The Dukes of Hazzard* anyway. Actually, it was specialized teaching. As a result of that, one of the casting directors at Warners who was teaching at this theater, the Chamber Theatre in North Hollywood, said, "You should teach a class as well." She was teaching commercials and she said I should teach acting for the camera, so they set up a class and I taught it, for maybe six months.

One of the students who went on to have an extensive screen career was Kathy Shower. She explained that Halsey invited her to join the class:

> I had done several guest spots on some television shows and I met Brett when I was on an audition for *The Dukes of Hazzard*. He was in there and we just started talking and he told me about this acting class that he was starting. He was sort of a mentor, I have to say, because I'd just arrived from Ohio and was naïve and he guided me in the right direction, right down to my name. Because my name is spelled Schaurer. He said, "You should change that so that people will understand and be able to pronounce it." And he was right, because for the first few auditions [when it was my turn to be called, it] was ..Uhhh, or just next, and next isn't always good, so Schaurer is not very memorable. He said, "If you just use the spelling…" and Shower would be phoenetic. And he was right—now I get, "I think of you every morning when I'm in the shower." People remember who you are, so it was great. So, he advised on many levels. He was a great help in guiding my career.

Shower described what it was like to be a student of Halsey's at the acting class:

> He's a wonderful teacher. When he's communicating, it's one on one. He's looking right at that person, making that

person feel important and bringing them in, and then they don't forget.

It was a small class but it was intense. It was intense learning, and it's something you do take with you and you don't forget. Then you don't *have* to keep going to a bunch of different classes, and it's *specialized*. The thing that he did was to teach *everything*. At some classes you sign up for, like at these acting schools, it would be, "Oh, we'll teach you how to do cold readings" and you pay a lot of money to learn how to do cold reading. You go to another one, they'll say, "Oh, we'll teach you how to do theater"...a lot of money for that.

Brett taught all of it, how to read, how to audition; film, television, theater, all of it. And it was intense but you learned. It was teaching technique: cold readings, how to audition, voice projection, every facet actually. Brett will take the trouble if he knows someone is listening and comprehending and taking it in, but he won't waste time either, which I admire. It's "You know what, I'll spend time with you, you can be in this class,

Art or Instinct in the Movies...

but if you don't listen and you don't respond, then I have nothing further to help you with." And that's true. You could tell the difference. He appreciated and saw which students were going to go further from that class and the ones that were just in there either to find a date or just to tell someone they're in class. A lot of people do that in L.A. It's like the thing to be, an actor in a class. But he saw the difference and so he wouldn't waste time. If he knew you would focus in, and you got it, you were better when you left. I was definitely better.

Halsey considered Kathy one of his best students. She commented:

They're his best students for various reasons. They're not just the best students because they sit and hang on every word, no. They're his best students because he realizes that they are going to take all that information and do something with it—it's not a waste of teaching. And I admire that so much.

The class was for a couple of hours in the evening:

Sometimes, depending on what we were doing, if we wanted to run over, we would. And there was another thing, he wasn't one to look at his watch and go, "Oh, well, sorry folks, it's come to five to seven. Bye. I know we're in the middle of a scene, but we have to go."

And then, afterward, he was so great because he would take us to a little restaurant called Micheli's right on the corner, down the street from the school. It's on Cahuenga in North Hollywood. It's still there. Everybody would sit after class, maybe just have a glass of wine or a little something to eat or a coffee and the waiters were performers at this restaurant. They were singing and it was just a way to end a class. It was a camaraderie where, again, you felt like you learned something and you'd take it with you and then you went to this Micheli's afterwards and it was such fun. You didn't feel it was like you were going just to college and then let go of it. You could talk about it longer. I'd talk about it longer, because you want more of his wisdom; you want to ask him more. You want to learn more. And things that maybe you're apprehensive about asking in class, you might ask outside of class. And he was always available for that. It's been of benefit for me, it really has.

Soaps

Daytime dramas, known as soap operas, put Halsey back onto American television screens and earned him a new audience who had most likely never even seen an Italian film. But Halsey's soap opera roles were artistically the least satisfying period of his career, plus the daily grind is stressful and the work difficult. They were lucrative compared to low-budget movies, but the end result was here today and gone tomorrow.

Halsey's soap opera resume comprised *Love is a Many Splendored Thing* (CBS), *Search for Tomorrow* (CBS), *General Hospital* (ABC) and *The Young and the Restless* (CBS). It was during this period that Halsey found himself devoting more time to his writing, even utilizing his experiences in fictional form for his second novel, *Yesterday's Children*.

Halsey explained to *The Oregonian* (January 28, 1978) what drove him to soaps: "I was competing with contemporaries who had a high Q rating [a measurement of audience recognition], while I had none."

When producer John Conboy offered Halsey the role of Spencer Garrison in the soap *Love is a Many Splendored Thing*, Halsey accepted the part even though it was filmed in New York. It was an established character and Halsey was taking the role over from another actor, Ed Power. It meant leaving home and family in Los Angeles and settling into an apartment just off Central Park West. He tried on weekends and holidays to get back to L.A. as often as possible. He did not know New York other than having visited for some long weekends, but went there to test for the show. As he told Patti Obrow in the April 1973 *Afternoon TV*:

> When I was here to test for the show, I decided to go out for a little walk, to get a feel of the city. I went back to the hotel and called my wife. I told her, "You know, I get a little feel of London." She nervously said, "You don't mean you went out walking. Don't do that anymore—you're going to get killed." I guess if all you know about New York is what you read in the European press—it's a jungle.

Halsey Joins 'Soap' Staff

NEW YORK — Brett Halsey has joined the cast of the ABC Television Network's daytime dramatic series, "General Hospital," in the newly created role of Dr. Adam Streeter.

Dr. Streeter is a widower with two young children. He joins the staff of Geneal Hospital as the Chief of Obstetrics.

Halsey is familiar to daytime television viewers from his recent role as Clay Collins on the serial, "Search for Tomorrow." He also played the role of Spencer Garrison on the former series, "Love Is a Many Splendored Thing."

Halsey was friendly with Steve Fellouris, owner of nightspot Casino Russe, who helped him find his way around New York. Halsey would much rather have been making films and came to detest working on soaps, but never let on his true feelings in interviews, telling Obrow that the show was rewarding for an actor and that all his colleagues were "extremely talented":

> Bibi Besch is very good. We had a short scene—I had trouble getting it—but when we finally clicked—it was an intimate moment between the two of us—it was so nice. I was lucky. I was through for the day. But she had to go on and on about some family tragedy. But it influenced the rest of her performance—the fact that we hit that nice moment in the scene. She told me about it afterward. I guess that's what acting is all about.
>
> Actors are basically the same everywhere. Some of the actors that I've talked with here have a misconception that Hollywood is some distant place and Hollywood actors are something else. Acting is the same if you are on television or in

films. The techniques may be different, but the difference is slight. It's something you can learn easily if a person *is* an actor. The techniques he can always work out. Doing this show, once I become acquainted with it, will be like doing a movie for a year or two.

Halsey once wrote a little piece to illustrate how actors can appreciate each others' problems and be cooperative. His memoir related to actor Lawrence Tierney, who came out of the obscurity of retirement for a plum role in *Reservoir Dogs*:

> Larry Tierney burst into screen stardom playing Dillinger in the 1940s. A drunken, brawling, tough-guy offscreen as well as on, his career quickly slipped into near oblivion. The point of this story is that, no matter what the situation, actors can relate very well to the problems of other actors.
>
> I first met Larry when he came to play a guest role on my series *Follow the Sun*. It was one of his dry periods in the early 1960s, and everyone was cheering for him to stay on the wagon, because when he was sober, his acting was magic. Out of the hundreds of actors I've had the pleasure of performing with, Larry was one of the very few who gave me a great lift, just from the pleasure of acting with him.
>
> After *Follow the Sun*, I went to Rome and, some years later, I ran into Larry on the Via Veneto. I knew he had come to Rome, because the stories of his drunkenness and brawling quickly made their way through the foreign film community. He had acquired the reputation of being a sucker-puncher. A sucker-puncher is one who will sit beside you at a bar quietly brooding over a drink, then out of nowhere and for no reason, he will make a fist, and crack you in the jaw. Most people quickly became wise to Larry and stayed out of his range. There were other times like the afternoon in Jerry's Bar, when George Williamson saw it coming and beat him to the punch. Tough as he was, like most drunks, he probably lost most of the fights he initiated.
>
> He had been drinking, but he was sober enough to recognize and greet me like a long lost friend. Because Roman winters were always cold, and Larry was without a coat, I invited him inside Doney's for some lunch. When I asked him why he wasn't wearing a coat, he mumbled something about his luggage being stolen. Anyway, the next day, I found him and gave

him a coat—then I didn't see him again until much later when I was in Paris, making a movie.

It was mid-morning when I crossed the Champs-Elysees, heading for a late breakfast in a small café next to the Crazy Horse nightclub. I saw Larry sitting a little unsteadily at the bar. He wasn't terribly friendly as I sat next to him and ordered my breakfast. He was quiet, as though brooding over some decision. "Oh, oh," I thought, as I watched him a bit more carefully. He tensed up. His hand, which was resting on the counter, rolled into a fist.

" Larry," I said.

" Yeah, " he responded.

" You can't hit me. "

" What? " he answered with some confusion.

" You can't hit me, " I repeated.

" Why not? "

" Because I'm in the middle of a picture. I can't get my face messed up."

" Oh. Yeah. That's right, " he replied. His tension drifted away, his expression lightened. In the midst of it all, and through his drunken stupor, Lawrence Tierney was still an actor who understood and respected other actors' problems. I have never forgotten him for that.

Halsey took seriously the characterization of the lead role in *Love is a Many Splendored Thing*. He told Obrow:

> What we're trying to do is to adapt him to myself as much as we can. He has basic things about him, for example. He is a senator, he's a lawyer, he is a good, honest person. It's the humor that I intend to inject. I didn't know the actor or the character before, so in this case, I will create my own character to an extent. I'm trying to play the character with a lighter touch. Generally, from what I've seen, the men on soap operas tend to get bogged down in the tragedy of life.

Later, Halsey admitted to D. Hood in the September 1977 *Afternoon TV* that the prospect of a regular soap opera was daunting after the lack of discipline in Italian filmmaking:

> I tell you, I didn't think I was going to be able to do it. I had signed the contract, so I thought, "Well I'm going to try." But

it was such a foreign medium to me, learning all those lines and just the general discipline of it. It's the hardest work I think an actor can do.

He told Tony Rizzo in the June 1977 *TV By Day*:

> It was the most terrifying experience I ever had in my life. Two nights before I started work, and after observing from the control room for a week, thinking, "How do they remember all that dialogue?," I was out on the town with Lloyd Bridges. We had a few drinks and he kept saying, "How do you do it? I don't know how you do it. I could never do it." I kept saying, "Lloyd, I haven't done it yet. Will you leave me alone?" But I guess I did it okay; I'm still around. I froze a few times, but I'm still working. I got through it.

Love is a Many Splendored Thing was canceled in March 1973 when John Conboy left. Although *Inside Hollywood* states Halsey then went back to Italy to make a movie called *Castle of Horror*, that information is incorrect.

When Halsey had completed *A Country on the March* in Costa Rica, he bounced back in another soap, *Search for Tomorrow*. Tracy Brooks Swope thought Halsey's acceptance was funny: "They had just written *Ryan's Hope* for me, and Brett told me, 'Oh, don't do another soap opera'."

Joins Cast

Brett Halsey, well-known movie and television actor, has joined the cast of the CBS daytime serial, "Love Is a Many Splendored Thing," in the role of Sen. Spencer Garrison, formerly played by Ed Power, who left for other career interests.

This time he played villain Clay Collins. Halsey was happier with this role and explained to *The Oregonian*:

> I played Clay Collins, the heavy, a mean bastard who continually beat up his wife. I once tore the dress off her in a bar. I philandered with my brother's wife. I left that show when I was deservedly stabbed to death in the back.

Tracy said, "He was very good in that role...very good. He's always very real and very relaxed. He's like a big cuddly bear."

Better still, Halsey negotiated a deal whereby he would only work three days a week. That gave him three days for full-time writing and one day off. This was a formula that seemed to work well for him. In the cast of *Search for Tomorrow* was an undiscovered Morgan Fairchild, who would soon go on to bigger projects and well-deserved fame.

Today, Halsey thinks *Search for Tomorrow* was the best, or at least the least-worst, of his four soaps, but he told Tony Rizzo in the June 1977 *TV By Day* that he was not upset to be killed off:

> I wasn't out of my mind with happiness on the show and I think the powers that be killed the character off when they did to make all of us happy. I stayed in New York four hours after my death scene and came right home. I didn't like New York too much.

Back home, Halsey spent some time writing his first novel *The Magnificent Strangers*, before accepting a part on a soap that was made in Hollywood. Working on *General Hospital,* Halsey played brilliant surgeon Dr. Adam Streeter. By now Halsey was easily recognized as the Old Spice Man from a series of popular television commercials. He interviewed for the commercial and wound up playing a rugged sailor whose seductive aftershave helps him land an exotic beauty on each arm. In the 1976 Old Spice commercial, Halsey walks off a ship and meets a beautiful girl while a boy of about 14 watches enviously. It ends with the sailor tossing the boy a bottle of Old Spice Cologne. Halsey also did commercials for Lincoln-Continental and Harlequin Books. The commercials paid very well and offered wide exposure. *The Gold Miner Dispatch* (July 9, 1976) reported that he was under consideration for a role in the feature film *MacArthur.* Lynda Hirsch (in the October 30, 1977, *Youngstown Vindicator*) reported that he was slated to do a movie in Bogota. The writers of *General Hospital* decided to capitalize on this movie offer by having Dr. Streeter travel to Colombia and set up a clinic there. Halsey was granted four weeks' leave of absence from the show. Then the movie producers postponed the start date

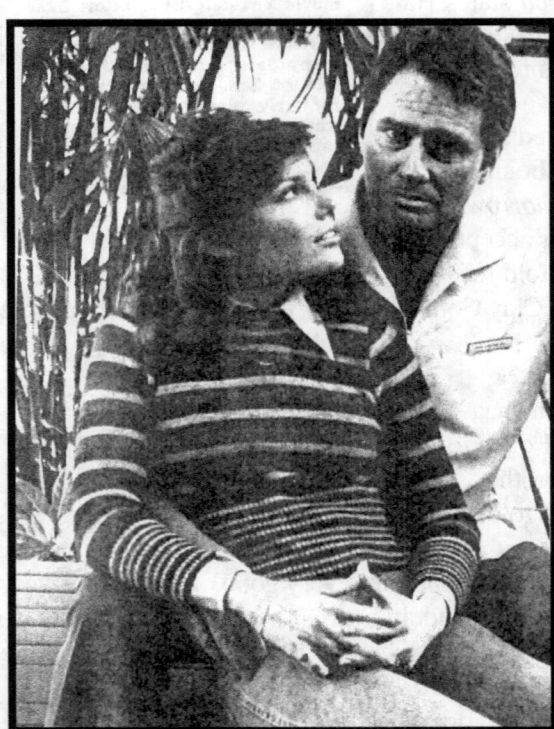

Halsey with Karen Purcell in *General Hospital*

and Halsey was due back on *General Hospital* by the time the movie was due to start. He used the leave of absence to promote his first novel.

Halsey did not really enjoy working on soaps like *General Hospital*, which are often looked down upon by media snobs. Halsey explained why they were constricting for an actor: "There was no room for improvisation, because timing was so critical. They timed them right down to the second." It could happen that an actor could wing it if he forgot the scripted lines, as long as he conveyed the information necessary to move the plot along: "If you could do it quickly, because, also, you have to have the cue for the other actor. In Mexico, they have speakers in the ear." Halsey developed a way of surviving: "I learned to rely on technique and tricks." But the popularity of *General Hospital* did lead to the formation of a Brett Halsey fan club, whose president was Marilyn Elliott of Kernville, California. An exclusive interview with Halsey appeared in the first issue of the newsletter, where he discussed his career in the soaps:

> I like being on *General Hospital* much better than *Search for Tomorrow* for various reasons; the main reason is that *General Hospital* is in Los Angeles, at home. Being away from Los Angeles was the main reason that I left *Search*. I wanted to be home in Los Angeles where my family is and I wanted to work here.
>
> Also, the character I was playing was a heavy and, in soap operas, either heavies get their just desserts or they are reformed, and very often it is good drama to have a heavy pay severely for his crimes and that is really what happened. They decided that Clay Collins was a bad enough person that he really should die, so I no longer had a character to play.

Halsey was not sure how long he would be on *General Hospital*:

> This is something that I don't have any control over...The show is going to have new writers and sometimes, or rather very often, they will eliminate old characters to create new characters that they are more familiar with. Adam Streeter is a creation of the former writing team, the Pollacks. I do know that there will be a lot of drastic character changes within the next six months.

In the end, it was Halsey who asked to be written out. *General Hospital* began as a half-hour show, so Halsey had time to write. Then it stretched to a full hour—the cast had to work 10-15 hours a day, and Halsey had no time for writing. Halsey told *The Oregonian*:

One of the girls on the show said to me the other day that life on *General Hospital* was overpowering her real life. Of course, some people have the knack for learning lines rapidly. One friend of mine had to memorize 30 pages of dialogue a day.

Halsey, Georganne La Piere and Richard Dean Anderson attend a *General Hospital* reunion.

Generally the actors get their scripts a week before the episode is to be filmed. They then have time to learn the dialogue, and this also gives them a chance to work on their characters—it is up to the actor to ensure their character's consistency.

Medical authenticity was one of the difficulties about *General Hospital*. Halsey recalled for John Archibald (in the February 20, 1978 *St. Louis Post-Dispatch*): "When you are doing an episode a day, you don't have too much time to study your script and it's important to be technically right when you're dealing with medicine. There are many viewers who are waiting for you to make a mistake." Halsey remembered some medical terminology by stashing notes in the bodies.

The show's director Ken Herman once explained in the magazine *Daytimers*:

> The first time the actors and I get together on a script is the morning of the day we're going to shoot. At seven in the morning the actors arrive and we take it act by act and go through the staging. I may say, "OK, at this point we'd like you to move over to here and maybe sit down at this point." While he's doing that, I want her to do this, move to that point and so on. I talk it through with them and the actors are taking notes on their scripts at the same time...It takes approximately two hours to run through the show act by act.

This was followed by rehearsals and a dress rehearsal at 1:15. The show was taped, as if live, at 2.30, and the actors went home at 3.15. Halsey had a good relationship with Ken Herman and respected his professionalism.

Halsey left his options open when he left the show:

> I was kind of eased out of the plot. After [my character's] unhappy love affair, I requested transfer to another hospital across town. This always gives me a chance to go back if I fail as an author. It's much better than getting killed off.

In later years, Halsey frequently made jokes about *General Hospital*—"You know, they called me this brilliant surgeon, and every one of my patients died." And he said to Hank Werba, in the January 26, 1988 *Variety*, that the soaps "were not that exalting but the problem is, they pay you so much money." Looking back in 2005, he said, "I don't have anything against soap opera other than I don't like to do them. But I don't disparage what they do."

Halsey's final soap role was on *The Young and the Restless*, after which he called it quits on soap operas for good. In *The Young and the Restless*, he played John Abbott, the president of a cosmetics firm called Jabot. Abbott was characterized by Halsey as a good guy but a ruthless businessman. But Halsey found this the least enjoyable of the four soaps: "The show was well-produced, the people were friends, but I didn't like that sort of work." Halsey left the show when his option was not renewed. He was not sorry. Halsey started dating a girl called Terry Janes, in a relationship that lasted several years, and she told him years later that she was glad he had left the soaps: "Thank God, you couldn't have survived another year." Halsey had found being a soap actor an unsatisfying experience. He was more and more motivated to write.

Italian Renaissance

Suddenly there was a renaissance in Halsey's Italian career. So much so that he would take an apartment in Rome. Halsey noticed a big difference in Rome, though, the second time round:

> The movie industry had died. In Italy, the population grows tremendously but the infrastructure doesn't, so there are too many cars. They would pass laws, such as alternate days for entering Rome according to the number of the licence plate. It would last a few days: the Italians would get two number plates.

Halsey noticed more racism and hookers on his beloved Via Veneto rather than la dolce vita. Even the social activity was "on a different level": "The first time, everyone used to dress well. I had three tuxedos, I wore them all." Now people wore jeans.

Halsey with Blanca Marsillach in *The Devil's Honey*

Producer Vincenzo Salviani had hired Halsey to star in Lucio Fulci's *The Devil's Honey*, which was shot in Spain, and was interested in working with him again when he directed the film *Flying* (1988, also known as *Velvet Dreams*). This starred Halsey and his former student, Kathy Shower, in what is the closest Halsey came to appearing in soft porn. This surprising career turn happened by mistake, Halsey explained: "What happened was, the producer/director went broke. After the actors had finished shooting, he went back later and shot some erotic scenes with other actors." A similar trick led to Vincent Price appearing in explicit nudity in continental versions of Jeremy Summers' *House of 1000 Dolls* and Sir John Gielgud sandwiched between scenes of hard porn in Tinto Brass' *Caligula*.

Halsey commented about Salviani: "He never should have directed. I think he directed only to save money, so he wouldn't have to hire anybody. He just wasn't a very good director. He was terrible." Halsey considered Kathy "very good."

Kathy Shower remains grateful to Halsey for recommending her for this film, which her fans rate as possibly her best work. "It played on cable here. I still get fan mail from that movie. The *most* comments, the most praise, the most interest is in this movie." Halsey wanted Kathy in the movie:

> Without him, I would not have been in the movie. He introduced me to the director, Vincenzo Salviani. Vincenzo was in L.A. at the time and Brett introduced me to him and said that I would be great for that part. I was just Playmate of the Year and I was doing a television series at the time, *Santa Barbara*, and I was doing another film, and they said, "Well, if you're going to be in Europe, this would be a good film for you to be in." And it was. It was the best experience of my life, working in Europe. It wasn't for Brett, unfortunately, I don't think, but it was for me. Because I think he and Vincenzo had creative difficulties and there were monetary problems but, for me, it was wonderful. Again, Brett was advising me, always telling me what to look for. It was a really good experience, because he helped me so.

She explained the effect of the film running out of money:

> When it came to the critical part, when you need to have the looping and where there are sound problems and you need to bring people in to make that work, they just didn't do it. And it's unfortunate, because the film suffered for it, really suffered.

It hurt that Salviani brought in other actors:

> Exactly, and even voice wipes. Any of the looping and the dubbing, sometimes you have to go back and do it. It wasn't Brett or I. And that destroyed the movie. It was upsetting for, I'm sure, Brett and myself. You go and you just get so annoyed, because people will go and see it and go, "God, that's them." And it's not. It was not us. Visually, but that's it. And that was really the worst part. It was disappointing because it could have been great. It was based on the book by Erica Jong, *Fear of Flying*: relationships and the fear factor, and things that happen in relationships. It was great.

Kathy agreed that Salviani was not a good director:

> I have to admit, if it wasn't for the director of photography and everybody else who knew what they were doing, it wouldn't have happened at all, I don't think. Brett would speak the script and he knew what to do, and the camera angles. There were things that we shot and Brett said, "No, we didn't cover that. You need to cover this." And Salviani would say, "Oh no, he's right. I'll do what Brett says." He basically directed as well. He did. He was looking out for me, even in scenes he wasn't in. He was very aware of how the film looked, how it came out. Which shows the professional person that he is.

The film is steamier than Halsey would usually accept. Kathy recalled:

> I am in a changing room, in a boutique, trying on my shopping, and Brett comes in and wants to make love there for kicks. I say, "Not here in the store" but do it to please him.
>
> When they approached Brett, they explained what this was, where the project would shoot and asked if he was available. He did have a lot of creative input, I think. They allowed him that. So it was a very attractive project for Brett.

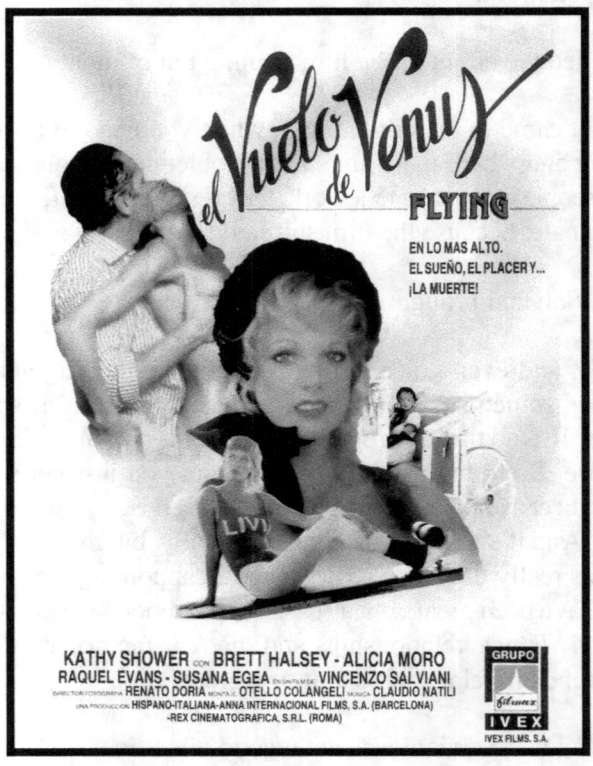

Although the film ran out of money and the release was long delayed, Kathy did not have difficulty being paid:

> Not for me. I had no difficulty at all. Again, I think Brett was instrumental in that, because he looked out and he said, "Hey, I'm gonna make sure that she's taken care of," but I do understand that some of the other people involved in production all the way down the line—make-up artists down to other performers—did not get paid and are still waiting to get paid for that film.

Kathy witnessed how Halsey took this little movie very seriously:

> He taught me that—to embrace whatever comes to you. He definitely taught me to embrace a project. Sure, there's going to be negatives, sure there's going to be problems, but he really taught me to embrace it and said, "You know what? Make it your best. You do well in it, you stand out in it, and it will be a success." And it's true, especially working in Europe. His vast experience has helped me tremendously and he knows that. He knows that. He should take credit for a lot of the credits on my resume , because he definitely was a part of that.

Halsey and Kathy also spent much of their offscreen time together:

> I remember the first cup of coffee I had on the Ramblas. It was so unfamiliar, and Brett and I sat at this lovely table and watched all these lovely people walk by. I just felt so good and so happy to be there. It's like he knew what he was doing, so I felt safe. The thing I must say, working with Brett on anything, I feel safe. Even if I have a project now, I'll call him on it. That's kind of a good feeling and a rare feeling for an actress, to feel that way.

Halsey had a meaty death scene in the action film *The Commander* (1988), and he played the campy death scene for all it was worth. Antonio Margheriti directed the film, shooting Halsey's scenes on the Amalfi coast. He has very little memory of Margheriti:

> Probably I don't relate much to the experience because everything went the way it's supposed to go. These Italian directors who *are* efficient at getting things done, you don't pay attention

to it. It's like, if something is done right, you only really know when something's wrong, then you concentrate on it, you focus on it. But when it's right, it's just the way it should be.

The thing I remember most about the picture was my wife at the time, Firouzeh. She hated the fact that I was an actor—I don't know why we were together in the first place. She always wanted me to get out of the business and do something serious. She was visiting. One of her first experiences on a movie set, and Lee Van Cleef in his spare time was telling her how he had overcome his alcoholism—he had a problem with alcohol—and, all the time, all day long, Lee was drinking beer.

And then Gore Vidal had a house near the location, where we went to dinner with him. He's kind of out there. I talk politics with him a lot. She thought that all the movie people were nuts.

Dorris Halsey pointed out that Firouzeh was of the Iranian royal family, "so one doesn't consort with actors." When Halsey took her onto the set of Lucio Fulci's *Touch of Death*, and she saw the graphic horror effects, she thought Fulci was "really crazy."

Luckily, Italian filmmakers remembered Halsey from the first period. He worked with Duccio Tessari and Lucio Fulci. And it was a blast from the past

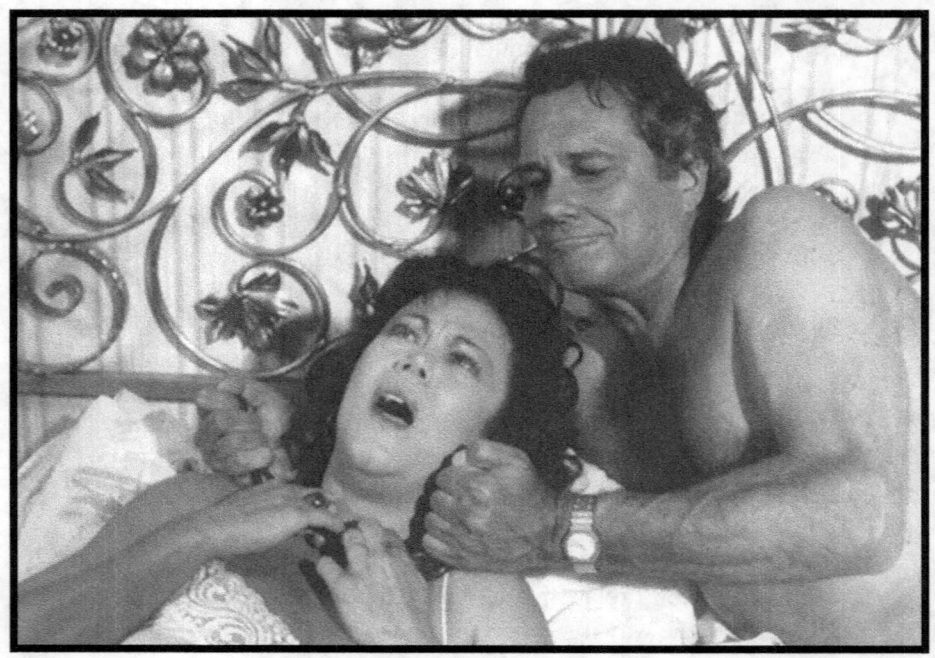

Halsey is a real lady killer in *Touch of Death*.

when Dario Argento cast Halsey in a role in his television show *Giallo* (1988). The show was a strange mixture of chat, variety and film inserts, including a typical Argento whodunit, *Turno di Notte: L'Impronta del'Assassino*. Halsey had a part in this short film that was directed by Argento associate Luigi Cozzi, and which was very much in the style of Argento's *gialli*.

In the first half, a girl is murdered in an indoor swimming pool and Halsey is a suspect. After various other items of chat and variety, part two is shown and the killer is revealed. Halsey's character was a red herring. The clue to the murderer's identity was the way a robe was folded, left to right, so the murderer was female, as men would wear the robe folded right to left. Except...Halsey laughed at the memory: "It didn't actually make sense, because no-one noticed I had done up the robe the wrong way, left to right, because my car keys were in the pocket of the robe on the left and I wanted to be able to get to them."

Luigi Cozzi was impressed with Halsey's work in the short and cast him in his feature film *The Black Cat* (1989), which was itself a tribute to Argento's *Three Mothers* project. Unfortunately, the film is an incoherent mess. Halsey did not have any confidence that Cozzi knew what he was doing, although in *The Dark Side* film magazine, Cozzi later praised Halsey's acting. Told of this, Halsey wryly remarked that he must have learnt *something* over the years.

Perhaps the worst picture Halsey made in Italy during this period was Bruno Mattei's *Cop Game* (1988). The film's stars, Brent Huff and Max Laurel, were unknowns, and Halsey is not even credited, despite having seven significant scenes as U.S. General Morris, who is in Saigon during the final days of the Vietnam War to investigate a mysterious Army killing. Strangely enough, spaghetti Western actor Alan Collins *is* credited and he doesn't appear in the film. Possibly Halsey replaced him at the last minute and the credits were not adjusted. Mattei is credited as director under the name Bob Hunter, one of his pseudonyms, but his real name is used as the editor credit. Mattei had previously edited one of Halsey's pictures, *Kill Johnny Ringo*. Mattei has a small cult following for his outrageously sordid pictures such as *Porno Holocaust*. *Cop Game* has its share of sleazy girly bar scenes. Even the action scenes are somewhat ham-fisted, though this may reflect the tiny budget.

Halsey is always convincing in uniformed roles and interacts well with Italian actor Romano Puppo, who began his career being shot by Eastwood in *The Good, The Bad and The Ugly*.

Rose (1986) was an Italian television film trilogy based on the theme of the older woman-younger man relationship. Halsey's episode paired him with Valerie Perrine in a rare romantic role at this later stage of his career. He looks smart and sophisticated in the luxury hotel settings of Rome's Hotel De La Ville, and there is a wonderful moment when, as he is romancing Perrine, he impulsively swings around a pole in the street. Halsey commented: "It was like something Fred Astaire did."

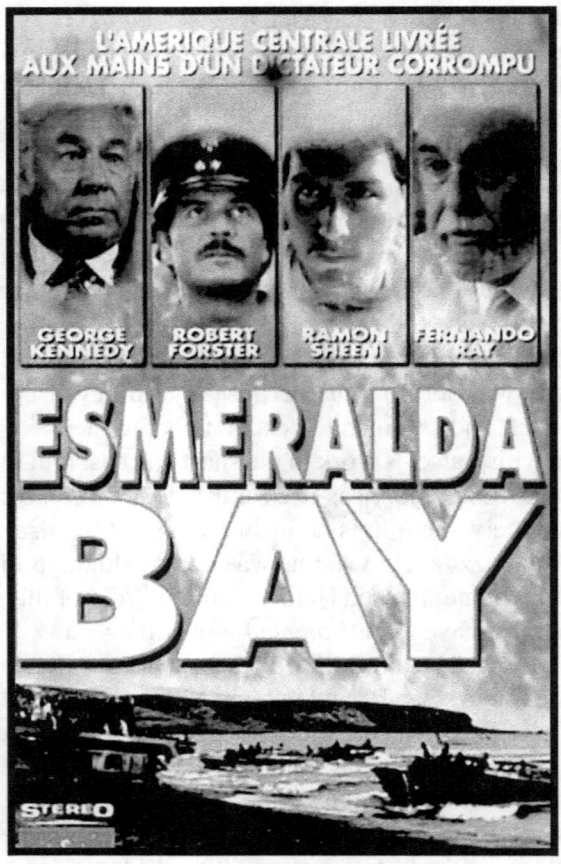

Halsey did a small role for Clint Eastwood back in Hollywood in his production of Sondra Locke's *Ratboy* (1986): "Clint put me into that. He called me and said, 'You want to do this?' I didn't audition. It was kind of a joke. I played Fritz Manes, who was the producer of *Ratboy*, so I was parodying the producer of the picture and it was kind of an in-joke." Although successful in France, the picture is virtually unwatchable.

Esmeralda Bay (1989) reunited Halsey with former *Espionage in Lisbon* cohorts Jess Franco, who directed this picture, and actor Fernando Rey. Halsey got the job offer when he bumped into Franco at the Catalonia Film Festival, where his two Salviani pictures were being featured. Halsey had no idea who Franco was and was unaware of his porno past and his involvement in *Lisbon*, although Franco knew Halsey. Franco offered Halsey a part, even though he could not offer much money. He would pay him in cash, and no agents were involved. The picture itself was a muddle, though Halsey praised Franco for his calm approach to directing action scenes of U.S. commandos landing on the beach to put down a rebellion. Halsey, who played a rebel, said, "I didn't really understand it. I don't think any of us did." Halsey's character endlessly chews on a cigar in a number of shots: "They didn't pay me much, so I insisted they buy me Cuban cigars."

The film was obviously low budget and used a lot of stock footage of U.S. commandos and warships, forcing the actors to imagine the action:

> That film was really very funny because we had this big armada, supposedly, an invasion, of all these ships and everything, and we didn't shoot anything. We're on this beach with nothing, shooting this way, and the armada was this way.

Lucio Fulci

Halsey first met director Lucio Fulci on the set of *The Devil's Honey* (1986), which was shot in Sitges near Barcelona. From the start, Fulci and Halsey found a mutual respect. Fulci spoke of *The Devil's Honey* in the book *Spaghetti Nightmares*: "I tried to make a movie about the misery of sadomasochism, but nobody understood it."

The Devil's Honey

The Devil's Honey is perhaps the most interesting of the Halsey/Fulci collaborations. The film falls outside any identifiable genre and is quite a peculiar piece of erotic/psychological drama. Although bold in its treatment of sadomasochism, the film is hardly titillating and does not function as pornography, nor is it horrific, albeit disturbing. The characters are unsympathetic and not particularly engaging. Fulci seems to be casting a cool, detached eye onto the characters' mistakes, leaving the viewer emotionally confused: how is the audience meant to respond? It is these elements, plus the above-par performances from Halsey and Blanca Marsillach, that make *The Devil's Honey* an interesting film and borderline-arty work, harking back to the early artistic pretensions of Fulci films like *A Lizard in a Woman's Skin* and *Don't Torture a Duckling*.

Fulci had been ill with stomach problems and thought he was going to die. Halsey feels that was the reason he took his time on this film, using more conscious artistry than exploitation. Predictably, the film was not commercially successful and for years was only available on a 2-disc video CD from Hong Kong.

Halsey's controversial role in *The Devil's Honey* required nudity and the depiction of perversion. The shy, slightly inhibited characters portrayed by

Halsey in his early Hollywood films such as *The Girl in Lover's Lane* and *Desire in the Dust* were replaced with a forceful personality grappling with explicit adult themes.

With the gradual loosening of restrictions in the cinema, old colleagues of Halsey's found work making hardcore porn, including Jess Franco and his partner, the luscious Lina Romay. Dario Argento was at the forefront of films featuring the pornography of violence—*Suspiria* and *Tenebrae* being prime examples.

Halsey's characters evolved through the years. Mario Bava's *Four Times That Night* included a risqué episode of attempted seduction by a nearly naked Halsey and, generally through the 1970s, his movie characters were becoming harder and more cynical. Even Richard in *Perversion Story* is more bitter and worldly wise (he is clearly uninterested in the seductive temptations of young Romina Power) than George Farrel in *Espionage in Lisbon* or Bert Morris in *Spy in Your Eye*. The cynicism inherent in the spaghetti Western—due to the crucial influence on the genre of the *Dollars* trilogy—lent Halsey's screen persona a harder, more ruthless edge that remained even after the spaghetti Westerns had faded out. That characterization deferred the shock presented by his explicitness and awareness of sexual deviancy in *The Devil's Honey*. It is ironic to bear in mind that Halsey's first wife once described him as "like a child."

Although Fulci was still fragile while working on the film, producer Vincenzo Salviani did not interfere. Halsey confirmed: "Not in anything artistic, no. He would just make sure everything was going. He was a line producer. He didn't have anything to do financially with that picture. He was just a production manager." Halsey's main memory of the film is of problems working with the lead actress Blanca Marsillach: "I didn't particularly like the girl...I don't like to work with people who take drugs."

Fulci starred Halsey in *The Devil's Honey*, *Touch of Death*, *Demonia* and *Cat in the Brain* (though thereby hangs a tale). Halsey has his own thoughts on why Fulci put him in lead roles in four pictures:

> We worked well together, he was open to my ideas and I really liked the way he used his camera. I learned a lot from him. In

my teaching, I teach his camera technique…he had very little sense of dramatic rhythm, but his camera was always interesting…He didn't get involved in working with actors. That's why we got along, because, without blowing my own trumpet, I knew what I was doing. If an actor didn't know what he was doing, Fulci would yell at him.

Halsey as Lester the cannibal in *Touch of Death*

Touch of Death (1988) impresses more with every screening, and Halsey's performance, ranks as one of the outstanding of his later career. The film at first seems baffling—were scenes that seemed funny supposed to be funny? But the humor was intentional and, in a way, the whole point—the film is, in fact, a black comedy and becomes an admirable low-budget achievement. It is competently written and directed, with a meaty role for Halsey as a deranged but charming cannibal.

Due to the collapse of the Italian film industry, the film was quickly shot for Italian television, and completed in a mere three weeks. Halsey's fee was only about $15,000. Like Don Siegel's *The Killers* (shot for American television), it was then deemed too violent for the small screen, resulting in a long delay before it was eventually screened. Alan Jones wrote in *Eyeball* that the film was unlikely to be released, "due to some impossibly complex lawsuit." According to Halsey, the lawsuit boiled down to the fact that the distributors refused to release it because they had given the production company $2 million to make it, and Fulci only spent $500,000.

Halsey's depiction of madness makes this one of the more interesting performances in his later films, and also proves Fulci was not a spent force, even though his peak years (*The Beyond*, *City of the Living Dead*) were now long behind him.

Touch of Death helps show how Halsey matured as an actor since early roles like *The Atomic Submarine*. Particularly chilling is his matter-of-fact depiction of Lester's descent into schizophrenia.

Lucio Fulci used Halsey three times (technically four), and there probably would have been more jobs with Fulci if the director hadn't passed away in 1996 at the age of 68.

Fulci had gained renown in the horror genre with the stunning success of *Zombie Flesh Eaters*. The trio of films he made starring Halsey revitalized

Halsey's Italian career and brought him to the attention of a whole new audience — younger film fans who had missed out on his earlier career. Fulci had great faith in Halsey's talents, letting him do more and more on the creative side, from introducing irony to the purely evil scripted character Lester in *Touch of Death* to rewriting the dialogue and managing the production on *Demonia* while Fulci was away. Fulci told supporting actor Grady Clarkson that Halsey was the boss.

Despite the beautiful Monte Castello locations in Sicily, *Demonia* (1990) is the weakest and least interesting of the Fulci/Halsey films. One reason is what Fulci deemed the "very bad photography" — as a number of shots suffer from excessive glare from the hot Sicilian sun. Halsey tries hard to rescue what dramatic possibilities the film offers, but the unoriginal storyline sinks beneath a welter of poorly executed gore effects.

Fulci and Halsey in *Demonia*

The plot of *Demonia* bears a superficial similarity to the plot of films such as Amando de Ossorio's *Tombs of the Blind Dead*. It is the hoary old horror cliché of revenge on the living by spirits unjustly killed centuries ago. This plot staple underpins dozens of classics like Mario Bava's *Black Sunday*, Michael Reeves' *Revenge of the Blood Beast*, Peter (Fillipo Walter Ratti) Rush's *Night of the Damned*, John Moxey's *City of the Dead*, Corrado Farina's *Baba Yaga, Devil Witch*, Herschell Gordon Lewis' *2000 Maniacs,* and so on.

Sadly, *Demonia* is not in the same league as any of the above. Even Lewis' trashy film works better. The genuine frisson of fear evoked by the creepy Knights Templar in Amando de Ossorio's film and its three sequels is entirely absent from the badly made-up naughty nuns of Fulci's film. Their appearance is unintentionally comic, even conjuring echoes of the famous British comedy *Carry On* film series, which is fatal in a horror movie. Indeed, the film resembles one of Jess Franco's feebler attempts at religious transgression (in movies like *Exorcism*) or even Walerian Borowczyk's softcore nunsploitation epics like *Be-*

hind *Convent Walls*. Fulci even obliges with a very tame orgy sequence, which is simply yawn-inducing. Halsey is absent from such scenes and sometimes seems to be in a different film altogether—and a better one.

Halsey's best moments come in his professional execution of dialogue scenes. Particularly interesting is his acting opposite Lucio Fulci himself, an old ham who could not bear to remain behind the camera, although Halsey declares it was probably also an economy measure, to save paying another salary. Halsey believed Fulci would have been an actor, though, if he could not have directed films. *Demonia* is so low budget that Halsey supplied his own wardrobe. In any event, Fulci acquits himself honourably in the role and is no worse than other supporting actors.

Halsey recalled the difficulties of shooting the film in Sicily: "Every day in the Sicilian newspaper, *The Daily Sicilian*, there was a photo of someone shot in his car." The film was threatened with closure at one point because the Mafia demanded to be paid for shooting in Sicily. "Everyone had to be paid," Halsey said.

If *Demonia* is less interesting than the two previous Fulci/Halsey films, it may be because Fulci "lost his enthusiasm" on this film. Halsey also criticized actress Meg Register for her lack of attention to her role and for bringing her boyfriend on location: "A mistake. She was looking off… 'Oh, look, my boyfriend is climbing the hill.' She blew a chance at an Italian career because she didn't appear to take it seriously."

Halsey often tells the story that Fulci "did not dress well" and was "not terribly clean" and he was astonished when he invited him once to a screening of one of Eastwood's pictures, attended by Clint, and he turned up in a nice blazer looking "spiffy."

Fulci was an old rogue. A fourth film starring Halsey came out without Halsey's knowledge or any payment. *Cat in the Brain* (1990) used footage of Halsey from *Touch of Death* added to scenes from other horror movies and tenuously linked by the story of a director (played by Fulci) being driven mad from making horror movies. Halsey saw *Cat in the Brain* around 1996 and was appalled by the quality of the movie: "The movie's crap. He's good at setting up gory

effects but Fulci's got no sense of narrative pace." He also was understandably dismayed about the pirating of his work in *Touch of Death*: "You can't do that. I should talk to my lawyer about it." Halsey thinks that this movie's release is the reason Fulci stopped taking his calls, assuming Halsey wanted to ask for payment.

Fulci himself once said of *Cat in the Brain*: "It's an extraordinary film. I play a horror film director so tormented by his nightmares that he has to put them up on the screen." It is indeed extraordinary—extraordinarily bad. This shambles should not really be regarded as a Brett Halsey movie at all, as he never acted in it, only in the far superior *Touch of Death*.

Lucio Fulci died from complications from chronic diabetes. His status as a filmmaker is hard to assess. He had the discernment to see Halsey's star quality but frequently compromised his own talent.

He was born in Rome June 17, 1927, and studied filmmaking under no lesser figures than Visconti and Antonioni. One can only imagine what they would have made of his body of work, yet in his own way, Fulci *was* a dedicated artist, claiming, "The cinema is everything to me. I've dedicated myself to making films. It's a very intense experience. I give everything I've got right up to the end, and then forget about it."

Halsey commented:

> It's a pity when someone's got *nearly all* the qualities needed to be a great filmmaker but just is lacking one element. Fulci wasn't interested in narrative. He was only interested in set-

ting up the next effect. Now, *Mario Bava* knew how to tell a story.

Halsey was quite amused by one aspect of *Cat in the Brain*: "I didn't know that he was such a lecherous old guy. I didn't know that he had sex on the brain, even though his other pictures had it, but this was just sex all the way through."

Fulci made a commercially successful version of Jack London's *White Fang* in 1973, and Halsey once tried to make another version. Julian Ludwig was involved with this and remembered:

> We wanted to do a story about *White Fang*. We thought we had the rights but the agent was not too honest. He sold the option to someone else for a higher price.

In fact, there was a little more to it, as Halsey explained:

> The script was very good. We bought the rights to the script. David Brown at Fox was a good friend of Julian Ludwig. We had a deal at Fox, but Fox was distributing Lucio Fulci's film, so they couldn't be in competition with that. We were going to train the wolves for six months. Fulci's film was crap, he used dogs. They never did release it in the end.
>
> Then the writer thought he'd get a better deal at Warners, but I had a good friend at Warners and he killed the deal. I told Fulci about it, not knowing he had done *White Fang*. He said, "That's *my* film."

The Desert Lion

On June 5, 1990, Halsey went to Morocco for 12 weeks to film the Italian TV mini-series *The Desert Lion* (later released as the feature *Beyond Justice*). He told Sylvia Train of *The Toronto Sun* (April 23, 1990):

> I didn't think I'd be doing the series. I really wanted more time here. It means I won't be here for signing the final papers for the home my wife and I bought in Bayview Village...My agent Margo Lane turned down the first money they offered, but they came back with an offer I couldn't refuse. It would be nice to be home for a while...but I always feel I'm a Torontonian wherever I am. I played the part of a University of Dublin professor in the film (*Demonia*) I did before *Godfather III*. I made them change it to the University of Toronto and I wore a Roots jacket.

This quote is quite revealing, I believe, demonstrating Halsey's chameleon-like ability to fit in with his surroundings, whether Rome, Munich or Costa Rica. Halsey had always considered himself a Californian—even, on occasion, a Mexican, but he clearly saw his future then in Toronto and wanted to be accepted there. Today he is back in Los Angeles. Halsey told me a few times that he left Toronto because he could not bear the weather. Then again, it could also simply reflect politeness to his host country.

Halsey wrote to Dorris Halsey on May 7, 1990, from Ontario, Canada:

> Dear Dorris,
>
> I am writing to show you my latest Torontonian publicity and let you know I'll be working on a three-part mini-series in Morocco until the beginning of July, then in Rome until around July 25th. I have told Hilsinger-Mendelson that I'll be available to go out and sell books any time after that.
>
> The series is called *The Desert Lion*, is being produced by International Dean Film of Rome—directed by Duccio Tessari—and I am co-starring with Carol Alt, Rutger Hauer, Omar Sharif, Kabir Bedi and Elliott Gould.
>
> I will finish *Godfather III* in New York on Friday [May 11] and will fly immediately to Paris, where I will make a connection Saturday morning to Ouarzazate. They are picking me up in Ouarzazate for a three-hour drive to Erfoud where we will be filming until the end of June. After Erfoud, we have about

10 days in Casablanca, which should be a lot more fun.

I am looking forward to seeing you [August]. If you want to contact me with personal dirt or business stuff—or if you want to send me something which might be interesting to read while I'm camped out on the Sahara, make note of the address below.

With love and kisses
Brett

Beyond Justice (1990) is an old-fashioned desert adventure, a modern *Beau Geste* with a spaghetti flavor. Halsey spent three months in the Moroccan desert, near the border of Algeria, for Italian director Duccio Tessari, whose career stretched back to directing peplums with Steve Reeves, writing and co-directing *The Avenger of Venice* and uncredited script work on *A Fistful of Dollars*. The role did not require great acting from Halsey—it is just good knockabout fun—but he throws himself into the physical action of gunfights with surprising gusto. *Beyond Justice* is in some respects closer in lineage to the swashbucklers Halsey made early in his Italian career, such as *The Magnificent Adventurer*, in which he was praised for his athletic performance. Halsey explained, "I was a little old to do the running, but all the crew remembered me as an action star."

For reasons of age, Halsey had realistically begun to accept supporting roles and was not the star of *Beyond Justice*; that was Dutch actor Rutger Hauer. But Halsey has a satisfyingly large part and works very well onscreen alongside Hauer as a member of his crack team sent on a desert rescue mission. Halsey rarely shared the screen with another male actor. The closest he came to a buddy movie was possibly Mario Bava's *Roy Colt and Winchester Jack*, where he was paired with little-known actor Charles Southwood, but the teaming was not particularly memorable and was not repeated.

Halsey wrote an interesting memoir of the filming of *Beyond Justice* in Erfud, Morocco on his birthday, June 20, 1990:

> The sun rose out of the nearby Algerian horizon to brighten this little corner of the Sahara Desert and begin the celebration of the day of my birth.
>
> It began in my room at 06:00 in the morning, with a cup of room-brewed American instant coffee, a few Moroccan butter biscuits, and some quiet thoughts about birthdays past. This wasn't the first time the acting profession had taken me away from home and family on my birthday, but June 20, 1990, was not a day to be regretted...
>
> The day's shooting schedule called for The Four Invincible Mercenaries to escape from the Evil Sheik's (Omar Sharif) castle and, in the process, lay waste to all the persons and property that might be foolish to think they could stand in the way of our mission.
>
> At 07:00 I went next door to awaken The Kid (Stewart Bick) of The Invincible Four and was greeted with an exclamation of Happy Birthday and the dubious pleasure of seeing The Kid attempt to out-shine the brightness of the sun by dropping his jeans and mooning me with his skinny butt.
>
> At 07:30 we left our digs at the Hotel Salam (which is famous among the tent-living nomads for its gracious charm and service) and headed across the bleak desert for the Evil Sheikh's castle, locally known as El Rissani. The Big Guy (Rutger Hauer) almost always zoomed out alone in his car. The general consensus was that he was in secret training for an upcoming Dutch Destruction Derby. The Brit (Peter Sands) rode with The Kid and me. The three of us discussed how fortunate I was still to be alive after my many years in action films and, when that subject became boring, combined our artistic abilities to delve into the hidden meanings and subplots of the scene in which we were about to perform.
>
> The Invincible Four were magnificent, to say the least. Armed with only machine guns, hand grenades and a Stinger missile launcher, we killed more unfortunate Arab combatants than our military does in an entire week.
>
> We might have done better, but we were constantly interrupted by the special effects people who had to unjam our guns; our inability to run more than ten meters without tripping over our own feet or the bodies of the many dead victims of our

bloodthirsty assault; and our escape Jeep, which had a dead battery and had to be pushed to get started. The hot, dry wind and the blinding, blowing sand didn't help much, either. Nor did the realization that the temperature was hovering around 52c (125 f) in the shade.

Camera problems allowed The Invincible Four to take an early break from the carnage to enjoy a delightful birthday lunch in our aluminium-clad, air-conditioned trailer. The tepid pasta and boiled potatoes were accompanied by toasts with a barely chilled, very interesting young Moroccan rose wine. It was while looking out upon a group of Tuareg tribesmen with their tethered camels that I reflected on the fact that, although this was not my first adventure on the Sahara, I still had never ridden on a camel. While my fellow mercenaries were witty and entertaining, they paid scant attention to my musing. They were more interested in their discussion of our good fortune to be almost finished with our work in the desert and our impending move to the fabulous legendary city of Marrakesh, but they were careful not to reveal a word about the unforgettable birthday celebration they had planned for the end of the day.

The afternoon ended with the slaying of 20 or 30 more Arab warriors and the explosive destruction of the castle gate. When the director yelled, "Cut, Print," we drove our vehicle through its flaming wreckage and returned to our trailers, where we changed into our less-threatening civilian uniforms.

The balance of the afternoon was spent with a dip in the Hotel Salam's sparkling pool and a siesta in my spacious suite, which looked out over the quaint, fetid Erfud canal.

While resting and keeping an expectant eye on the phone in anticipation of a call from one or more of my distant families, I received a call from The Cute Blonde (Catharine Daily). The Cute Blonde assumed her most casual voice to inform me that I was expected to appear in the lobby at 19:30 and I was *not* to ask any questions.

The Cute Blonde barely mentioned the pain in her neck, which was the result of an unfortunate encounter with a native burro in the fabled Todra Gorge, and revealed nothing about where we were going or how long we were going to be away. Overhearing me tell the hotel telephone operator that I expected to return by 22:00 (the hour at which calls from home were usually attempted), The Cute Blonde gently suggested that we may not return until around midnight.

I was amazed by this piece of information. What could we possibly do that could last until midnight? Erfud at night is normally about as exciting as listening to four hours of high-speed Morse Code on my shortwave radio. During the day, a trip to the local Post Office had become an eagerly anticipated social event.

The Cute Blonde led me out of the hotel, where a driver was waiting with one of the production's sleek Peugeot sedans. She was a bit indefinite with her directions, but the driver seemed to understand and headed out into the desert on the semi-paved road to Ourzazate.

After about 15 minutes of watching the passing desolation and listening to The Cute Blonde's muttering about the rapidly disappearing sun, I remembered that The Big Guy and Our Beautiful Star (Carol Alt) had been very enthusiastic in their description of a spot they had discovered to watch the most impressive sunsets in the entire world. My suspicion was partially confirmed when we came upon The Big Guy behind the wheel of his customary Peugeot, with The Kid at his side.

At the sight of our car, The Big Guy gunned his Peugeot onto a rocky, rutted track, which apparently led to the crest of an escarpment which looked like it had been violently torn from the deepest bowels of mother earth. After a jolting five or 10 minutes, we arrived at the summit where The Brit was putting final touches to a beautifully laid table-setting, which he had arranged on a massive, naturally formed, square-cut stone. He had placed an exquisitely carved, silver Moroccan tea-set and a colourfully decorated birthday cake on a crisp white tablecloth, which had to be weighted down to protect the table-setting from the constantly blowing wind.

The sandy dust, which had been raised by the wind, partially obscured the sunset, but the panorama, which spread out below the escarpment, was spectacular. In the fading daylight we gazed down on the near and distant sand dunes, oases, mud villages, and the twinkling lights of Erfud. The Brit poured measures of Scotch from the tea service and raised a toast in my honor. We shared a rare moment of warm good-fellowship as we savored the whiskey and reflected on the good fortune that brought us together in this place, at this time. Our little group was unexpectedly joined by two Berber tribesmen who suddenly appeared from somewhere down the mountain. An offer of cake and wine brought smiles to the strangers and they sat down to join us.

At some point during this intimate little gathering, I was touched and grateful to learn that the tea service was a birthday gift from my friends.

Darkness fell and blotted out our panoramic view, so we packed up to retrace our tracks to Erfud and the Film Company's Tent of Gastronomic Delights, which had been pitched next to the Erfud Canal, behind the hotel.

Our host at the tent, Lauradonna, served an unforgettable meal (a wonderful pasta dish followed by something equally wonderful), topped off with another, larger, more elaborately decorated birthday cake. This celebration was shared by the balance of our cast and crew, which now included The Evil Sheikh and The Evil Sheikh's Son (Kabir Bedi). The Big Guy made sure there was a copious amount of J&B and fine wines to accompany the birthday cake, and a good time was had by all.

But wait. It wasn't over.

I had begun to think so until The Little Prince (David Flosi) mentioned something about a belly dancer. A look at the chagrined expressions on the faces of The Cute Blonde, Our Beautiful Star and my fellow mercenaries led me to believe that another secret had been leaked. The Little Prince wanted to kill himself when he realized what he had done, but I didn't care. Why should I? There was more to come.

I was informed that the only genuine limousine in Erfud was awaiting my presence at the hotel entrance to carry me off to Act III of my birthday celebration. Not wishing to keep anyone (least of all myself) waiting, I seized a bottle of J&B by its slender neck and hurried along the bank of the Erfud canal, crossed its picturesque bridge and approached the curved driveway in front of the hotel's wide, welcoming doors.

My friends were delighted at my utter surprise when I was confronted by the truly unexpected. A tall, young, blond, attractively attired *camel* was waiting for me to climb into the saddle on its firm, well-shaped hump.

I felt like an Admiral of the Saharan fleet as I cruised down Erfud's main street on my magnificent ship-of-the-desert, leading a procession of merry-makers to the banquet room of one of the village's lesser-known, mud brick hotels.

At the primitive hotel entrance we were greeted by Erfud's equivalent of the University of California's Marching and Dance Band. The band led the way up some stairs to a balloon-filled banquet room, where our group, plus the rest of the

Art or Instinct in the Movies...

film's crew, and the inevitable party crashers drank and danced our way into the night.

It was long after midnight, and well into someone else's day of birth, by the time my happy head hit my pillow. I had missed a call from home but their birthday card had arrived by mail the preceding day. There was a telegram waiting at the reception desk from Wife III and Daughter II. The call from home came through first thing in the morning, as well as a telegram from son III.

After more than a half-century of birthday celebrations, most of them have blended into a mist of hazy memories. June 20, 1990, will always remain vividly in place as one of the most memorable of them all.

Canada

In the 1990s, Halsey was working in Canada and had less choices offered to him than he would have in Hollywood and was now working for whoever would hire him as well as working in independent films. This meant working for inexperienced and incompetent directors on occasion. Halsey named Milad Bessada as the worst director he had ever worked for:

> My worst experience of a director was on a Canadian film made in Egypt, *Search for Diana* [1993]. The director had directed the Santa Claus parade in a town near Toronto. His wife was the female star. The picture was a tribute to his wife. I was a professor and she was a student. His wife was too old to play a student. I really tried to help him. He was an amateur. He had mortgaged his house to raise the money. He'd make terrible mistakes in placing the camera. He'd have me with my back to the statues of Karnak and pointing them out to her when they were behind me. The camera crew started to laugh. I told him, "You can't shoot that." I was trying to guide him, "Put the camera here." He wouldn't listen. We'd shoot the mistakes. The film only showed in Egypt and in Montreal for the Egyptian embassy.

Halsey believed the film was unreleasable, as the looping was not done, but in 2006 it began playing on a Canadian digital channel. Hearing of this, Halsey quipped that they must be desperate for product.

Halsey's view on amateurs who use their own money to make films and then lose the lot is simple; you would not call yourself a dentist without training in dentistry, so why do people think they can direct films without any experience? Halsey's other memory of this unfortunate project is that Cairo "was not nice."

Much better was a very nice performance Halsey gave as Judge Thomas S. Kirk in *Switching Parents* (1993), which is an overly sentimental and not especially interesting little film. Halsey underplayed with subtlety and gravitas, coolly demonstrating what a marvelous screen actor he is. Halsey was unimpressed by the director Linda Otto. His role was small but he was on the set quite a bit:

> I didn't think she was very good because she wasn't prepared. There was so much we could have done with that…so many more shots she could have gotten, but she didn't have time, because she couldn't make up her mind. She'd come to work unprepared and then she and the director of photography, who was also a woman, kept getting into these long conversations about what they were going to shoot. Well, you don't do that on the set. You do that before you come to work.

Small as it is, Halsey's performance is a key one from this period and could well have led to a career playing judges. He commented:

> The problem with doing these things is I don't like auditions and I haven't been pursuing it and I really should, because playing judges is easy. One of the things that you could do is, you're sitting up there and you could have the script in front of you, because all the shots are up.

Halsey did not do any research on how to play a judge as he felt he did not need to: "If you watch television at all, you can see how a judge behaves. *Law and Order*, shows like that." In 2005, Halsey was looking forward to doing jury duty to which he was summoned and which he thought might be effective for research, though in the end he was not required.

The movies Halsey made in Canada had little impact:

> No, they were just work, to make money. That's one of the reasons that I left the business for the time I was in Costa Rica. In the picture with Jim Brolin, *Backstab* [1990], what happened was we get to the climax of the picture where we're all in this room and somebody shoots somebody—I don't remember exactly what happened—but he has his gun and I have my gun and then we stopped and said, "Wait a minute, where does this second gun come from?" It wasn't indicated in the script at all. All of a sudden, a gun appears out of nowhere. It was a mistake in production. So we had to stop. We lost half a day while they got back to figure out where this gun came from, maybe write it.

Halsey does have one quietly excellent moment in *Backstab* in a courtroom scene when he is answering questions on the witness stand and nicely hesitates in simply saying "No" and uses his eyes to express the character's emotions. Halsey joked when complimented on his playing: "Maybe I couldn't remember the line. It's the actor's job to make as much of it as you can, without going overboard."

In *Terminal Rush* (1995), Halsey plays a security guard taken hostage by terrorists who are threatening to destroy the Hoover Dam. Halsey's role does

Brian Dennehy and Halsey in *To Catch a Killer*

not offer much of an acting challenge—his main function in the film is to play the father of the hero, Don "The Dragon" Wilson. His performance does display a caring paternal quality . The film suffers from martial arts expert Wilson's inexperience as an actor—he makes Jean-Claude Van Damme and Steven Seagal look like members of the Royal Shakespeare Company. In this author's opinion, *Terminal Rush* only comes to life when Halsey is onscreen. Halsey brings credibility and professionalism to any film project and he has been the saving grace for many a dire movie. And in quality films like *The Godfather: Part III*, he simply adds an extra touch of class.

In the television movie *To Catch a Killer* (1992), Halsey has a small character role as lawyer for the deranged mass murderer John Wayne Gacy. Brian Dennehy gave a powerful performance as Gacy.

Halsey's concerned pleading with the shifty, monomaniacal Gacy offsets Dennehy's depiction of repulsive smugness very well and makes for an effective scene and a quality interaction between the two performers. Not that Halsey saw it that way:

> That was not enjoyable, because I was working with an actor who didn't want to be there. He's had a wonderful career and he's probably a good actor, but in the scene or scenes we had together, he didn't want to be there. He wanted to be elsewhere. I don't know if he was going to go play golf or what the hell he was going to do, but I had no sense that I was working *with* someone. We were just saying lines back and forth so that he could get the hell out of there.

Halsey played opposite Rob Lowe in the thriller *First Degree* (1996) and was a suitably sleazy villain, quite unlike his usual smooth image, but the film brought him little notice and was not a hit. He said: "I only have one good scene in the shootout at the end." The film plays frequently on U.S. television. Halsey recalls asking Rob Lowe for an autograph for Firouzeh's daughter, who was a fan, and his gracious agreement.

Halsey seemed visibly bemused by the silliness of the script he was performing in the sci-fi adventure *Expect No Mercy* (1995) and was dismissive when recalling it. Kathy Shower, who kept in touch with Halsey, although she was in Barcelona, was sure that it was in Canada that Halsey began to get disillusioned about his acting career:

> That's where it all started. You read a project and you think, "Oh, I could make this really good" and then you get involved with people who are not professional. They don't know what they're doing. I can see why he would be a little despondent. I don't think he could ever give it up, if something came across his desk.

In addition to acting during his Canadian years, Halsey acted as a talent consultant, giving advice on casting and so on, for some Canadian production companies, L.E.G. Productions (1994-96), Evolution Productions (1989-90) and Norstar Productions (1995-96). He also sold ideas and scripts to these companies.

Halsey's most recent movie credit is also a Canadian production, the thriller *Risk Factor* (formerly *Into the Heat*). Halsey shot scenes for this in 2003 for successful independent Frank Caruso, who became a friend. The film was not entirely completed, however, until 2005, when Caruso raised a final $50,000 to shoot some additional scenes, for which Halsey returned to Toronto. Halsey knew it was a low-budget production and adjusted his artistic and financial expectations in accordance, flying economy for instance ("First-class would have been the end of the budget.") but thought he did some good work in the movie.

Risk Factor

Frank Caruso explained how he came to cast Halsey:

I met Brett back in 1994 through a literary agent who was representing his scripts. I was looking for a dramatic screenplay that could be produced for a reasonably small budget and the agent pulled several off his shelves but none appealed to me.

He remembered another title, *Grave Misunderstanding*, but couldn't find a copy, so he picked up the phone and called the writer—Brett Halsey. Brett had a copy in his apartment, so I drove over and met with him. He was a big charming man with a quick smile. Within minutes he made me feel so comfortable that I felt I had known him forever.

As we talked—mostly about the film industry—I noticed a poster of Kathy Shower, actress and former *Playboy* Playmate of the Year (1986). I had always admired her and was envious of the fact that she had personally autographed the poster.

He seemed amused by my rather boyish crush on her and informed me that he knew her quite well, very, very well. It turns out that they had been an item at one time and had managed to remain friends over the years. I informed him that I had a film project that she would be perfect for, so he picked up the phone and called her. The first thing he said to her was, "I have a friend who wants you in his next film. Here, you can talk to him yourself."

I was shocked. First of all, he called me a friend and I had just met him that day. Secondly, he passed me on to the girl of my dreams. As soon as I picked up the phone, Kathy (in her wonderful Ohio/Southern California accent) screamed, "HAAALLLOOOOWWWWW. Any friend of Brett is a friend of mine." I was totally on Cloud Nine. Thanks to Brett, Kathy did come up to Toronto and we made a wonderful little film called *Love Letters, A Romantic Trilogy,* which has been playing on Canadian television since 2002.

Over the years, Brett and I managed to stay in touch and got together as often as our busy schedules allowed us—even when he was teaching in Costa Rica. I recently cast Brett as a dashing but very dangerous arms dealer in my feature film *Into the Heat.* Brett's scenes were brilliant. He was charming, funny and still managed to convey that element of danger that was so necessary in his role. He never overplays. His subtlety is quite remarkable—and that makes his characters so believable.

El Profesor, Costa Rica

Halsey first made contact with the University of Costa Rica around 1973 when he went there to write, direct and produce a documentary television series for Classic Films Int. on the Presidential election there. The series was called *A Country on the March*. This led him to make more contacts there and reinforced his love for the country, which was first kindled back in 1956.

In one of the most unusual entries in his extensive filmography, Halsey had been hired to appear in a short film that seems to have been the closest he ever came to art cinema. *Afternoon of a Faun* (1956) was set to the music of Debussy. Every shot was synchronized to the music. The director, Albert De Goyen, was a Costa Rican of Dutch ancestry who had gone to the USC Film School and used $50,000 of his family's money, derived from coffee plantations, to fund the short. Halsey explained that, unfortunately, the price of coffee fell and then the cost of the film kept increasing. They spent three months filming but it was never completed. A German company, Quintental, was also involved.

Halsey explained why the cost of the film escalated: "The director was crazy. He'd want to wait for days for clouds to be just right. Then he'd want smoke on eight mountains. We'd burn all the used tires in Costa Rica."

Halsey got his friend Mike Steckler onto the film as an assistant director and recalled they passed the time plotting a fantasy revolution, until some of the crew got seriously interested: "We dropped it immediately."

Halsey was being paid, but only a small amount. He would have earned much more back in Hollywood in the course of three months, and he had his first child on the way, but the film appealed to him and he fell in love with Costa Rica. He was also reluctant to work on a film and not complete it, but he made immediate arrangements to return to L.A. when Charles, Jr. was born. The money was running out just then and they could not pay Halsey any more. Halsey told De Goyen he would have to leave, but he would come back to complete the film if more funds were raised. Sadly, they weren't and the uncompleted film is now believed lost. De Goyen and his sister, who also worked on the film, are now deceased.

Many years later, Halsey would bump into De Goyen one more time in London, where he was directing commercials. He never made any more movies.

Halsey started teaching Acting for the Camera in Costa Rica in 1997 and took whatever film work came his way. He loved Costa Rica because he found it "like Tahiti—less civilized." He had returned to Costa Rica to live, buying a beach property, and decided he would love to do more teaching. He applied to the University of Costa Rica and as soon as Manuel Ruiz, the director of the School of Dramatic Arts, looked at his curriculum vitae, he said, "You're hired."

Afternoon of a Faun

It was not easy to teach Spanish-speaking students, but Halsey had an assistant who helped to translate and most of his fourth-year students spoke English anyway. Halsey found that teaching the students also taught him more about acting for the camera than he ever knew as a leading man in starring roles, and he began to wish he had taken acting more seriously himself.

Halsey went to live in Costa Rica "to slow down," but found himself becoming a respected professor in the Latin American academic world, with offers coming from outside Costa Rica. The son of the Head of the Film School in Havana is a big fan of Halsey's and asked him if he would be interested in acting in a film for him. In 2001 Halsey was invited to Cuba to give a master class at the Escuela International de Cine y TV, which is rated as one of the top five film schools in the world and invites some of the best professionals and academicians from all over the world. Halsey worked with Sandy Lieberson and producer Paul Maslansky, and had a great time in Havana.

Halsey explained how he taught acting for the camera in Costa Rica:

> I was teaching in a theater school but I was teaching fourth year students who were already trained actors. I taught them that, on camera, you must think—think of something—because the eyes will show what you are thinking. I taught them to be honest and learn how to move. I never believed in The Method because, in addition to staying in character, you must remember the blocking and the lines.

Dr. Dagmar Werner and Halsey in Costa Rica

Halsey's preferred textbook is Tony Barr's classic *Acting for the Camera*, first published in 1982. He actually went to Costa Rica as an "escape from the craziness" of Hollywood and show business and "to get a better perspective on life in general—a lot of what we go through here is not necessary." Halsey was "fed up." He was going to auditions for jobs he did not want and felt "no satisfaction getting them:"

> Most casting directors used to be frustrated little girls who couldn't get movie stars' autographs, so they became casting directors to get their revenge.

Halsey began to hate auditions because he could not stand being asked by some 25-year-old, "What have you done?" Kathy Shower, on her return to L.A. after eight years in Spain, agreed:

> We both support each other on that. We're both in the same situation as far as having left and then come back to it. So he's trying to tell me, "You have to do this." At the same time, he's not wanting to do it, either.

It may seem, on the outside, a very strange choice for Halsey to go to Costa Rica. Jay Bernstein stayed in touch with Halsey by phone and gave his own summation of his motives: "It has to do with the fact he is a gentleman and he is intelligent. To be an actor, unless you are a major star, acting is not intellectually stimulating. I think he found it not intellectually stimulating doing TV guest shots. He went to Costa Rica to contribute in a way that was fun for him and positive." Halsey agreed he was "tired of episodic TV":

> It's one of the reasons I went to Costa Rica, because I got tired of just doing the same old thing for money. Just get the check, get the money and go home. Really, that's why I went to Costa Rica, because I was fed up with the business as it was.

Tracy Brooks Swope, now Tracy Avildsen, was pleased that Halsey went to Costa Rica, knowing that he liked peaceful places:

> Costa Rica? I was really happy for him because that's a place where he can really thrive, away from all the hustle and bustle. The simple life…Brett doesn't need a lot to be happy. Never has. We stayed in one room at the beach, during a summer. We were staying at a friend's house on Carbon Beach and we were happier than we'd ever been. I think if you can get along with someone, you just like being with them, it doesn't matter where. You can be in a mansion or a castle and it's never big enough for two people that aren't getting along.
>
> It wasn't surprising when he decided to go to another country to teach at the university. I thought it was wonderful for him because that's how he operates, really. He's so smart and so articulate and after a while all the noise in our world can become like white noise—you know, how we live—and for him it's distracting for his psyche. In Costa Rica he has so much more to give, because he can do it in a way that he's *heard.* For him, it helps him to focus. He can help create a whole new generation with his gift for teaching acting, and with his writing skills, and with people really able to listen to him and respect him as he deserves. I was happy for him because he so much enjoys peace, like fishing in Kernville, just the simple life. He's one of the few people that do. A lot of people say they do but they can't.
>
> On another note, you can also take Brett anywhere. I think that's why we got along, too. We can both go anywhere and we are able to fit in. He can do the Italian suit and the whole Gucci thing but I think he would really just love to have a loose open shirt on and his flip-flops and just hang out—have

a glass of great wine, make some dinner, and just enjoy life. That's who Brett is.

A student called Michelle Jones was selected by Halsey as his most promising student and, on a visit to him in Los Angeles, stated that for all the students, it was "wonderful and great to have Halsey there to teach us the way of film" and "very inspiring" and he is now "much missed by the students." In 2007, she developed a script with Halsey called *Not Tonight Josephine*.

Not all of the students were aware of Halsey's distinguished screen career, but some were. Adriana Mora was one of his students:

> When I first met him, I had no idea who he was. This was the day I auditioned to be accepted into the senior theater. All I knew then was that there was a *gringo* in my audition. And, since I spoke English, the teacher had asked me to audition in English, so Brett could join the process more effectively. This just made me a bit more nervous.
>
> Some weeks later I heard on the radio that they were commenting that a famous actor was living in Costa Rica and that he was going to teach at the University. The presenter mentioned some of his movies. When he said *The Godfather* and filled in some of his background, I almost had a heart attack. I knew then that this was the *gringo* that had seen my audition. I wanted to die. If I had known this then, I am sure the audition would have been a total mess. I would have been too nervous.

Another favorite student was French Canadian Gabrielle Houle:

> I didn't know what type of career he had had when he was living in the United States and I don't know if any of my classmates and colleagues realized how big a career he had behind him. Brett and I developed a friendship from the year 2001 to 2002, the time I spent in Costa Rica. I think we immediately got along because both of us were from Canada and we could speak English together and share similar references to politics, television and so on. He was my teacher in two Acting in Front of the Camera classes and the main consultant on a television series project, a collaboration between the University of Costa Rica and a local television station. This was quite an experience. The passion Brett has for show business and movies was very evident from the first time we met and I believe it was

contagious. We, the students, were always working with him in quite small groups. Brett brought me to my first audition and he was advising and preparing other students for such things. His passion for show business was radiant.

Cesar Delgado attended Halsey's class, too:

> When I first met him, I already knew he was a well-known actor in American soap opera, Italian horror movies and spaghetti Westerns, who had won a Golden Globe once, so I got kind of scared, since I didn't know what to expect from him. I thought he would be a self-conscious person who would not want to give away any secret or trick. Boy, I was wrong. He was one of the most open and loving people from the business that I have actually met. He was always encouraging people to go for the best in their field.

Halsey's course was not obligatory, Adriana observed:

> When students are in the last years, they can choose which classes they are more interested in. For example, if they want more directing or more acting classes. So I think that more of the students who signed up for Brett's classes knew who he was...the ones that did know felt a lot more motivated in the class because we knew that for us this might be a once-in-a-lifetime opportunity to learn. I doubt that someone with Brett's background will ever again be willing to come to Costa Rica and teach in the University for the salary Brett accepted. Of course, he was not there for the money, that is for sure.

The students appreciated Halsey's enormous movie-making experience, said Adriana:

> He knew how things were done and how they were not to be done. And he knew because he had done it a thousand times before. It is different when you have a teacher that knows things because he/she has read them and studied the subject. In this case, it was the years of show business that were contributing to our education.

The course was purely practical. Adriana explained:

His classes were not full of theory at all. We worked in this class. And we learned through work and mistakes. The few times when he had something a bit longer to say, he would ask someone to translate. The big secret is that Brett does understand and speaks Spanish perfectly well, he just does not want to.

Cesar Delgado was invited to the class after helping Halsey shoot and edit a video project. Adriana complained, "The problems, here in the Third World, are always the technical resources. Students don't have camera or editing equipment or sound equipment. It is very hard to develop the projects."

One of the videos Halsey made with the students, *Cita en Setiembre* (1999), had, she recalled, "terrible audio problems, so it could not be made public, which is too bad." Halsey commented that because of the poor sound, the looping was not done. The video actually belongs to the University, and Halsey was slightly annoyed that the students never bothered to re-dub it. He did not feel it was his job to do that, it was the students' job to do that: "I don't direct, I just supervise."

The video actually looks very professional, good enough to play on television. This is partly because the film is a dialogue between two mature people, a man and a woman, and the acting is very good. This is because they had the services of two professional actors, Marcelo Gaete and Sara Astica, who did it gratis. Halsey was "really happy" with their performances. The whole budget was only about $50, which included the videotape. Halsey said he would offer screen credit in exchange for free lunches.

The piece was an adaptation Halsey made of a Russian play, *Autumn Appointment*. He pointed out the restrictions involved in filming. The cameras were necessarily fixed and the students couldn't control the light, because they did not have the right sort of lights and had no light meter. Despite these problems, Halsey used these productions to teach all aspects of making pictures, such as having the actors' looks crossing over. He was teaching with shooting, as he only had two four-hour classes in two weeks.

Another production, *Cartas de Amor* (1997), an adaptation of *Love Letters*, featured the student actors themselves and is more obviously an amateur effort. Some of the acting by the young students is inadequate. The co-directors were Marta Apuy and Jean Marten, with Halsey simply credited as Professor. The first shot of the production (shot as usual on video) pans from the sky downward to two kids. The kids bookend the film, which ends with a sweet final shot of the two children, a boy and a girl, running from the camera hand in hand. Halsey had wanted to open up the text of the stage play by taking it into the open air. Nancy Parke-Taylor spent some time visiting Halsey in Costa Rica and is glimpsed briefly in this production as an extra. For such a small and cheap production, the film has extensive final credits and Halsey explained that this was a joke. He was spoofing Hollywood films that have long lists of credits.

Cesar was lucky when Halsey selected him to direct:

> I remember that since I was not an official student from the University, just someone that Brett had allowed to listen to his class, I was somewhat inactive until he offered me the task of directing the short film we were going to make. I was in shock when he told me. There were people in the class who were almost graduating but Brett picked me. He said that he saw something in me that the others didn't have that could help boost the film to a higher level.
>
> At first, I felt very insecure about certain things, like directing actors or camera placement, but he gave me the confidence to follow my instincts without listening to what other people, who would never accept me as a director, would have to say. That gave me so much confidence and strength that sometimes I got into certain arguments with Brett.
>
> These little discussions we had were merely style issues. I wanted to direct the movie like an MTV-type of video, with fast pace and weird camera angles, and Brett wanted me to make a more *academic* film. We had a fight once about a scene in which I wanted to switch story time and he wouldn't let me. I was able to convince him to let me do it, even though he was still not sure about it. We finished shooting the whole movie, and not a lot of people had much faith in it, but I did, thanks to the advice and trust Brett gave.
>
> At the end of shooting, I edited the movie along with its producer. We spent three weeks in the editing room, I got really obsessed about it, and then showed it to the entire class and some management from the school. They loved it. Amazingly, the people who were always arguing with me loved it too. The most interesting point was when Brett saw it. I won't forget what he said, "You made me feel old-fashioned." It was one of the best compliments I have ever had in my life. The film was the official selection of the Costa Rican film festival the following year. It did not win but it was sure a marvelous experience.

Halsey's class was friendly and fun. Adriana commented:

Brett is pretty funny. I remember one time sitting next to him during an acting test. The test was very, very long and the acting was not exactly involving. After about two hours, the test finally ends. I turned to my right. I knew Brett would have plenty to say. He looked at me with absolute tranquillity and said, "You know, there was just one thing lacking." I was amazed. Maybe Brett did not find this test as painful and as bad as I did. So I asked, "One thing?" And he said, "Yes, anything good. Now let's go for coffee." And that was it.

Halsey developed a friendship with these students. Cesar said:

He would always call me to fix his computer. His computer was always giving him trouble and he didn't like the technical stuff, so he would always say, "If I have a problem with my machine or I need to buy something for it, I will leave it to you. That's what you are here for." We would all laugh. We had the best of times when Brett was around.

Adriana agreed:

Every year Brett would invite us over to his house to watch the Oscars. He would make many copies of the voting ballot. We would each get a ballot and then put money in a jar. Then we would each guess who would be the winner of each nomination. Guess who always took our money at the end of the night? Every single year he would win. Obviously because he knew a lot more about who is who and about the movies, but we all had a blast getting ripped off.

Halsey poses with his 2002 class.

Halsey laughed: "I only did that *one* year. Everyone put in a dollar each. Whoever gets the most correct wins the pot, the least gets the stupid prize."

Jay Bernstein was astonished by Halsey's generosity: "I heard stories how he'd have these Costa Rican kids to his house and cook dinner for the students. Why would he do that?"

He did it because, as Gabrielle Houle pointed out, Halsey was "not only a teacher but a friend and a career advisor to us":

> We would organize dinners many times a week at his place when he would tell us anecdotes about his time in Hollywood. I was in charge of cooking and Brett was supervising and entertaining everyone. He would often tell me, and other actresses he believed in, to start behaving like ladies, and not young girls any more; that it would help us in the acting environment and would help us with our self-confidence. I didn't believe Brett at the time he told me that, but now I perfectly understand what he meant and his advice does help in building self-confidence.

When the teaching terms ended, Halsey would return to Toronto and do any work his agent could offer, including commercials. In fact, he liked doing radio commercials and television commercial voice-overs, because they were easy: "You don't have to learn anything." Once he arrived home on a Friday and Nancy told him he had an interview for an appearance in a Budweiser beer commercial the following morning. Halsey wondered how his agent knew he'd be there. Later he learnt she had heard he *might* be back and gone ahead and booked him for it. The Budweiser commercial proved lucrative and Halsey was amused looking back at his nonchalance during the interview. The director asked Halsey if he could play it like he was talking to a complete idiot. Halsey replied "Sure, I'll play it like I'm talking to you." Fortunately, the guy saw the joke and Halsey got the job.

While in Costa Rica, Halsey kept his hand in as a film actor. He was involved with the Film Commission in Costa Rica and, through that, met filmmakers Oscar Castillo and his wife Maureen Jiminez. They used him on television in Spanish-language TV series, *La Pension* and *El Barrio* and in small roles in two features, *Asesinato en El Meneo* and *Mujeres Apasionadas*. He worked on a Fox Kids Network production, *Mogli The New Jungle Book*, which was shot in Costa Rica.

Halsey used his language skills in *La Pension* where he plays an American speaking Spanish. Halsey enjoyed the job because he found it a challenge to act in Spanish. *Asesinato en El Meneo* is ably directed by Oscar Castillo. Clayton Halsey was the editor and got the job because he met the Castillos on visits to his father in Costa Rica and, ironically, Clayton's name is on the poster and Halsey's isn't. It is a witty comedy about a killing in a nightclub. Halsey got his part because:

> I fit that part, and we're friends. It was another case of, "Do you want to come down and do this?" It's such a small community that everyone knows everyone else.

The film has been sold to Latin America:

> "It's commercial. It will probably sell in the U.S. on the Spanish-language network but there's been some problems with the sales rep that they had for the U.S. He went broke or something. The Mexicans have a lot on the market, that's the problem.

The Castillos do aspire to international sales for their films and not just local consumption, Halsey explained:

> The local market is too small to support feature film production. I remember now a figure I heard that the top money anyone can expect to earn in Costa Rica would be about $85,000. You can't make a movie for $85,000, so you're totally dependent on foreign sales.

When he left Costa Rica to return to Los Angeles, Halsey spent some time, on behalf of the Film Commission in Costa Rica, trying to get co-production deals going with foreign partners but found it impossible. Producers insisted on the films being in the English language, so they could sell them in domestic markets. In return for investing millions of dollars, producers would want insurance and the guarantee of a sale. Nevertheless, Halsey was optimistic about the possibility of a future for pictures in Costa Rica: "I send the Minister of Culture, who's a friend, clippings from *Variety*. We are trying to get a co-production agreement with the U.K. and Canada, but in Costa Rica there is no law governing co-productions, so there can be no co-production agreement until a law is passed." Halsey could still see a future for Spanish-language productions, possibly in genre cinema.

At a party in 2005, Halsey met legendary producer Roger Corman (who had been executive producer of *The Cry Baby Killer*) and proposed he invest in Costa Rican features but later heard that Corman told the producers he wanted all the rights in return, to which they would not agree. Halsey had now all but given up trying:

> It's too difficult, because with most co-production agreements that exist in the world—Canada has about 30 or 40 of them—the agreement itself is based upon the law. In Costa Rica they haven't passed yet the law. They're just not that interested in promoting art.
>
> When I was in Nicaragua the first time visiting a friend of mine who has a school there, he was talking about my teaching there and I said, "Well, what kind of equipment do you have?" "We don't have anything." I said, "What about the government?" He said, "The government has a choice. Either they can support art or they can buy beans." Beans win.
>
> Costa Rica has a lot to offer but the organization is just so difficult. You need the financing to make really good pictures. They make pictures there and some of them go to festivals, but the last two made by local people weren't very good. They just don't have the knowledge or the experience. The only way these people can get good experience is to get out of the country and work, come to L.A. or go to Spain or somewhere and assist on bigger productions.

Mujeres Apasionadas, directed by Maureen Jiminez, did not fare as well as *Asesinato en El Meneo*. Halsey commented, "It started out to be a comedy and then they decided it was going to be a story about women's problems and so it became a drama midstream, so in the end it was kind of nothing. It just didn't work."

While in Costa Rica, Halsey considered getting involved in the setting up of a Green Iguana farm with Dr. Dagmar Werner, who tried to move from the Central American jungle to Costa Rica and who reminded him of Dian Fossey of *Gorillas in the Mist* fame. The project fell through after her backers withdrew, but Halsey considered her story as a possible motion picture and wrote a synopsis, *The Dragon Lady*.

Halsey stayed in Costa Rica until his work at the University came to end in late 2003. In January 2004 he went to Los Angeles and stayed with his friend

Stanley Winston while looking for an apartment. He looked in various parts of L.A. including Hollywood and the San Fernando Valley, before finding a pleasant area in the south of Beverly Hills.

It was University politics, basically, that led to Halsey leaving his professorship. One of the other professors needed more time for teaching. Halsey taught two four-hour classes, one was theory (how to) and one was practise (doing it). He lost one and there was not enough time to do both theory and practise, which made teaching difficult. Then he lost the power to credit students who attended his classes informally, as only fourth and fifth year students could take his classes, when they later joined the course. To cap it all, he was starved of resources and found he was subsidizing the course himself:

> I was spending my own money on a lot of materials. Once, the class made a film I wanted to enter into a festival in New York, so the students could compete abroad. The entry fee was only $25, and I had to pay it. Finally, I gave them an ultimatum: either more class time and more resources or I'll quit.
>
> I left in November 2003. I had been lobbying for two to three years for a $20,000 budget to make a short film. The dean approved the money after I quit. The only condition was, he said, "Any money you spend, *you* have to requisition." I said, "But I won't be here." So they said, "No money."

The parting was not acrimonious, though, and the University invited Halsey back in the summer of 2005 to hold workshops. Manuel Ruiz described Halsey to me as "this good fellow." When Halsey left, he retained his beach property. He bought land and considered building a house. He liked the steady climate there, which is between 68 and 72 degrees. He was hoping to spend more time in Costa Rica in future. On the other hand, he had no plans to retire: "Retire? Retire from what? It's fun. I seem to have done all this work but I don't feel tired. I had a lot of time off."

Creative Writer

Edward Palmer, who was a friend of Halsey's, helped him get started as a novelist. Ellis Kadison convinced Halsey to turn his stories of life in the Italian film industry into a book, but it was Palmer who offered him practical help in finding a publisher:

> We've had a friendship through the years. I helped make the deal for the first novel, with Bantam Books, because I had a working relationship with them on motion picture deals. I knew Mark Jaffe, president of Bantam. I told him Brett could do the job. I was the broker. I thought it could have been made into a Jacqueline Susann–type of mini-series or movie. It may have been a mistake that no actual script was ever written for the movie. That may have been what was needed to get the wheels turning.

Halsey has always taken his writing seriously and it began remarkably early. On his own account, he had been inspired early on by the writings of Budd Schulberg. The first script he recalls working on was as early as 1956. He wrote in the 1961 Fox profile: "I've been writing a screenplay for about five years. I just work at it awhile, then put it away, not in a hurry about it. It isn't good enough really, some day I'll do the whole thing over again."

The script was "an unintentional precursor" to Halsey's most recent novel *Halfbreed* and by 1961 he was preparing it as a pilot script for a projected Fox television series to be called *El Camino Real*. Halsey remembered:

> It was centred around a crossroad trading post in early Southern California and its premise was based upon the conflict brought on by the coming together of the Yankee and Californiano cultures. The trading post was run by a young Easterner and I was to play a young Californian vaquero, living on a rancho owned by his uncle, who was to be played by Cesar Romero. The Head of Fox TV at the time was William Self. It was at the time when Fox was on the verge of bankruptcy, because of the *Cleopatra* financial fiasco. Self told me he was confident my show could be a success, but he had financing for only one pilot and that was *Twelve O'Clock High*, which ended up on the air from 1964 to 1967.

Halsey got into scriptwriting in a bigger way when he went to Italy and found himself welcomed to rewrite terrible dialogue, which was the result of literal translations from Italian into English. His first seriously completed script was co-written with Italian writer Gino Mancini, in English and Italian: "It was a caper story, about smuggling drugs into Italy, that was optioned by an Italian producer but never made." Then Halsey rewrote the scripts of pictures like *Kill Johnny Ringo*.

Halsey's success as a writer and then as a production executive, following a distinguished acting career, led to his gaining an industry reputation as an all-round creative picture-maker. A rare example of someone who could do everything in the filmmaking process. This led to an occasion where he was approached to save a picture that was in trouble. The producers had shot a picture in Israel with a female director and decided that it did not work. The story made no sense.

The story concerned an impotent Jewish man in the 1920s who took a wife. She mysteriously became pregnant and had a baby. As the baby could not be his, he became furious and killed her, but his village pardoned him because she must have been at fault. But then he remarried and the same thing happened again. Now the village was becoming disturbed. The third time he married, his wife got raped and fell pregnant. The man was unwilling to have a baby with a woman raped by someone else. Finally, the Head Rabbi advised him "Maybe you shouldn't be married!" Jewish humor!

Unfortunately, the cut of the film Halsey saw failed to deliver the irony of the situation. It simply did not work. Halsey spoke to the director, who resisted his efforts to salvage the film. Eventually, in frustration, Halsey gave her an ultimatum: "Either work with me, or I'll fire you!"

However, her contract gave her final cut of the picture and she refused to alter the film. The resultant film was a disaster. Halsey thought it had the potential to gain an international release if she had taken his advice, but she would not budge. He ruefully recalled, "The picture was never finished properly. The investors never recovered any of their money."

Perhaps Halsey's major writing project was his Western script *West of Hell*. This project was Halsey's first major attempt at a screenplay and he devoted a lot of time and effort to it, to superb effect. Amos Powell came out to Rome to help Halsey with it and, such was Halsey's faith in the property, he later bought out Amos' interest in the script for $7,500.

Halsey also asked a friendly acquaintance, writer George Bacos, for his opinion of *West of Hell*. Halsey often asks friends what they think of his scripts. Bacos recalled, "I did read it. We agreed there were two storylines in it and it was too convoluted." He suggested some changes, with which Halsey agreed. Bacos said there was "a clique of friends" around Halsey but "we became closer over the script."

It is perhaps Halsey's most successful movie script, in that it is the most easily translatable to the screen. It has all the classic elements of a solid Western and is easy to visualize on the big screen, allied to a very interesting twist in characterization. The supposed heroine Nicole is slowly revealed to be the catalyst for the various misfortunes of the characters involved in the search for gold statuettes. Halsey actually envisaged her as a teenage temptress who leads men to their ruin: "She's the Devil. Ideally, she should be played by a 14-year-old, but you can't do that." The part needed a very good actress who could suggest innocence, vulnerability, Machiavellian evil and greed all at the same time. Unsurprisingly, Halsey sold various options on this script over the years. Recently it was optioned by producer-director Ron Joy with a view to shooting in New Mexico, under the new title *Fool's Gold* [not to be confused with the new 2008 film *Fool's Gold* starring Kate Hudson and Matthew McConaughey].

In 1978 Halsey published his fictionalized memoir of his years in Rome, *The Magnificent Strangers*, which was originally entitled *Exiled in Wonderland*. Halsey had to agree to change the title because the publishers had recently published an unsuccessful novel with the word "exile" in it.

This steamy account of life among the American expatriate film community in Rome contained portraits of real-life figures — Rex was an exaggerated portrait of Gordon Scott. Some of the main characters are clearly based on friends, such as Sandy the agent and Marilu the actress. The novel also contains actual mentions of Steve Reeves, Lex Barker, Paul Maslansky, Luciana Paluzzi and even Brett Halsey.

Halsey told Dorothy Austin (*Milwaukee Sentinel*) when it was published:

> I thought at the time that Rome in the '60s was like Paris in the '20's, Hollywood in the '30s, San Francisco in the '50s. It

was a time and place that never was before and never would be again, and I thought it ought to be recorded.

Although mentioned in the book, Halsey does not appear in it as a character because, he explained, he "did not wish to be that introspective." Halsey sold the book to Charles Bloch, senior editor at Bantam Books, by submitting an outline. They liked it but were initially sceptical because he was an actor and asked for some sample pages, so Halsey wrote 32 pages and they bought it immediately. It took two years to write, on the days when he was not doing television. Halsey reminisced to Ruth J. Gordon in the February 1978 *Soap Opera Digest*:

> When I started on the book, I went to Charles Bloch and I said, "I think I will go to UCLA and take an extension course in creative writing so at least to have some idea"—and he said, "Don't you dare. You just write the book. That will just screw you up. You can write well." He also said, "If you have any problems with grammar or whatever, we will take care of that."

Halsey first met his literary agent, Dorris Halsey (no relation), at Bantam social occasions. Dorris recalled, "I was instrumental in having his books published. Charles Bloch was a friend we had in common and Judy Hilsinger the publicist, and so on." She did not think his being a movie star was much to do with the success of his books:

> In New York, it doesn't mean much. Not New York, in L.A., yes. It is what he has to say that counts. In *Yesterday's Children* [Halsey's second novel], of course, that was very much a part of it, because he was a soap opera star and therefore he knew whereof he spoke; and the same with *The Magnificent Strangers*, because he spent so much time in Italy when Cinecitta was the queen of it all.

Dorris was aware of Halsey's stardom when they met and considered him "better-looking" than Tyrone Power: "He is terribly likeable."

Julian Ludwig said of Halsey's first two novels: "He is a good writer. The books are terrific. They are mostly stories of things that happened to him." This is certainly true of the first two novels. Halsey told John Archibald in the February 20, 1978, *St. Louis Post-Dispatch* how he came to write about his time in Rome in the 1960s:

> I was always making notes, mentally if not on paper. Most people knew that I had a book in mind. Recently the woman

I used as a model for the character of Ellen saw me in New York and she screamed, "You told me 11 years ago that I'd be in your book, and I am."

When *The Magnificent Strangers* was published by Bantam, they got behind it—Halsey received an impressive $75,000 advance—and sent him on a promotion tour. It won the *West Coast Review of Books* Silver Medal Award and warm praise:

> Halsey shows himself to be a first-rate novelist who knows the subject he's writing about. This is his first novel and it is totally absent from cliché and predictable formulas for commercial success. It is this honesty which permeates his work.

The book is rather racy, and Halsey told C.W. Skipper (February 27, 1978, *Houston Post*): "I did not intend to write a dirty book. Why, I sent a copy to my mother....I'm a little nervous."

The novel became a bestseller. The *L.A. Times* reported producers David Merrick and Carlo Ponti bidding for the film rights. Halsey later rewrote parts of the novel on his laptop while filming *Beyond Justice* (1990) in Morocco, as he had come to feel the original was a bit amateurish and the revised book was published by i-Universe. *The Toronto-Sun* (May 8, 1992) reported that there were plans for a six-hour mini-series based on the book to be co-produced by Gene Kirkwood (*Rocky*) and Silvio Berlusconi. Halsey was quoted saying, "They're talking to Clint Eastwood and Michael Anderson about directing."

Halsey followed it in 1984 with another novel based on his own experience, this time of working on daytime television, *Yesterday's Children*: "I wanted a title that would *sound* like a soap opera." Halsey did a lot of research about breast cancer and was forced to do a major rewrite when the publishers vetoed the theme. Three hundred pages were cut and the rest of the novel had to be rewritten to exclude the material.

Halsey was philosophical about the wasted effort. When he was a development executive at Paramount later, he was amused when a writer sent in a script devoted to what happens to a writer's manuscript when it is submitted.

Bantam Books were keen to repeat the success of *The Magnificent Strangers* and offered him an advance of $15,000 if the manuscript was accepted, but they did not like the manuscript Halsey submitted and it was rejected. To this day, Halsey does not know why. His agent Dorris Halsey then placed it with a new firm, Knightsbridge Publishing, who produced a handsome hardback. This came with a ringing endorsement on the dust jacket from Clint Eastwood: "In *Yesterday's Children*, Brett Halsey has given me a fresh understanding of soaps and the people who make them."

There was also a quote from Burt Reynolds. Halsey had been friendly with Burt, and Dick Clayton, who had gone into partnership with Burt in a production company, asked him for a quote for the book jacket. Halsey noted of Burt: "I haven't been friendly with him in recent years. He had a medical problem that helped to separate him from a lot of friends." Halsey's friend, actress Madlyn Rhue, also wrote an endorsement for the book, which did not appear on the book jacket: "Brett's book may be all about daytime television, but his writing is strictly Primetime... I can't wait to see the movie."

Halsey hoped to emulate the success of his first novel with this one. He promoted it to *The Star* (March 21,1978):

> I have always believed that the lives of the people who make the soap operas are vastly more interesting than the people they play.
>
> There are tremendous rivalries and power struggles: secretaries trying to become producers, jealousies between stars.
>
> Two of my main characters are a young woman producer and an older woman star who are fighting for control of the show.
>
> Another character is a girl who plays a heavy in a soap and is harassed by fans.
>
> There have been real cases where actors who play bad guys get such hate mail that guards have to be sent in.
>
> I have about a dozen leading characters and they all have their love affairs. Because I'm modeling my book's characters on real people, I don't want to get too specific.
>
> But people in the industry will recognize who I'm writing about...A lot of marriages come out of working together and a lot of fooling around. And, therefore, I guess a lot of divorces.

In publicising *Yesterday's Children*, Halsey told Joseph Finnigan of *Inside Hollywood*:

> I model my characters after composites of real people. It's not an expose of daytime television, but is a little more explicit about what goes on than one normally reads in daytime TV fan magazines. There are things that are constantly complained about in TV that I get my knife into.

Tracy Brooks Swope helped Halsey with his books:

> He's just an amazing guy, just with his writing and acting. I spent many hours helping Brett edit his books, beginning with *The Magnificent Strangers*. That was real fun. He's a perfectionist. He would write it and I would go through it. Very, very good writer. Brett wrote his second book *Yesterday's Children* and based one of his leading characters on me and our soap opera days. He dedicated the book to me. I was touched. We were very comfortable with each other. It was an effortless, wondrous union, physically, emotionally and spiritually. I will always hold a special place in my heart for Brett.

Halsey began another novel, *My Soul to Take*, a modern take on Helen Hunt Jackson's 1886 novel *Ramona*, which concerned the problems faced by Indians in early California and has been adapted for plays, movies and television. He finally completed it in 2008 as *Halfbreed*. The novel was a long time in gestation. Halsey began working on it when he was at Warners in the 1980s and wrote a long treatment then. Halsey renamed the novel in 2004 at the suggestion of Dorris Halsey, who encouraged him and agreed to represent it, a little reluctantly at first:

> I discouraged him before. I said, "Come on, it has been done a thousand times in many different ways." But he's absolutely stubborn about it, and so, if he must do it, let him do it. I reluctantly said I would try again. It's time that the young adults learned about the injustices that this country has inflicted on both the Mexicans and the Indians.

Halsey took the original *Ramona* and stripped it down, completely rewriting it in a modern idiom and adding many new characters and incidents. It is virtually a new work. It was the first of Halsey's novels to be imagined completely outside of his own experience. He increasingly found the internet a more useful research tool than libraries and spent a day reading an excerpt on clipper ships. By now, Halsey described himself as "not as prolific as I used to be" and would some days do no writing as such, just "a lot of research and thinking about things." Sometimes, writer's block set in. When I first met him, he said: "I hit a wall last week." He named one character in *Halfbreed*, Cleo Cordero, after a girl he once had a crush on in school.

When demand for Halsey's acting was slow, he did more writing: "I have had a number of scripts optioned, not made." Titles include his 1960s project *West of Hell*, a thriller/rock 'n' roll/romance *Date With Fate* and his favorite script *War and Pizza*.

Halsey passed *War and Pizza* to Clint Eastwood:

> It's a period piece during the time of the Czars and I have this Italian Prince that gets involved in local Russian politics. Actually, it's relevant today because of the war with the Muslims. It's a big dress comedy. I gave it to Clint and he read it and said, "I really liked it. As a matter of fact, I started it and I couldn't put it down until I finished it. But why did you write it? No one's ever going to produce this."

Another unmade script was the romantic comedy *Pierrot*, which he wrote for Mindy Productions in Rome. Halsey wrote the script from an original story about clowns between Capri and Naples.

Halsey spent a year in London with the Sun Entertainment Group, writing and preparing a science fiction picture *Silverworld*. The music was all recorded by Kenny ("Under the Boardwalk") Young, whose original story it was, but the picture was not made because it would have been too expensive in the days before CGI. The company put him up first at the Knightsbridge Apartments and then at the house in Flood Street, Chelsea. Halsey sometimes took a bus from the King's Road up to the West End.

Halsey wrote the script for *Safari* (1986), a made-for-TV action picture, about the black market in medicines, which was funded by RAI, the Italian state broadcasting company. It was shot in Zaire but the production was troubled. The famous director Roger Vadim was hired to direct and producer Roberto Manelotti hired Halsey to write the script from a story by Luciano Vincenzoni (who wrote *The Good, the Bad and the Ugly*). Halsey noted, "The producer knew that I was a writer. And he wanted me also to play one of the parts, but my disagreements with Vadim were so strong that we didn't want to work together."

Halsey explained the conflict:

I respected Vadim before we started this project, but he was just so far off the intention of the project. If he wanted to do an intensely personal little story with people, that would have been fine, but that wasn't the story that he had. It was supposed to be like a pilot for a series but it just failed so miserably.

It was made for TV. It was supposed to be the first co-production between all the major European television networks. What happened was, Vadim was the wrong choice as director. I think the producer hired him on his name and reputation but Vadim said to me time and again, "I don't do action films, I do personal stories." And so, we had many disagreements and the producer didn't back me up, although the producer said, "Yes, that's what I want." I would write action. *Safari*... you would expect some action. But Vadim wanted to cut all the action, so we had some real disagreements. As a matter of fact, we disagreed so much that I didn't go on location. And Vadim shot what he wanted to shoot and it wasn't what the producer wanted. Vadim shot only close-ups, he forgot to shoot masters, so they couldn't cut the film together. The producer had to go back. The producer lost a lot of money because he had to go back and do a lot of re-shooting and it kind of blew the deal because they weren't finished in time for this launch of this European co-production.

Halsey was shabbily treated. His name is not on the picture. It wasn't that he requested it be taken off: "No, no, no. It was because of the disagreements. I wrote the script from an original story. They credited the writer of the original story on the screen as having written the screenplay but he didn't have anything to do with the screenplay. I could have sued, but suing in Italy is extremely difficult." Manelotti also withheld the last payment to Halsey: "It was only two thousand dollars." Halsey regarded the film's completion difficulties as a form of revenge. He never saw the film, which did not emerge until 1991.

He sold a proposal for a TV sitcom about Italian WWII prisoners of war to Evolution Entertainment in Toronto, using again the title *War and Pizza*, because he likes it as a title. He even ventured into the horror field with the scripts *Wolf Woman* and *Grave Misunderstanding*, which was optioned by Columbia. In 2005, he had an idea for a TV pilot *Juana of the Jungle*, in the mould of *Medicine Man* and *Sheena, Queen of the Jungle*.

He was well aware of the odds against having a script made: "At Warners, 4,000 scripts a year are reported on. Maybe 40 are optioned. They will buy maybe 15 to 20 and make maybe four to five." But he remained optimistic:

"If you keep slinging enough mud, some of it will stick." These days, Halsey is totally committed to writing and unconcerned about his acting career.

Halsey had no plans to retire from acting but he was not exactly keen to get back into the rat race of auditioning, as he came to hate auditions, and turned down an offer when he returned to Los Angeles from Costa Rica to read for the soap opera he did in the 1970s, *The Young and the Restless*. He did not like soap opera and felt he did not need it any more. He had his pension and ideas for writing. He would have considered a small regular role in a series, but not something as demanding as a lead in a soap. More pessimistically, Dorris Halsey felt Halsey had "reached an age, as I have, where we don't really exist any more in this town."

Kathy Shower, still in regular touch with Halsey, completely understood his attitude when she returned to L.A. from years in Barcelona:

> There's a lot of bubblegum projects. It's just fluff and you have to go in and deliver those lines. You're working with the flavor of the month. You do have this vast experience, you have these multi films behind you, and people such as Clint Eastwood. You have credibility. And you go in and you read with a reality star from *American Idol* that week and you lose it all. You lose the desire. You stand there and you say, "This isn't what it's about." Once you've had the experience that Brett has had in moviemaking, you don't want to go out on *that* memory.

Now back in L.A., Halsey encouraged students like Cesar Delgado to go to L.A. to seek a big break and wondered how he could sponsor them to do so. He was even considering putting them up on his apartment floor. He hoped to revive his Hollywood career but also to finish the long-cherished dream to complete his novel *Halfbreed*. He bought a computer and set to work, not bothering to call his agent Don Gerler for over six months as he got engrossed in the writing.

He also re-established contact with old friends like Tracy Avildsen, Jay Bernstein and Clint Eastwood. Eastwood said, "Brett, anything I can do...."

He gave Halsey a small part in *Million Dollar Baby* (2004) and considered whether he could offer him something in *Flags of Our Fathers* (2006), but did not have a role suitable as the majority of the parts were for younger men. Halsey worked in *Baby* for a day and a half but the scene did not make it into the final cut of the picture. Halsey was disappointed but the film was too long and his scene, as a doctor attending Hilary Swank, involved an anal procedure that was felt to be tasteless. Eastwood had the courtesy to call Halsey in person and apologize. He told him, "Gee, Brett, I had to cut me and Morgan, too." This made Halsey feel better and he voted for the film in all categories in the

Oscars, as a voting member of the Academy of Motion Pictures Arts and Sciences. Halsey would never let such a small matter affect his friendship with Eastwood, which went back so far. On one occasion, they went to the House of Blues on Sunset Boulevard to hear some music, but the nature of the clientele meant that a separate room had to be constructed to give Eastwood and Halsey their privacy. Eastwood has frequently helped out old Universal colleagues with parts in his movies. Halsey told a story about his loyalty to his friends:

> Nicky Blair was a close friend of Clint Eastwood and Steve McQueen. Nicky was an actor who could handle little roles but was a better restaurateur. When Steve was dating Ali [McGraw] while still married to Neile, Steve was with Ali at Nicky's when Neile came in. Nicky had to hide them in his office, and Neile wouldn't leave.
>
> When Clint and *Unforgiven* were up for Oscars, Warner Bros. decided to have the Oscars party at Spago. Clint said to Warner Bros., "Fine. You have your party at Spago. I'll have mine at Nicky Blair's." So Warners had to change it to Nicky's. Clint was being loyal to a good friend.

Shortly after the filming of *Million Dollar Baby*, Eastwood's Malpaso production office rang Halsey to ask him about his screen credit. They said,

Halsey and Morgan Freeman on the set of *Million Dollar Baby*

"How would you like your name on the credits?" Halsey replied, "You know, above Clint's—and before the title." They said, "We didn't mean that." Halsey laughed, "No, I didn't think you did." They just meant the spelling.

Halsey quickly shrugged off not being in the final version of the film. At this time, he was so absorbed by completing his latest novel that he expressed the desire *not* to work, so that he could concentrate on his writing. He put in long hours on the novel and did not waste a minute during the day. He sent *Halfbreed* to Clint, who loved its depiction of the history of California and phoned Halsey twice to say how much he was enjoying the novel.

Halsey stayed busy with his writing and his Costa Rican students would send him scripts they were writing, seeking his advice. Oscar Castillo asked him to help edit a movie script he was preparing.

It Ain't Over Till it's Over

Halsey was living alone in his apartment in 2004 but said he was "never lonely" because he had his characters around him as soon as he got started writing. Dorris Halsey said of him,

> This style is exactly what he wants and this life is what he wants now. He is not looking for a lot of money. He is very happy with what he has. He is doing well. And he does what he wants. I don't think he wants to be attached any more. He doesn't want to be a couple. He wants his freedom and yet when he wants companionship, he can have it, easily.

When Dorris said this in 2005, no one could have predicted that Brett Halsey would get married a fifth time.

In fact, things were not even then quite as they seemed. Halsey was enjoying a varied social life, which included television's *Hee-Haw* singing star Marianne Rogers, former wife of country star Kenny Rogers. When they met at a party, she found him vaguely familiar, though she didn't know anything about his career, but she did remember thinking him "a good-looking guy." Later, he showed her some of his films, beginning with a gruesome Lucio Fulci movie. It did not stop her throwing a fabulous party for his 72nd birthday at her apartment in 2005. Marianne also accompanied Halsey to a special revival of *Gunman's Walk* at Hollywood's Egyptian Theatre in October 2004, which was also attended by its stars Tab Hunter and James Darren. Halsey had forgotten how small his role was: "I had to look to see me in it."

In 2005, Halsey visited the Egyptian Theatre to see a restoration of Michael Reeves' classic *Witchfinder General*, a film he had never seen. With his professional eye, he was able to see past his personal knowledge of director Reeves and star Vincent Price and said he would have edited the film more tightly. Halsey met old friends at the screening such as the film's producer Philip Waddilove, his wife Susi and veteran actor Clu Gulager.

Jay Bernstein was not surprised that Halsey at 71 still found it easy to date attractive women:

> The kind of women that he would want, he would be their first choice. They are the most beautiful of women that would be attracted to older men. Any woman 45 and above would want him.

Kathy Shower praises Halsey's "gorgeous stature and everything": "Brett is still a very handsome man. It's that charisma. If you have that, it modifies but it doesn't really go away." Tracy Avildsen says: "He's the sweetest guy. Very smart too. A very good friend and a very good boyfriend."

Unusually active for his age, Halsey circulates in Beverly Hills at celebrity events, seeing old friends like Jane Fonda, and at premieres such as Clint Eastwood's *Flags of Our Fathers* and goes to private screenings for members at the Academy of Motion Picture Arts and Sciences. When attending the local cinema, he sees the likes of Quentin Tarantino in the audience. Tarantino would be aware of Halsey — he dedicated *Kill Bill* to Lucio Fulci. He has his own website. He considers offers to teach in Costa Rica and Latin America; goes to celebrity signing events (as far away as Charlotte, North Carolina) and he sees old friends. He collaborated with Frank Caruso in setting up an acting school for film and television called AIM (Actors in Motion), with Frank Caruso running the headquarters in Toronto and Halsey running the L.A. branch. He generously fields enquiries from film scholars and writers seeking information on topics as varied as the history of the Universal Talent School and the role of Mario Bava in the films of Riccardo Freda. He continues to create wonderful scripts and field them to potential producers.

He seems pleased when writers and critics tell him his screen career has been fabulous and enjoys giving advice to young actors and screenwriters at the start of their careers. He seems as contented as he could possibly be, if given to moments of sadness when he thinks about the past. He ambles about locally, chatting to people as if he were not the great 1950s Hollywood and 1960s European celebrity "Brett Halsey." Just occasionally, he gets recognized, usually by "older women," he laughs. He describes himself now, when asked, as "a writer who acts" rather than, as he used to be, "an actor who writes." He works tirelessly to expand his gift for writing, continually coming up with new story ideas. In March 2005, Halsey got a nostalgic reminder of his beginnings in the industry. He accompanied Dorris Halsey to the 60th anniversary party at CBS for Head of Business Affairs, Ann Nelson. Dorris reported, "He was very well-dressed. Brett got up and spoke, even though he doesn't know Ann. He said, 'I preceded Ann here. I was on this stage. Stage 46. I was a page'."

After surprisingly long years of critical neglect — Halsey was not even listed in the early editions of Leslie Halliwell's encyclopaedic *Filmgoer's Companion* — fanzines such as *European Trash Cinema*, *Giallo Pages*, *Fangoria* and *Psychotronic* finally interviewed him at length about his amazing and unusual career. Halsey was interviewed by Bob Murawski and Jeff Burr for a new DVD release of Fulci's *Cat in the Brain* and I was allowed to suggest some questions. He was also interviewed for DVDs of *The Atomic Submarine* and *Return of the Fly*. Late in the day, Halsey is finally being given the kudos his talent deserves.

Halsey himself does not dwell unduly on his past achievements but prefers to think of new adventures, any opportunities to visit Costa Rica, Cuba, Chile,

even Paraguay, countries that clearly appeal to the Spanish blood in his lineage. Leaving Halsey after discussing some revisions to this book in June 2005, I watched him walking back to his apartment, this tall, greatly distinguished man in a Hawaiian shirt, looking a little, as Tracy Avildsen affectionately said, like a bear. The phrase came to mind because he had just bought a gun to fight off bears in preparation for his first ever trip to Alaska. His adventurous spirit may be traceable to his childhood love for travel author Richard Halliburton who wrote adventure travel books and lived for a time in Costa Mesa, where Halsey grew up. In the 1920s, Halliburton was a bigger selling author than Hemingway, and Halsey has expressed a desire to do a movie about him.

But what is Brett Halsey's location in the acting pantheon? It is beyond question that he has earned a high position. This author sees him as a true successor to Montgomery Clift and Robert Walker for the subtlety of his playing, his spiritual qualities and complexity. He is a worthy contemporary of that great powerhouse actor of American film and television, his old page boy colleague Robert Vaughn, albeit even more at home with lightness and comedy than Robert—witness effortlessly funny moments in Bava's *Four Times That Night* and even as early as his amiable performance as the son in *Ma and Pa Kettle at Home*.

If the general public does not have this overall perception of his achievements, it is because Hollywood restricted his possibilities onscreen more than the Italians did and his Italian work was not so well distributed. The DVD era is beginning to rectify that situation. Movies long unavailable have become easy to locate for fans who only know of Halsey's Fulci-era movies. Even *The Magnificent Adventurer* can be purchased on a shiny DVD-R as *The Burning of Rome*. Halsey himself has been able to see early movies like *The Cry Baby Killer*, which he had never caught before. A reappraisal of Halsey's magnificent career is long overdue from the critical establishment and the public at large.

And, as for Halsey personally, how does he feel at this point in his life, with so many exciting things behind him? He wrote this for some friends, adapting it from someone else's work to fit his own situation more closely and it makes a fitting coda to this book:

> Old age, I decided, is a gift. I am now, probably for the first time in my life, the person I have always wanted to be. Oh, not my body. I sometimes despair over my body—but I don't agonize over it for long. I would never trade my amazing friends, my wonderful life, and my loving family for less gray hair or a flatter belly. As I've aged, I've become kinder to myself, and less critical of myself. I've become my own friend. I don't ride myself for eating that extra cookie, or for not making my

bed, or for buying that silly doodad that I don't need, but looks so wonderfully goofy in my living room...

I will dance and sing along with those wonderful tunes of the 50s and 60s, and if I, at the same time, wish to weep over a lost love, I will. I know I am sometimes forgetful. But there again, some of life is just as well forgotten and I eventually remember the important things. Sure, over the years my heart has been broken. How can your heart not break when you lose a loved one, or when a child suffers? But broken hearts are what give us strength and understanding and compassion. A heart never broken is pristine and sterile and will never know the joy of being imperfect...

I like the person I have become. I am not going to live forever, but while I am still here, I will not waste time lamenting what could have been, or worrying about what will be. For the first time in my life, I don't have to have a reason to do the things I want to do. If I want to play games on the computer all day, lie on the couch and listen to old CDs for hours or don't want to go to the beach or a movie, I have earned that right. I have put in my time doing things for others, so now I can be a bit selfish without feeling guilty.

Afterword
Brett Halsey —
Art or Instinct in the Movies...

Brett Halsey today is especially revered in specialist circles for his work in spaghetti Westerns and Italian adventure films, while a wider public knows him well for Hollywood classics like *Return of the Fly* and *Return to Peyton Place*.

When one examines the Hollywood classics and the European genre movies together, it becomes clear that Brett Halsey has fashioned an impressive body of work. This film lover has no hesitation in claiming Halsey's screen career to be one of the great, undiscovered achievements of post-War cinema. It is astonishing that an actor can be so outstanding in so many excellent pictures without receiving widespread popular recognition at the level of, say, Jack Nicholson. It is generally the film buffs who truly value Halsey's contribution to film rather than the mass audience who will simply enjoy his performances when they catch them on television.

I put this partially down to limited American distribution of some of his very best work, often for Italian directors like Freda and Fulci, and partially down to the unusual pattern of his career. Halsey himself acknowledged the latter: "I've been comfortable out on a limb, following less conventional paths."

These less conventional paths reaped rich artistic rewards. Some of Halsey's performances are magnificent.

I first experienced Halsey's very singular screen impact in one of his Italian pictures when I was a child and have all my life been intrigued by what made him stand out so prominently from other Hollywood expatriates like Ray Danton and Gordon Scott, who starred in similar genres.

As I came to see more of Halsey's work, I became interested in understanding the qualities that make Halsey, in my opinion, the ultimate movie star. The questions that suggested themselves were: Could Halsey's movies reveal the ingredients for that intangible known as star quality? Can one say more than simply that Halsey's charisma is down to one of those mysteries of personality whereby the camera confers a spiritual grace on certain performers?

In their book *The Eurospy Guide*, Matt Blake and David Deal praise Halsey's "somewhat languid aura." Languor is a correct but insufficient characterisation of Halsey's screen impact, which is more complex, although languor is an attractive part of it and certainly evident in his laid-back, lounge lizard-type performances as early as his television series *Follow the Sun* in 1961 and as late as the Italian romantic drama *Rose* in 1986.

Matt Blake and David Deal are spot-on, however, in drawing attention to Halsey's screen persona, which I believe is the essence of his movie star greatness.

The aura that envelops Brett Halsey onscreen offers an innate superiority drawn from personal qualities that transcend simple notions of looks or talent.

Of course, it is impossible to overestimate the crucial part looks and talent play in the composition of that impression, which is made up of elements both obvious and not so obvious. Physical appearance is the most obvious.

As a moviegoer, I pay tribute to Brett Halsey as one of the most handsome male stars to have graced the screen, right up there with Cary Grant, Marcello Mastroianni and Alain Delon. Fellow actor Clu Gulager witnessed Halsey's early years in Hollywood and describes him as the best-looking young actor around in that period.

However, I would not wish to suggest that is where his true value lies. In his early B movies and television shows, Halsey had much in common with sensitive, dedicated young actors like his friend James Dean, who recommended Halsey for a role he could not take. The evidence is there in television shows like *Gunsmoke* "Helping Hand" (1955) and movies like *The Girl in Lovers Lane* (1959) which, despite its low budget, offers a performance by Halsey that would have made Dean proud. Halsey's work was intelligent from the start and, as he matured, an intellectual quality came to the fore—brooding, thoughtful, sensitive performances that began to bring him serious recognition within the industry.

There is perhaps an analogy here between Brett Halsey and Robert Taylor. The young Robert Taylor principally offered masculine good looks in his early romantic leads. It is clear, though, that he soon began to take the art of movie acting seriously and develop his latent talent into fine dramatic capability. The dramatic core of Taylor's talent came to eclipse his looks in downbeat films like Mervyn Le Roy's *Waterloo Bridge* (1940) and David Miller's *Billy the Kid* (1941). In his darker screen moments, Taylor's looks no longer came into the cinematic equation; he was simply a very convincing conveyor of grief or worry or evil, his former charm neutralized by a sinister avoidance of smiling.

Brett Halsey seems to have undergone the same process. Halsey smiled a lot in early movies like *All I Desire* (1953) but in later movies, like *Web of Violence* (1966), he was giving more melancholic, complex performances that did not rely on looks or charm. Then, with the advent of the spaghetti Western, with its pervasive themes of greed and revenge, Halsey became a powerfully suggestive actor of darker emotions. In one superb example, the Western *Today We Kill...Tomorrow We Die* (1968), it is not just his rougher, bearded look that downplays his physical appearance but also his psychologically unsettling, brooding stares into the camera. These go beyond the Sergio Leone–type stares then fashionable in the Italian Western, and hark back to older templates, such as Arthur Kennedy's troubling stare into the camera in Fritz Lang's *Rancho Notorious* (1952).

Going beyond Robert Taylor's achievements, Halsey created brooding qualities you would not find in the script. His vengeful cowboy Bill Kiowa is hard as nails, almost psychotic, and yet Halsey's interpretation does not lose sight of the fact that Kiowa is a victim. Halsey's characterisation is oddly sympathetic, suggesting almost spiritual qualities to the role.

This dimension is most perfectly realized in Halsey's character Richard in the strange giallo *Perversion Story* (1969), exemplified by his unusually quiet and sorrowful demeanour, which is of course appropriate to the dramatic context of investigating his sister's mysterious death.

I believe this quasi-spiritual dimension to Halsey's best work is one of the personal qualities that make up his unique screen aura. To explain Halsey's aura more fully, we would have to examine questions of the origin of his evocation of fundamental traits of human personality such as honesty, bravery, decency, because these transmit so forcefully in Halsey's work, whatever he is playing, e.g. there is an honesty that comes across even when he is playing dishonest characters, perhaps because of the earnestness of his performance. Having come to know him personally, I believe these qualities transmit so strongly through the medium of celluloid because Brett Halsey is an artist, committed to truth and excellence, as he has demonstrated in teaching his acting classes.

Brett Halsey has always been more interested in self-fulfilment than in fame or money. We have seen how he turned down the role of James Bond and completed pictures where he was paid very little or paid in a barter arrangement. I would certainly argue that there is in his work a center of truth—an interest in verisimilitude in his acting—that is not so readily apparent in his contemporaries. I put this down to Halsey's excellent dramatic grounding at the Universal Talent School in part but also to an instinctive desire for quality. I believe his best performances demonstrate that instinct can transcend even the most carefully applied art.

Halsey's approach to action movie heroes reveals an awareness of the dynamics of screen acting, which is probably instinctive and therefore exhibits an appealing naturalness, for all that it is informed by considerable awareness and investigation of the craft. When Halsey became one of the iconographical heroes of the spaghetti Western, he brought to the screen rich dramatic sensibilities that distinguished him from the likes of less complex spaghetti Western actors such as Anthony Steffen and Montgomery Wood.

Spiritual qualities and artistic truth play a dominant role in the composition of Halsey's screen aura, yet there is more. Halsey's gift of capturing the viewer's attention derives from a quality beyond his highly professional execution of an actor's skills in fluff like *Bang Bang* (1967), his only musical comedy. His talent is a necessary, but not sufficient, condition of the further dimension to which he takes what is understood by star quality.

In his best roles, Halsey transcends the mechanics of screen acting—focus on character, concentration on serving the script, good interpretation of dialogue, clear delivery, lithe physical movement, mobility of facial expression—principally because the screen is Halsey's natural home.

There is no question that he is a born movie star—intended by nature to grace the screen—and I think the satisfying truth of his screen performance is essentially a by-product of our recognition of an artist follow-

ing his true vocation. The naturalness evoked by his doing so creates an aura around Halsey that few other actors achieve.

There is one other element to Halsey's screen persona, an important one, that crosses over directly from the actor's own approach to life. As his screen talent matured, Halsey's burgeoning confidence permitted him to inject humor into straight scenes. I refer not to the in-jokes he perpetrated in *Today We Kill...Tomorrow We Die* and *Perversion Story* but to whole action movies like *Espionage in Lisbon* (1965) where Halsey's personality considerably lightened the tone. It was Halsey's suggestion that *Touch of Death* (1988) be played as a black comedy. Humor and pleasure-seeking elide quite naturally from Halsey's private life into his screen aura and add to its appeal. This becomes clear from reading his unusual life story.

When you have a generosity of spirit as rare as Halsey's, allied to powerful intellect, the creative possibilities are immense and Halsey's life has been about realising those possibilities as fully as possible, while having fun at the same time.

In my view, that marriage of motives, idealistic and hedonistic, is where Halsey's screen impact comes from, marrying dynamism and languor in an attractive cocktail that makes Brett Halsey the ultimate movie star—Hollywood royalty, indeed, in Jay Bernstein's phrase—and creator of half a century of movie magic.

Filmography

All I Desire (Douglas Sirk, 1953)
The Glass Web (Jack Arnold, 1953)
Walking My Baby Back Home (Lloyd Bacon, 1953)
Ma and Pa Kettle at Home (Charles Lamont, 1954)
Johnny Dark (George Sherman, 1954)
The Black Shield of Falworth (Rudolph Mate, 1954)
Naked Alibi (Jerry Hopper, 1954)–uncredited, as Employee
Revenge of the Creature (Jack Arnold, 1955)
To Hell and Back (Jesse Hibbs, 1955)
Three Bad Sisters (Gilbert L. Kay, 1956)
The Girl He Left Behind (David Butler, 1956)
Hot Rod Rumble (Leslie H. Martinson, 1957)
Lafayette Escadrille (William Wellman, 1958)
High School Hellcats (Edward L. Bernds, 1958)
Gunman's Walk (Phil Karlson, 1958)
The Cry Baby Killer (Justus Addis, 1958)
I Want to Live! (Robert Wise, 1958)
Submarine Seahawk (Spencer Bennett, 1958)
The Atomic Submarine (Spencer Bennett, 1958)
Speed Crazy (William J. Hole, Jr., 1959)
The Girl in Lovers Lane (Charles R. Rondeau, 1959)
Blood and Steel (Bernard L. Kowalski, 1959)
Jet Over the Atlantic (Byron Haskin, 1959)
Four Fast Guns (William J. Hole, Jr., 1959)
Return of the Fly (Edward L. Bernds, 1959)
The Best of Everything (Jean Negulesco, 1959)
Desire in the Dust (William F. Claxton, 1960)
Return to Peyton Place (Jose Ferrer, 1961)
Seven Swords for the King (Riccardo Freda, 1962)
Twice-Told Tales (Sidney Salkow, 1963)
Jack and Jenny (Victor Vicas, 1963)
The Avenger of Venice (Piero Pierotti, 1964)
The Magnificent Cuckold (Antonio Pietrangeli, 1964)
The Magnificent Adventurer (Riccardo Freda, 1965)
Espionage in Lisbon (Tulio Demicheli, 1965)
Spy in Your Eye (Vittorio Sala, 1965)
Lovers and Kings (Geza Radvanyi, 1965)
The Hour of Truth (Henri Calef, 1965)
Kill Johnny Ringo (Frank G. Carroll/Gianfranco Baldanello, 1966)
Web of Violence (Nick Nostro, 1966)
Bang Bang (Serge Piolet, 1967)

Anyone Can Play (Luigi Zampa, 1967)
One Day After August (German Lorente, 1968)
Today We Kill...Tomorrow We Die! (Tonino Cervi, 1968)
All On the Red (Aldo Florio, 1968)
The Wrath of God (Albert Cardiff/Alberto Cardone, 1968)
Perversion Story (Julio Buchs, 1969)
Kidnapping (Albert Cardiff/Alberto Cardone, 1970)
Roy Colt and Winchester Jack (Mario Bava, 1970)
Four Times That Night (Mario Bava, 1972)
Where Does It Hurt? (Rodney Amateau, 1972)
Coon Skin (Ralph Bakshi, 1975)
Crash (Barry Shear, 1978)
Power (Barry Shear, Virgil W. Vogel, 1980)
Scruples (Robert Day, 1981)
Devil's Honey (Lucio Fulci, 1986)
Ratboy (Sondra Locke, 1986)
Rose (Tomaso Sherman, 1986)
Players—unsold TV pilot (1988)
The Commander (Antonio Margheriti, 1988)
Flying (Vincenzo Salviani, 1988)
Touch of Death (Lucio Fulci, 1988)
Cop Game (Bruno Mattei, 1988) – uncredited, as 'General Morris'
Beyond Justice (Duccio Tessari, 1989)
The Black Cat (Luigi Cozzi, 1989)
Esmeralda Bay (Jess Franco, 1989)
Demonia (Lucio Fulci, 1990)
Cat In the Brain (Lucio Fulci, 1990)
The Godfather: Part III (Francis Ford Coppola, 1990)
Back Stab (James Kaufmann, 1990)
To Catch a Killer (Eric Till, 1992)
Switching Parents (Linda Otto, 1993)
Search for Diana (Milad Bessada, 1993)
Almost Golden: The Jessica Savitch Story (Peter Werner, 1995)
Kissinger and Nixon (Daniel Petrie, 1995)
Terminal Rush (Damian Lee, 1995)
Expect No Mercy (Zale Dalen, 1995)
First Degree (Jeff Woolnough, 1996)
Free Fall (Mario Azzopardi, 1999)
Asesinato en el Meneo (Oscar Castillo, 2002)
Mujeres Apasionadas (Maureen Jiminez, 2003)
Million Dollar Baby (Clint Eastwood, 2004) – scene deleted
Risk Factor (Frank A. Caruso, 2003-7)

Short Films

Universal musical shorts c. 1953: *Ray Anthony*; *Andy and Della Russell*; *The Four Aces*
Leave It to Harry (Will Cowan, October 25, 1954) — musical short starring Harry James, also featuring David Janssen
Afternoon of a Faun (Albert De Goyen, 1956)
When Money Talks (student film by Clayton Halsey, 1986)

Television Episodes as Guest Star

Waterfront (1954)
The Life of Riley (c. 1954)
Brave Eagle, "The Gentle Warrior" (Paul Landres, January 25, 1956); and two more episodes
Gunsmoke, "Helping Hand" (Charles Marquis Warren, March 17, 1956)
Studio 57
United States Marshall
Tales of the 77th Bengal Lancers, "The Hostage" (November 4, 1956); and two more episodes
The 20th Century-Fox Hour, "Smoke Jumpers" (Albert S. Rogell, November 14, 1956)
Highway Patrol, "Temptation" (Henry S. Kesler, 1957)
West Point, "Start Running" (January 18, 1957)
Matinee Theatre, "The Story of Joseph" (April 19, 1957) – as Joseph
Playhouse 90, "Winter Dreams" (John Frankenheimer)
West Point, "The Fight Back" (June 7, 1957)
Silent Service
Flight, "Bombs in the Belfry" (Jean Yarbrough, 1958)
Perry Mason, "The Case of the Cautious Coquette" (Laszlo Benedek, January 18, 1958)
Harbor Command, "Killer on My Doorstep" (February 28, 1958)
The Millionaire, "The Susan Birchard Story" (R. G. Springsteen, April 2 1958)
The Adventures of Jim Bowie, "Bad Medicine" (April 18, 1958)
Mackenzie's Raiders, "The Imposter" (Abner Biberman, 1959; cast included Leonard Nimoy); and two more episodes
Dr. Hudson's Secret Journal (John Brahm)
Studio One, "The Last Summer" (John Frankenheimer)
Highway Patrol, "Breath of a Child" (Henry S. Kesler, 1959)
Death Valley Days, "Eruption at Volcano" (Paul Landres, February 14, 1959)
Sea Hunt, "Diving for the Moon" (February 15, 1959)
Bat Masterson, "River Boat" (Walter Doniger, February 18, 1959)
World of Giants, "Feathered Foe" (Nathan Juran, October 17, 1959)

Five Fingers, "Thin Ice" (Lamont Johnson, December 19, 1959)
Brock Callahan, "The Silent Kill" (George Blair, 1959)
Adventures in Paradise, "Passage to Tua" (James Neilson, April 11, 1960)
Alias Smith and Jones, "Return to Devil's Hole" (Bruce Kessler, February 25, 1971)
Columbo, "Death Lends a Hand" (Bernard L. Kowalski, October 6, 1971)
Alias Smith and Jones, "The Day The Amnesty Came Through" (Jeff Corey, November 25, 1972)
Toma, "Crime Without Victim" (Daniel Haller, October 18, 1973)
CBS Daytime 90, "Once in Her Life" (Robert J. Shaw, February 14 1974)
City of Angels, "The Losers" (Barry Shear, April 6, 1976)
The Bionic Woman, "The Antidote" (Don McDougall, January 21, 1978)
The Love Boat, "The Last of the Stubings/The Million Dollar Man/The Sisters" (February 4, 1978)
Fantasy Island, "Let the Goodtimes Roll/Nightmare/The Tiger" (November 4, 1978)
The Dukes of Hazzard, "The Rustlers" (October 5, 1979)
Fantasy Island, "The Chain Gang/The Boss" (Mike Vejar, October 19, 1979)
Buck Rogers in the 25th Century, "Cruise Ship to the Stars" (Sigmund Neufeld, Jr., December 27 1979)
Hart to Hart, "Murder, Murder on the Wall" (Tom Mankiewicz, November 11, 1980)
Charlie's Angels, "Attack Angels" (Kim Manners, June 3 1981)
The Fall Guy, "The Meek Shall Inherit Rhondda" (Sidney Hayers, November 11, 1981)
Fantasy Island, "A Very Strange Affair/The Sailor" (January 2, 1982)
Fantasy Island, "Forget Me Not/The Quiz Masters" (April 10, 1982)
The Dukes of Hazzard, "Eno's in Trouble" (Paul Baxley, November 19, 1982)
Knight Rider, "Give Me Liberty…Or Give Me Death" (Bernard L. Kowalski, January 21, 1983)
Matt Houston, "Whose Party Is It Anyway?" (January 23, 1983)
Mike Hammer, "Sex Trap" (March 24, 1984)
Automan, "Club Ten" (April 9, 1984)
Matt Houston, "Caged" (Cliff Bole, October 26, 1984)
Airwolf, "Sins of the Past" (Donald A. Baer, October 27, 1984)
Cagney & Lacey, "Insubordination" (John Patterson, October 29 1984)
The Dukes of Hazzard, "The Dukes in Hollywood" (George Bowers, November 2, 1984)
Half Nelson, "Uppers and Downers" (April 5, 1985)
Mike Hammer, "Murder in the Cards" (December 3, 1986)
Giallo, "Turno di Notte – L'Impronta del' Assassino" (Luigi Cozzi, 1987)
Street Legal, "Blue Collar" (Allan Harmon, December 15, 1989)
E.N.G. (1990)

Top Cops, "Gene Ambs" (1991)
Sweating Bullets, "Dead Men Tell" (September 30, 1991)
Counterstrike, "Native Warriors" (October 26, 1991)
Street Legal, "The Good Lawyer" (Eleanor Lindo, November 29, 1991)
Forever Knight, "Dying to Know You" (Brad Turner, June 9, 1992)
X-Men, "Enter Magneto" (1992)
X-Men, "Night of the Sentinels, Part 1" (1992)
Secret Service, "The Assassin" (1993)
Matrix, "Lapses in Memory" (July 15, 1993)
Top Cops, "Mel McDougall/Dave Smith" (Paul Lynch, October 5 1993)
Kung Fu: The Legend Continues, "The Possessed" (Allan King, May 2, 1994)
Tekwar, "Unknown Soldier" (Allan Kroeker, December 29, 1994)
Kung Fu: The Legend Continues, "Plague" (Mario Azzopardi, January 30, 1995)
Kung Fu: The Legend Continues, "Target" (Jon Cassar, May 1, 1995)
Kung Fu: The Legend Continues, "Demons" (Jon Cassar, October 2, 1995)
The Associates, "Disclosure" (George Bloomfield, January 23, 2001)
La Pension, "Adios a la Vieja" (Oscar Castillo, 2002)
Mogli, The New Jungle Book (2002)
The Florence Henderson Show (2007) — talk show appearance

Television Series as Writer/Producer/Director
A Country On the March (Costa Rica, 1973)

Series' Starring Roles
Follow the Sun: 30 episodes, shared between three leads. Halsey was featured in eleven episodes, though credited in all. Some appearances were just a brief interaction with the other leads.

"A Rage for Justice" (Jules Bricken, September 17, 1961) – pilot episode
"Cry Fraud" (Francis D. Lyon, September 24, 1961) — Halsey does not appear
"The Highest Wall" (Ted Post, October 1, 1961)
"Journey Into Darkness" (Gilbert L. Kay, October 8, 1961)
"The Woman Who Never Was" (Felix Feist, October 15, 1961)
"Busman's Holiday" (October 22, 1961)
"Another Part of the Jungle" (Francis D. Lyon, October 29, 1961)
"The Longest Crap Game in History" (Felix Feist, November 5, 1961) — Halsey does not appear
"The Hunters" (Francis D. Lyon, November 12, 1961) — Halsey does not appear

"Little Girl Lost" (Ted Post, November 19, 1961)
"Night Song" (Felix Feist, November 26, 1961)
"The Primitive Clay" (December 3, 1961)
"Conspiracy of Silence" (Ted Post, December 10, 1961)
"The Far End of Nowhere" (Don Taylor, December 17, 1961)-Halsey does not appear
"Mele Kalikimaka to You" (Mitch Leisen, December 24, 1961) — Halsey does not appear
"The Girl from the Brandenburg Gate" (Felix Feist, December 31, 1961) — Halsey does not appear
"Chicago Style" (Mitch Leisen, January 7, 1962) — Halsey does not appear
"The Last of the Big Spenders" (January 14, 1962)
"Ghost Story" (January 21, 1962)
"Sergeant Kolchak Fades Away" (Jacques Tourneur, January 28, 1962)
"The Dumbest Blonde" (Robert Butler, February 4, 1962)
"Annie Beeler's Place" (February 11, 1962)
"The Irresistible Miss Bullfinch" (February 18, 1962)
"A Choice of Weapons" (February 25, 1962)
"Maine of the Month" (March 4, 1962)
"The Inhuman Equation" (Jack Donohue, March 11, 1962) — Halsey does not appear
"A Ghost in her Gazebo" (Leonard J. Horn, March 18, 1962)
"Not Aunt Charlotte!" (March 25, 1962)
"Run, Clown, Run" (Justus Addiss, April 1, 1962) — Halsey does not appear
"Chalk One Up for Johnny" (Leonard J. Horn, April 8, 1962)

Love is a Many Splendored Thing (1972-1973)
Search for Tomorrow (1975)
General Hospital (1977)
The Young and the Restless (1980-1981)

As Himself
Vico Auf der Donau (with Heidi Bruhl, German TV, 1968)

Novels
The Magnificent Strangers (1978)
Yesterday's Children (1984)
Halfbreed (2005-2008)

As Development Executive
Passport to Danger (c. 1984)

As Professor Overseeing School of Dramatic Arts, Costa Rica
Cartas de Amor (Marta Apuy & Jean Marten, 1997)
Cita en Setiembre (1999)

As Screenwriter
Safari (Roger Vadim, 1986)

Unproduced Scripts
El Camino Real (script for projected Fox TV series)
Pony Express
Unknown title: caper story co-written with Gino Mancini
Silverworld (from a story by Kenny Young)
West of Hell a.k.a. *Fool's Gold*
The Girls of Fashion Island (treatment)
The Bali Hai Boys
Grave Misunderstanding (U.S. and Canadian versions)
War and Pizza
War and Pizza (different story to previous entry, a TV series proposal re. WWII Italian prisoners of war)
Steve Martini (in Italian)
Date with Fate
Wolf Woman
Pierrot
Soulfire
The Dragon Lady (synopsis)
Juana of the Jungle
Lady Jane's School for Young Ladies
Yesterday's Children (synopsis)
The Magnificent Strangers (three-part TV series)
The Czarina's Favorite Cousin
Thomas Locke
Seven Lives
The Woman who Loved Too Much
Fancy Dress Party
Not Tonight Josephine (with Michelle Jones, 2007)

Unrealized Acting Roles
The Bullfighter and the Lady (Budd Boetticher, 1951)
The All American (Jesse Hibbs, 1953)
The Searchers (John Ford, 1956)
The 300 Spartans (Rudolph Mate, 1962)—Halsey confirms he was considered for this (probably the Barry Coe role) but was busy elsewhere

The Amazing Miss Bartlett —unproduced (1963)
Zorro —unproduced version (mid-1960s)
Romeo and Juliet (Riccardo Freda, 1964)
The Invincible Six (Jean Negulesco, 1968)—Halsey was considered for this (probably the lead, played by Stuart Whitman)
Castle of Horror—unproduced Italian horror (1973)
MacArthur (Joseph Sargent, 1976)
Title unknown—movie to be shot in Bogota, Colombia (1977)

Wrong Attributions (in periodicals and on the internet)

The Man from the Alamo (Budd Boetticher, 1953)—it is possible Halsey was considered for a small role but he is not in the film.
The Last Blitzkrieg (Arthur Dreifus, 1959)–often attributed to Brett Halsey but he is categorical that he was not in it.
Sangre en Montana (1966) with Gloria Osuna (reported in the French Press)– Halsey confirms he never worked with Gloria Osuna.
Bang Bang Kid (Giorgio Gentili, 1968)–confused with *Bang Bang*.
Cowards Don't Pay (Mario Siciliano, 1969)

Bibliography

Arce, Hector, *The Secret Life of Tyrone Power* (Morrow, 1979)

Balbo, Lucas; Blumenstock, Peter; Kessler, Christian, *Obsession: The Films of Jess Franco* (Graf Haufen & Frank Trebbin, Berlin 1993)

Baronas, Mike; Gavin, Kit, *Paura: Lucio Fulci Remembered* (forthcoming)

Barr, Tony, *Acting for the Camera* (Harper & Row, 1986)

Blake, Matt; Deal, David, *The Eurospy Guide* (Luminary Press, 2004)

Bogdanovich, Peter, *The Killing of the Unicorn: Dorothy Stratten 1960-1980* (Morrow, 1984)

Broccoli, Cubby, *When the Snow Melts: The Autobiography of Cubby Broccoli* (Boxtree, U.K. 1998)

Fentone, Steve; Ferguson, Michael, *Revenge is a Dish Best Served Cold: The Encyclopedia of "Spaghetti" Westerns* (privately published, c. 1996)

Fentone, Steve; Capicik, Dennis, *The Admirable Halsey: Spaghetti cinema stalwart Brett Halsey interviewed* (Giallo Pages Volume One, c. 1996)

Ferguson, Mike; Fentone, Steve, *Roy Colt Shoots His Mouth Off!: An Interview with Brett Halsey* (European Trash Cinema # 12, July 1995)

Frayling, Christopher, *Spaghetti Westerns: Cowboys and Europeans from Karl May to Sergio Leone* (Routledge & Kegan Paul, U.K. 1981; revised edition I.B. Tauris, U.K. 1998)

Gallant, Chris (ed.), *Art of Darkness: The Cinema of Dario* Argento (Fab Press, U.K. 2001)

Halsey, Brett, *The Magnificent Strangers* (Corgi, 1978; revised edition iUniverse, 2001)

Halsey, Brett, *Yesterday's Children* (Knightsbridge Publishing, 1984; new edition iUniverse, 2000)

Hofler, Robert, *The Man Who Invented Rock Hudson: The Pretty Boys and Dirty Deals of Henry Willson* (Carroll K. Graf, 2005)

Jones, Alan, *The Filming of Fulci's "Demonia"* (Eyeball 2, Summer 1990)

Jones, Alan, *Profondo Argento: The Man, the Myths & the Magic* (Fab Press, U.K. 2004)

McDonough, Jimmy, *The Ghastly One: The Sex-Gore Netherworld of Filmmaker Andy Milligan* (A Capella, 2001)

McGilligan, Patrick, *Clint: The Life and Legend* (Harper Collins, 1999)

McKay, Gardner, *Toyer* (Warner Books, 1998)

Meikle, Dennis, *Vincent Price: The Art of Fear* (Reynolds and Hearn, U.K. 2003)

Michalski, Michael, *Fly On the Wall & Fly Boy Brett Halsey* (Scarlett Street No. 46 & 48, 2003)

Murray, John B., *The Remarkable Michael Reeves: His Short and Tragic Life* (Luminary Press, 2004)

Murray, John B., *Robert Vaughn: A Critical Study* (Thessaly Press, U.K. 1987)

Negulesco, Jean, *Things I Did and Things I Think I Did: A Hollywood Memoir* (Linden Press, 1984)

Palmerini, Luca M.; Mistretta, Gaetano, *Spaghetti Nightmares: Italian Fantasy-Horrors as Seen Through the Eyes of their Protagonists* (Fantasma Books, 1996)

Pink, Sidney, *So You Want to Make Movies: My Life as an Independent Film Producer* (Pineapple Press, 1989)

Shickel, Richard, *Clint Eastwood: A Biography* (Vintage Books, 1997)

Slater, Jay (ed.), *Eaten Alive: Italian Cannibal and Zombie Movies* (Plexus Publishing, U.K. 2002)

Thrower, Stephen, *Beyond Terror: The Films of Lucio Fulci* (Fab Press, U.K. 2002)

Weaver, Tom, *Many Horror Returns & The Italian Jobs* (Fangoria 215 & 216, 2002)

Williams, Tony, *Brett Halsey: Interview by Tony Williams* (Psychotronic 40, 2004)

If you enjoyed this book,
check out our other
film-related titles at
www.midmar.com
or call or write for a free catalog.
Midnight Marquee Press, Inc.
9721 Britinay Lane
Baltimore, MD 21234
410-665-1198
(8 a.m. until 6 p.m. EST)
or MMarquee@aol.com

www.ingramcontent.com/pod-product-compliance
Lightning Source LLC
Chambersburg PA
CBHW071224080526
44587CB00013BA/1489